CAHUILLA DICTIONARY

By

HANSJAKOB SEILER
and
KOJIRO HIOKI

2006
MALKI MUSEUM PRESS
Morango Indian Reservation
Banning, California

1979, 2006
Malki Museum Press
Morongo Indian Reservation
Banning, CA

MALKI MUSEUM PRESS
P.O. Box 578, Banning, CA 92220
951-849-7289
951-8493549 FAX
www.malimuseum.org

Library of Congress Catalog Number: 78-71635
Printed in the United States of America

To

Katherine Siva Saubel

and

Alice Lopez

2006
PREFACE

Since the publication of this text in 1979 saving Native American languages is an even larger growing concern in the new century. The authors of this text are both from distant countries whose interest in helping Native Americans save, document and teach their languages is miraculous.

Museums in Germany and other European countries have some of the most extensive artifact collections and exhibits on Native American cultures and language that are to be found anywhere. We are thankful to people such as Dr. Seiler and Dr. Hioki and others from afar that are interested in preserving and working to help record invaluable Native American history.

Cahuilla is a Uto-Aztecan based language. Dr. Hioki once explained that it is sometimes easier for someone who speaks a more guttural language, such as Japanese or German, to learn to make some of the sounds in the Cahuilla language and therefore pronounce it correctly. This statement tells the importance of teaching languages to our young people at very early ages, while their vocal chords and voices are forming and while their minds are wide open for learning.

We have not updated this text; however we do want to make our readers aware that both Dr. Seiler and Dr. Hioki have continued to explore, interpret and write about the Cahuilla people and their language. Dr. Seiler has written numerous other books on the Cahuilla language available in Germany and still others here at home, in California, are also working on new Cahuilla language linguistic and grammar texts.

We are still here.

CONTENTS

INTRODUCTION

1. Acknowledgements

This work is intended to complete the description of the Cahuilla language and to facilitate access both to the Cahuilla Texts (Seiler 1970) and to the Cahuilla Grammar (Seiler 1977). The non-linguist interested in learning something about the 'words' of this language and about their use will find rich information concerning the ways of thinking, religious beliefs, social structure, medicinal knowledge, and the everyday life of these people. The linguist will hopefully find in this Dictionary a means for better understanding the Texts and a help for the illustration of many points discussed in the Grammar. The choice of the graphical representation of the words and the format in which all the relevant pieces of information are given are ultimately motivated by the structure of this language and by the scientific desire to convey a maximum of information to a maximum range of interested readers. The spelling of the words is phonemic and the account for our phonemicization is given in the Grammar (p.24 f.) A guide to the pronunciation of the phonemic symbols is presented at the end of this introduction.

As a typological characteristic Cahuilla words include much material which in English or other Western European languages would be distributed over several words within a clause or even within a complex of subordinated and main clause. To do justice to this very dominant property and to bring out all the relevant information connected with it, neither the full word form as it occurs in actual speech nor the abstract entity of the morpheme would be the proper format for representing the lexical entity. Instead, the stem has been chosen as the most satisfactory frame. The details of this representation are discussed in section 2.

For general information about the Cahuilla language and about the Cahuilla people as well as for acknowledgements to the native speakers and to the institutions and scholars who helped me in my work, the reader is referred to the relevant sections in the Grammar and in the Texts.

Part of the lexical material of this Dictionary has been extracted from the Texts, the Grammar, and from my extensive unpublished field notes. A considerable part, however, of the entries has been collected by my co-author Dr. Kojiro Hioki during two field trips (August-December 1972 and July-August 1973) in which he also re-checked the forms and meanings of most entries collected earlier. In this painstaking work he was fortunate to have the precious and unfailing help of our two Cahuilla friends to whom we dedicate this book. Hioki also was the first explorer into the as yet largely unknown fields of sound symbolism. As we think that it plays a rather important role in structuring the lexicon, especially in the realm of verbs, we present in a separate publication materials which might incite the interested specialist to do further research.

H.S.

2. Structure of the Dictionary

Orthography

The following phonemic symbols are used in this dictionary: occlusives /p t č k k^{W} q b d g/, voiceless fricatives /s š x x^{W}/, voiced fricative /v/, laryngeals /ʔ h/,

nasals /m n ñ ŋ/, liquids /l l̃ r/, glides /w y/, and vowels /i ii e ee a aa u uu o oo/, plus stress (for a fuller discussion of these symbols, see Seiler 1957, 1977; cf. also Bright 1965 and 1965a with slight deviations; the differences are commented on in Seiler 1977). The traditional arrangement of the Roman alphabet has been utilized for ordering the symbols in the dictionary, to the extent that this has been possible. Special symbols follow those which they most closely resemble graphically. An initial glottal stop as well as vowel length are disregarded. Thus the following order results:
a aa b č d e ee g h i ii k k^w l l̃ m n ñ ŋ o oo p q r s š t u uu v w x x^w y ʔ.

2.1. Lexical Entry

In principle this is a stem dictionary which provides detailed information on the morphemic composition of the stems. Morphemes are separated by hyphens. When a stem always occurs with a certain affix, the total form is segmented by hyphenation in the main entry. However, when derivational prefixes -če-, -pe- and -vuk- are obligatorily combined with certain verbal stems, then the stem minus the prefix is listed as the main entry in order to facilitate being looked up, e.g. "-hémi- v.itr. with -če- ..." is to be understood as 'the stem -hémi- v.itr. always occurs with the prefix -če-', and "-húqin- v.tr., also with -če- ..." as 'the stem -húqin- v.tr. may occur with -če-". Such treatment of the obligatory prefixes -če-, -pe-, -vuk- is justified on the ground that this prefixation is a productive morphological process in the language, so that the non-occurrence of the prefixless stem is merely a gap in the system.

The meaning of the derivational affixes is defined in the grammar; therefore only possible combinations, which are lexically conditioned, are entered in the dictionary. When the meaning of a derivative is unpredictable, the derivative form is treated in a sub-entry. The verbal prefixation -mu- is not treated in the grammar; the form -mu- apparently originates from -muˀ 'nose', and on account of its aspectual meaning 'head first' and its frequent occurrence it is listed under 'derivation'.

The term 'simplex' refers to a stem without an affix, e.g. -xélew- v.itr. A remark such as 'also with -če- (more frequent than simplex)' is to be interpreted as: 'the verb stem -xélew- can occur with -če-, and the derivative form with -če- occurs more frequently than the stem alone.'

If a restriction on the distribution of the main entry is given (e.g. that it may only occur with specified prefixes), the restriction is valid only for the stem entry concerned, not for derived stems, e.g. '-číki- v.itr. with -wen-' means: the verbal stem -číki- occurs always with the derivational suffix -wen-; this does not necessarily hold for its derivation, that is, e.g. -číškim- distrib. can occur in constructions with other suffixes.

Word classes are indicated by the usual abbreviations (see the list). The parentheses used in the classification, e.g. (gerund), express that the form is not unambiguously analyzable synchronically but has been identified as such on the basis of the productive morphological process, e.g. of nominalization of a verbal stem with the suffix -ve(l).

Person names are indicated by PN and place names by PlN. Only ethnologically important proper names are included.

Lexical forms are classified as sound imitation on the basis of statements by the informant. These forms always occur with the verb -yáx- 'to say, to be' thus forming a periphrastic construction (see below) which is marked accordingly.

Peripharastic forms are marked as periphr. They comprise two roots: the semantically central one and the dummy root -yáx-. The semantic difference between periphrastic and monolectic forms corresponds, roughly speaking, to that between 'partial' and 'total' (for a detailed comment see the Grammar).

The plural form, plur.. is listed in full when it is not predictable, e.g. ʔánet n., plur. ʔánt-em, otherwise the following representation is used: čípatma-l n., plur. -l-em, that is, the full form is čípatma-l-em (-l absolutive suffix, see below).

The stem may contain a submorpheme, submorph., which indicates a meaningful subpart of a morpheme. Submorphemes that may be mutually substituted are cross-referenced, e.g. -múʔaqi- v.itr. (=-múʔ-aqi- with submorph. -aq-, see -múʔaš-). For the morphological status see the Grammar.

'Construct' indicates that the form must occur with a possessive pronoun, e.g. -na n. [construct] father, where the hyphen indicates that the form na is preceded by the P_1 pronoun (see the Grammar).

The absolutive suffix is indicated by hyphenation; e.g. púč-il̃ n. eye, indicates that the stem púč- ~ púš- occurs elsewhere, namely in construct, né-puš 'my eye' or in derivation, -púš-l̃u-ni- 'to put eyes (in the doll)'.

Some nouns occur with a classifier, classif., instead of showing a construct state. The classifier then appears as construct, e.g., ʔáwal n., with classif. -ʔaš, dog ... né-ʔaš ʔáwal lit. my pet dog; my dog (for a detailed discussion of the classifiers see the Grammar).

'Allomorph', ALLOM., indicates morphophonemic alternation, while 'variation', VAR., either free variation or variation under unclear or unknown conditions.

'Nominal/verbal group' is a semanto-phonological unit consisting of more than one lexical form, in which the combination between the members is not as rigid as that between the members of a compound.

'Suppletive forms', supplet., are listed as separate entries with cross-reference, e.g., -čéx- v.itr. to die with plur. subj., see -múk-.

The Cahuilla dialects are abbreviated as Des.Ca. (Desert Cahuilla), Mt.Ca. (Mountain Cahuilla) and rarely Palm Springs Ca. (Palm Springs Cahuilla, including Chino Canyon) and Wan.Ca. (Wánikik Cahuilla). KS and AL refer to our more recent main informants: Kathy Saubel, representing the Mt.Ca. dialect, and Alice Lopez speaking the Des.Ca. If a lexicon entry was reported unkown to one or the other informant, this is marked as, respectively, KS dnkn and AL dnkn (does not know).

The English interpretation is intended to describe the morpheme's range of usage as far as possible,e.g. -múk- v.itr. ... 1. to get sick, weak (with suff. durat.) 2. to die (with suff. [+realized]). If necessary, grammatical information is also given. A literal translation may precede the normal correspondence, separated by a semi-colon. A cross-reference is given in certain cases, e.g. -púlin n. construct, plur. -púlamñ-am daughter (of a woman), cf. -súŋama (of a man), -méxan son.

2.2. Derivation

Derivatives are listed under the stem from which they are derived. Further subderivatives are indicated by indentions under the main entry so that the structural hierarchy can be shown:

-páw- v.itr. to get water

-páw-law- to go after water

-páw-law-pa- to go after water and return

By verbal distrib. (distributive) a process is considered to be a set of single realizations (see the Grammar).

Compounds are marked with + symbol between components, and if necessary a literal translation (lit.) precedes the normal (English) equivalent, e.g.

kú-t n. fire

-kut+múx- v.itr. lit. to shoot fire; to start fire (by friction)

Phrases, i.e. nominal/verbal groups, are marked with an empty space between the members, and in some cases, by secondary stress, e.g.

kùt níniwet n. fire-like wind

2.3 Miscellaneous

Synonym, SYN., designates either synonym or antonym.

Citations, CIT., are given in order to illustrate the meaning of the entry and its combinatorial possibilities; idiomatic expressions are also included under CIT.

Botanical identifications have in most cases been brought up to date by reference to BandS (Bean and Saubel 1972).

3. A Guide to Pronunciation

Orthography	Pronunciation
a	unrounded open vowel as o in not
aa	long unrounded open vowel as a in father
b	voiced bilabial fricative (in words borrowed from Spanish) as b in Spanish abuelo 'grandfather'
č	voiceless palato-alveolar affricate as ch in church
d	voiced dental fricative (in words borrowed from Spanish) as d in Spanish adelante 'forward'
e	unrounded front mid-open vowel as e in pen
ee	long unrounded front mid-open vowel as e in German Bär 'bear'
g	voiced velar fricative (in words borrowed from Spanish) as g in Spanish amigo 'friend'
h	voiceless glottal spirant as h in harm
i	unrounded front closed vowel as i in hit
ii	long unrounded front closed vowel as ee in bee
k	unaspirated voiceless velar stop as k in skill
k^w	unaspirated voiceless labio-velar stop as qu in squish
l	voiced alveolar lateral as l in German laut
l̃	voiced palatal lateral as lli in million
m	bilabial nasal as m in man
n	alveolar nasal as n in net
ñ	palatal nasal as ñ in Spanish mañana 'tomorrow'
ŋ	velar nasal as ng in sing
o	rounded back mid-open vowel (in words borrowed from Spanish) as o in boy

oo	long rounded back mid-open vowel (in words borrowed from Spanish) as aw in law
p	unaspirated voiceless bilabial stop as p in spin
q	voiceless post-velar stop as q in Arabic qāla 'he said'
r	voiced alveolar flap (in words borrowed from Spanish) as r in María
s	voiceless alveolar fricative as ss in kiss
š	voiceless palato-alveolar fricative as sh in ship
t	unaspirated voiceless alveolar stop as t in stop
u	rounded back closed vowel as u in put
uu	long rounded back closed vowel as oo in boot
v	voiced bilabial fricative (see /b/)
w	bilabial semivowel as w in west
x	voiceless velar fricative as ch in German Buch 'book'
x^w	boiceless labio-velar fricative as wh in American English which
y	palatal semivowel as y in yes
ʔ	glottal stop as the element separating the two parts of the exclamation 'oh-oh'

4. Abbreviations

+	**boundary in compound**
ad...	**refers to...**
adj.	adjective
adv.	adverb
AL	Alice Lopez
ALLOM.	allomorph
arch.	archaic

autom.	automatic
BandS	Bean and Saubel 1972
Ca.	Cahuilla
caus.	causative
CIT.	citation
classif.	classifier
demonstr.	demonstrative
Des.Ca.	Desert Cahuilla
distrib.	distributive
dnkn.	does not know
durat.	durative
imper.	imperative
indir.	indirect
indef.	indefinite
indiv.	individual
interj.	interjection
interr.	interrogative
KS	Kathy Saubel
lit.	literary
Mt.Ca.	Mountain Cahuilla
n.	noun
neg.	negative
obj.	object
periphr.	periphrase
pers.	person
PlN	place name
plur.	plural
PN	person name
postpos.	postposition
prob.	probably
pron.	pronoun
quantif.	quantifier
recipr.	reciprocal

redupl.	reduplicated, reduplication
sbdy	somebody
sing.	singular
spp.	species
Span.	Spanish
sth.	something
subj.	subject
submorph.	submorphemic
suff.	suffix
supplet.	suppletive
SYN.	synonym,
VAR.	variant
v.itr.	verb intransitive
v.tr.	verb transitive
Wan.Ca.	Wánikik Cahuilla

5. Bibliography

Bean, L. J., and K. S. Saubel	1972	_Temalpakh (from the Earth). Cahuilla Indian Knowledge and Usage of Plants_. Banning, California: Malki Museum Press.
Bright, W.	1965	"The history of the Cahuilla sound system." _IJAL_ 31, 241-44.
-----	1965a	"A field guide to Southern California Indian languages." _UCLA Archaeological Survey Annual Report_.

Seiler, H. 1957 "Die phonetischen Grundlagen der Vokalphoneme des Cahuilla." *Zeitschrift für Phonetik und allgemeine Sprachwissenschaft* 10, 204-23.

----- 1970 *Cahuilla Texts with an Introduction*. Indiana University Publications, Language Science Monographs, Vol. 6. Bloomington, Indiana and the Hague: Indiana University Press and Mouton.

----- 1977 *Cahuilla Grammar*. Banning, California: Malki Museum Press.

PART I.

CAHUILLA-ENGLISH

A

ˀáča-ˀe 1. adj., plur. ˀáˀča-am 2. adv. 1. good, fine 2. well, very

ˀáča-kʷe(n), VAR. ˀáča-ku adv. well, in a good way, satisfactorily

-ˀáča-kʷ- v.itr. to get better, to get recovered

-ˀáča-kʷ-eni caus. to fix sth. good

ˀáča-kʷ-enet n. being good

ˀáča-ˀika adv. to the right

ˀáča-ma adj. right, good, enough; thank you

ˀáča-ŋa adv. in a good way, in/on the good thing

ˀáča-ŋa-x adv. to the right

ˀáča-x adv. to the right

Cf. ˀelélema bad

CIT. ad 1. ˀáča-ˀe ñišluvel a good old woman, cf. ad 2 nišluvel ˀáča-ˀe a very old woman

hésun ˀáča-ˀe lit. his heart is good; he is a good man, cf. hésun ˀáča-ma lit. his heart is fine; he is glad

ad 2. náwišmal ˀélka ˀáča-ˀe the girl is very pretty

ˀáksaˀviš n. the youngest person

-ˀáku- v.itr. to lift up the chin (e.g., a chicken lifts up the beak to swallow water), to look up

-ˀálaˀ v.tr. to mock, to echo sbdy cf. -mémxive- v.tr. Mt.Ca

Cf. -kúkus- to make fun of sbdy

CIT. táxliswetem čemem-ˀáˀala-wen čemkúktašwenepa when we talk, the Indians mock us

ˀalaxčíŋˀa n. grass (like cabbage leaves)

ˀálukul n., plur. -am wild goose

ʔalwáa conj., VAR. ʔalawáa (excluded alternative) ..., so that ... not ...

CIT. nenéŋqal qáwiš húŋanax ʔalwáa piš netéwap I am hiding behind a rock, so that he won't find me

ʔálwamal̃ n., plur. -em crowlike small black bird

ʔálwet n., plur. -em crow

ʔálxawil̃ n. string of bow

-ʔámi- v.itr. to go/come down, climb down

-ʔámi-n- caus., Mt.Ca. -ʔámi-ñi- to let go, bring down; (for sing. obj., cf. -wíčexan- for plur. obj.) to throw away, toss, to leave wife or child behind

-ʔáʔmami- caus. and distrib. to throw away, drop repeatedly; (recipr.) lit. to throw down each other; to wrestle

tax-ʔámamni-vaš/-wet n. wrestler

-ʔámi-n-iči- to drop sth. on the way; to leave sbdy behind

-ʔámi-n-ŋi- to take somewhere; to throw away; to leave behind

ʔámi-n-at n. sth. that was thrown away; orphan

ʔámi-n-iš n. person who threw sth. away or left his wife or child behind

-vuk-ʔámi- v.itr. to go over, go down to the other side (e.g. mountain)

CIT. ʔáy hésuni pe-ʔámi-n-qa (pe-ʔáʔmami-qa) lit. he threw out his heart (... repeatedly); he sighed (... repeatedly/ sobbed)

ʔelélkʷiči neta pe-ʔámi-n-qal lit. he throws a bad thing on me; he does an evil thing to me

sékŋa pe-vuk-ʔámi-n-qal lit. on his back he let it go over (his shoulder); he carries it on his back

ˀámi-ka adv. to the side, on the side

ˀámi-ŋax adv. from the side

ˀáˀmi-ŋax adv. redupl. between

CIT. newéwenqal wíh káar ˀámi-ŋax I am standing between two cars

-ˀamíwoki n. construct Span. friend

ˀámiˀan adv. in the middle, halfway

CIT. ˀíl̃i penqívišnik ˀámiˀan I am going to cut the tree in half

ˀámna-ˀa n. big/great one; god; spirit

ˀámna-wet n. big/large one kíš ___ Big House (ceremonial), néma ___ lit. my big finger/hand; thumb

ˀáˀamna-wet distrib. (for not pluralizable nouns)

ˀáˀamna-čem plur.

ˀámna-k^{W}- v.itr. to get/grow big

-ˀáˀamna-k^{W}- distrib. to get bigger and bigger

-ˀámna-k^{W}-ni- caus. to make big

-ˀámna-k^{W}e-lu-ni- caus. to give power; to make big

ˀámna-ma adj. big, roomy (house, etc.)

CIT. ˀí kíˀat ˀámna-k^{W}-al, ˀávuqal, wélqal this baby is getting big, growing, and growing up

míyaxwen xél̃ay piš pe-ˀámna-k^{W}e-lu-ni-pi he has to make his clothes big

-ˀámu- v.itr., v.tr. to hunt

ˀámu-ˀat/-ˀil̃ n. hunting (season)

ˀámu-vaˀal: pa___ hunting place (habit.)

ˀámu-vel: pa___ place which was hunted

ˀámu-piš: pa___ place to be hunted

ˀámu-vaš/-wet n. hunter

ˀámul n., plur. -em   cactus (big and yellow like pumpkin, eatable by roasting); agave, cf. BandS p.31

ˀáñet n., plur. ˀánt-em ant, big ant, cf. kúvišnil̃ small ant

-ˀáqi- v.itr.   to open (blanket, curtain, door, etc.)

-ˀáˀqam-, -ˀáqa- distrib. to open back and forth

-ˀáqi-n- caus., also with -če-, to open a little

SYN. -hákuš- v.tr. to open

CIT. yáˀi ˀéleqal "curtain" ˀáq ˀáq yáxqal the wind blows and the curtain opens back and forth

ˀáqniš n.   sparrow

-ˀáqyaw- v.tr.   to rock a baby; to take care of a baby

SYN. -téček^{w}- v.tr. to take care of

CIT. kíˀati pentáwiqal peman wéey wéey néyaxqal pen-ˀáqyaw-qal I hold the baby in my arms, took it and take care of it

ˀáasia interj.   oh (expression of surprise both positive and negative, used only by men; cf. ˀeléle used by women)

-ˀásis n. construct   niece, i.e. brother's daughter

ˀáswet n. with classif. -ˀaš eagle; eagle feather: ˀáswet piš with eagle feather

ˀàswet séˀi   Eagle Flower PN

CIT. ˀáswet piš peemúxwen with eagle feathers they are shooting it

-ˀaš n. construct   pet, domestic animal

-ˀáš-l̃u- v.tr.   to keep as a pet

-ʔáʔaš-l̃u- v.tr. distrib.

ʔáš-l̃u-nax n. one who is supposed to keep a pet

ʔáš-l̃u-vaš n. one who likes to have pets

ʔáš-ka n. one who owns a pet

ʔáš-vik/ʔáš-l̃u-vik one who owns a lot of animals

-ʔáč-i peta/-ʔáš-ŋa on horse back

CIT. né-ʔaš ʔàswet my pet eagle

pe ʔ náxaniš ʔí ʔáʔwalemi mey-ʔáš-ka that man owns those dogs

-ʔáškay- v.tr. to fail to meet; to fail to hit the target in shooting

-ʔáškay-law- to fail to meet sbdy.

CIT. penmúxqal wíkikmal ʔáy pen-ʔáškay-ʔi I shot a bird, but missed it

čemtáwaswen pičem-ʔáškay-wenʔe píʔti we got lost and missed the road

SYN. -qátiw- v.tr. to miss

ʔátmal n., plur. -em a little worm (eats tree trunk)

ʔátukul n. greasewood (used for rheumatism)

ʔátukʷika adv. against the wall inside the house, to the corner; to the dark place

ʔátut n. chokecherry, cf. BandS p. 119-200

ʔávasil̃ n. willow, black willow, cf. BandS p.135

ʔávusil̃ n. a cactus plant

ʔáwa particle 1. (with negative particle kíʔi or kile) if not, otherwise
2. (at the head of the question) what about

CIT. ad 1. pál neˀékama ˀáwa kil̃ neˀékamaxepa ˀen-
mékanem give me water, if you don't
give it to me, I will kill you

ad 2. ˀáwa ˀíye míva híwqal what about your
mother, where is she?

ˀáwa-l n., construct -ˀáwˀa horn of an animal

-ˀáˀaw-lu v.itr. to put on a deer head for hunting
deer

-ˀáwa-k n. one with a big horn

CIT. péqi páˀvuˀul míyaxwen piš pe-ˀáˀaw-lu-pi súkat
ˀáwˀa-y only the great medicine man
can put on the deer horn

ˀáwal n., plur. ˀáˀwal-em, with classif. -ˀaš dog; ˀáˀwal-
em a lineage in Martinez

CIT. ˀáwal ŋáaŋqaleve wáw wáw yáxqal when a dog cries
(=barks), it says 'wáw' 'wáw'

ˀáwsun adv. above, way up

ˀáwsun-ika adv. way up

ˀáwsun-ŋa adv. above

ˀáwsun-ŋa-x adv. from above

CIT. kíš ˀáwsun above the house, on the roof

ˀáwsun ˀeemčíˀanwe lit. they put you high above
to sit; they respect you

ˀáwta adv. on the upper ground; PlN Nelson Camp
in Los Coyotes Reservation

ˀáwta-ika adv. to the upper ground

ˀáwta-ŋa-x adv. from the upper ground

ˀáwta-ˀat n. a family name (= Aug. Lomas) lit. one
which is on the upper ground

-ˀáwuwey- v.itr. with -sun 'heart' as 1st member of compound see -sun

ˀáy adv., VAR ˀáy-ax already

-ˀáy- v.tr. to pick from a tree (fruit, beans, etc.)

-ˀáy-ikaw- to pick here and there

-ˀáy-ˀa n. [construct] that which is picked; harvest

ˀáy-iš n. one who picked

ˀáy-ivaˀal n.: paˀ ___ picking place

ˀáy-ivaš/-iwet n. picker

CIT. nenékene nekíˀiway pen-ˀáy-ik I came to pick what I have been waiting for

ˀáyamal̃ n. raccoon

-ˀáyaw- v.tr., ALLOM. -ˀáyu-, -ˀáywa-, -ˀáyw- 1. to be fond of, to love 2. to want (to do sth.)

ˀáywa-nax n. one who is supposed to want to do

-ˀáyaw-ˀa n. that which one likes

ˀáyw-iš n. one who likes

CIT. ad 1. ne-ˀáyaw-ˀa wíwiš acorn mush is what I like

ad 2. pen-ˀáyaw-qal wíwiči I want acorn mush

pen-ˀáyaw-qal penméknik I want to kill him (going to do it right now)

pen-ˀáyaw-qal piš penméknap I want to kill (thinking about the possibility)

-ˀáyaw- v.itr. with a preceding verb stem as first member of verbal group to do almost

-ˀáˀyaw-an- distrib.

CIT. hemsèˀŋaxlaw ˀáyaw-ˀih they almost got late

-ˀáyax- v.itr., ALLOM. -ˀáyxa- in -ˀáyxa-ne caus., 1. to be alike, resemble 2. to seem that ...

-ˀáˀayax- distrib. many individ. subj.

-ˀáyxa-ne- caus. to make like, to fix in the way like

ˀínis ˀáyax-wen a little

CIT. ad 1. ˀí láapisi ˀáyax-wen this looks like a pencil

ad 2. qamívi ˀáyax-wen piš hílk^{w}iveh lit. what is it like that it is wide; how wide is it?

híšte henhíwniška ˀáyax-we I thought I was going to stay (but I am not)

ˀáyil̃ n. turtle

-ˀál̃mu- v.itr. to speak the Diegueño language

ˀál̃mu-ka(t) n.,plur. **ˀál̃mu-kat-em** a Diegueño Indian

ˀál̃mu-at n. Diegueño language

ˀày qapév adv. (AL known but not used), VAR. ˀayqapév almost

CIT. ˀayqapév píčik he is almost going to arrive, it is about the time for him to arrive

ˀày qapév súpl̃i táwpaxiš nánvayaqa piš taxčemtéewive it is almost a year that we saw each other

-ˀáˀalxe- v.itr. to tell a true story

ˀáˀalxe-at/-il̃ n. a true story

ˀáˀalxe- vaš/wet n. story-teller

ˀáˀalxe-wen-et n. true story, story telling

Cf. -sel̃nliščе- v.tr. to tell a tale

CIT. níye čemik ˀáˀalxe-qal my mother tells us a true story

ˀáˀalxe-at piyk míyaxwen there is a story about it

ˀáˀamivam, see ˀáˀavuˀwet

-ʔáʔas- v.itr., ALLOM. -ʔás- in caus. to bathe, take a bath
-ʔás-ni- caus. to bathe sbdy
-ʔás-ni-law- caus. to take sbdy to bathe
ʔás-ne-ʔil̃ n. baptism
ʔáʔas-vaʔal n. bathing place

ʔáʔaviva VAR. ʔáʔayviva elder

-ʔáʔavuk- v.itr. to grow; to get old
SYN. -wél- to grow
CIT. ʔí kíʔat ʔáʔavuk-qal wélqal this child is growing and getting big

ʔáʔavuʔwet n. supplet. sing., ʔaʔamivam plur. elder; aged person
CIT. néʔ ʔéiy ʔeta hen-ʔáʔavuwet I am older than you

ʔáʔawet n. fly, cf. píʔpiš horsefly

ʔáʔčaʔčem PN a clan's name

C

ča adv., ALLOM. čaqe just
čaqe múka lit. just die in doing sth.; barely do sth., cf. péqi yáxik
CIT. čaqe támay penčewáqinpulu I just could tear apart the jaw
čaqe múka penkʷáqaʔle ʔúmun I barely ate it all

-čáʔ- v.itr. to choke

*There are no words in Cahuilla that begin with "B".

čá?-iš n. one who chokes, one who has got sth. stuck in his throat: blue jay

čačáaka n., plur. -tem, VAR. čahčáaka one who is lively, delightful

Cf. muš?íval lazy person

-čáčawa- v.itr. to have T.B.

čáčawa-yl̃ n. T.B.

čáčawa-š n. a T.B. patient

CIT. čáčawa-yl̃ neyáwqal ne?ú?uxqal lit. T.B. gets hold of me, so I am coughing; I have got T.B., so ...

čáh n. tea

SYN. tútut indian tea

-čáka- v.itr. (AL uses -kávaqi-) to lie sideways; to incline sideways (of the new moon)

Cf. -kávaqi- to lie sideways, -túmkaw- to lie on one's belly, -táča- to lie with face up

-čál- v.itr., v.tr., ALLOM. -čáčal- autom redupl. v.itr. to pop off, to come off (as corn, paint); v.tr. to scrape in a short stroke (as dry goods); to shell (as corn grains by twisting two husks together)

čál-va?al n.: piš ___ scraper

SYN. -číl̃ay-

CIT. ?enwéesi pensísayqal pen pen-čáčal-qal I am peeling off the walnuts and shelling them

čálaka n. horned toad

-čáli- v.itr. to hatch (eggs as bunch)

-čášlam- distrib.(many bunches here and there)

-čáli-n- caus. to hatch (eggs as bunch)

-čášlam-i- distrib. and caus. (bunches of eggs here and there)

CIT. gaíina hétiqal wéevuˀum meta me-čáli-n-qal a hen sits on eggs and hatches them

čámiš n. tall wild cherry (prunus helissofolius), BandS p. 119

-čánaa- v.itr. to be curved round (a new moon, dog's tail)

-čančánaa- redupl.

SYN. -káyvaa- to incline being curved

CIT. páŋiš ménil̃ čánaa-qal the new moon is getting round

-čáŋaa- v.itr. to stand up (hairs); to be jagged (rocks)

SYN. -sakʷaa-, -yáŋaa-

-čáŋal- v.itr. also with -pe- (more frequent than simplex) to get stunned (of body); to get weak (esp. dying)

SYN. sám yáx-

CIT. táxaw čáŋal yáxˀe his body got stunned

-čáŋin- v.tr. with -pe-, ALLOM. -pe-čáŋi- with -wen- to stick, to prickle

-pe-čášŋame- distrib.

-čáčaŋ- distrib.

CIT. čúŋal ne-pe-čáŋin-qal a sticker sticks in me

čáŋˀalaŋiš n. plant (tea for ulcers)

-čápi- v.itr., also with -če-, ALLOM. -čáp- in caus. and distrib. with -ʔi to split, to crack (trees, etc.), cf. -pe-xéki to crack (stone, glass, etc.)

-čápayn- distrib., caus. and distrib. with -ʔi

-čášpam- distrib. to split (many subj.)

-čápi-n- caus.

-čášpame- caus. and distrib; VAR. -čáčap- to split (many indiv. obj. into many parts)

-vuk-čápi-n- caus. to split with a stroke

CIT. ʔúmun kélawat če-čášpam-wen many trees are split in many parts

čáqapa interj. so what!

SYN. mínčaʔan

čaqaʔéil̃ adv. Mt.CA., VAR. čaqe-ʔéʔil̃, see čeʔéʔnil̃ Des. Ca. in secret, in a sneaky way

CIT. čaqaʔéʔil̃ nesésemqa I am laughing in a hidden way

-čávayal: he-puš čávayal, see púč-il̃

-čávi- v.itr., supplet., with plur. subj. and with sing. of collect noun, see -púli- for sing. subj. to fall, drop down

-čávi-law- to fall way off

-čávi-ni- caus. to make fall

čávi-iš n. that which is fallen down (leaves, etc.)

color term base + čávi- to fall in a certain color

CIT. yúyat tèviš-čávi-qal the snow falls in white

čáwa-ʔal n., plur. -čáwa-ʔam, construct -čáwʔa rib

-čáwa-ŋa adv. on one's rib, side

-čáwa-ʔi peta on one's rib, side

čáwal n., ALLOM. čáwul that which is jagged (rocks, mountain)

kìš čáwal PlN. lit. house which is jagged; jagged rocks; Whitewater

qàwiš čáwul a jagged mountain

-čáwaqe- v.itr. (=-čáwa-qe- with submorph. -aq-; see -čáway-) to get on hands and knees (about to crawl)

-čáwaqa-n- caus. to make sbdy stay on hands and knees

mu-čáwaqe- v.itr. to get in a crawling position with head first

-mu-čáwaqe-l̃ew- v.itr. to fall on one's hands and knees headfast

-čáway- v.itr.(=-čáwa-y- with submorph. -ay-, see -čáwaqe-) 1. to crawl, 2. to climb (mountain, tree), 3. to ascend (of road)

-čášway- distrib. to climb up and down

-čáway-law- to climb up to the top

-čáway-ni- caus. to make sbdy climb

-pe-čáway- to climb up quickly

pít čáway-wen-et the steep road

pít čáašway-wenet the road which goes up and down; the bumping road

CIT. ad 1. séwet čáway-qa témaŋa the snake is crawling on the ground

ad 2. ʔáwal penémeqal gáatuʔi pe-čáway-qal kélawat piš/peta the dog chased the cat, which climbed up the tree quickly

ad 3. pít čáway-wen the road is steep

-čáwi- v.itr. to become clear, level (sky, land)

-čáwi-n- caus. to clear, to level off

čáwi-wen-et n. an open place

SYN. -čéxi-, -táwi-

CIT. témal čáwi-wen the land is level

čáwiš n. Indian shoes, sandal

CIT. čáwiš newákˀa lit. Indian shoes my shoes; my Indian shoes

-čáx- v.itr. to melt (ice, etc.)

-čáx-ne- caus. to melt

Cf. -séy- to melt **(lard)**; -kéy- to melt (overripened fruit); -xáš- to thaw (snow, ice)

čáxal sound imitation, in periphr. Mt.CA: čáxʋ to splash a little (e.g., a frog jumping into the water)

čáxasiwet n. a monster who lives in Idyllwild

čaxčáaka n. see čačáaka

čáxuu sound imitation, in periphr., see čáxal Des. Ca. to splash; to somersault

čáxwal n., plur. -em lizard (brownish, living among rocks)

-čáy- v.itr., with -sun 'heart' as first member of verbal group, ALLOM. -čáay-, -čáčay- distrib. emphatic more frequent than -čáy- to be happy, to have a good time

-sun+čáy- to be happy

sun+čáay-il̃/-wenet fun, merrymaking

CIT. nésun káviičiwe nésun čáy-we I was surprised and happy

čémsun čáčaay-qa čempáˀweneve páˀvaˀli we are having a good time drinking wine

čáyal n., plur. -em mistletoe, cf. BandS p. 101

-čáyaqi- v.itr. 1. to stick out (out of hole, water, etc.) 2. to peek out

-čáyaq-an caus. to stick sth. out

color term base + čáyaqi- sth. sticks out in a colored appearance; tul-čáyaqi-wen sth. black is stuck out

SYN. -čéki-

CIT. ad 1. híčemi čáyaqi-we pepéeliŋax sth. is sticking out of the newspaper

ad 2. kíˀat čáyaqi-wen kímul pax the kid is peeking through the door

-čáymu- v.itr. to speak Cupeño language

čáymu-at n. Cupeño language

čáymu-ka n., plur. čáymu-kat-em Cupeño Indian

CIT. čáymu-at-i peyˀéˀnankatem they are going to learn the Cupeño language

-čáyu- v.tr. to put on as earrings, to use as earrings

-čáyu-ne- caus. to put earrings on sbdy

čáyu-l n. earring

-čáyu-vi- v.itr. to have earrings on

CIT. qénxətmi men-čáyu-qaˀle I had the beads on as earrings

čáˀa-l n. 1. sieve, 2. trap

CIT. ad 1. penyáčinqal kʷíñili ne-čáˀa-ŋa I sift acorns in my sieve

ad 2. qáxalmi meemhéhwanwen čáˀal pa they trap the quails with a trap

-čáˀaqi- v.itr. (=-čáˀ-aqi- with submorph. -aq-, see -čáˀaš-), ALLOM. -čáˀi- in periphr. to go up, rise (of the sun, smoke, etc.)

-čáča^ʔaqe- distrib. to go up and down, to go up one after another

-čáʔaqa-n- caus. to raise, to lift up

-čáčaqa-n- caus. and distrib.

čáʔaqi-vaš/-wet n. one that typically goes up (e.g. airplane)

CIT. ʔáy támit čáʔaqi-wen the sun is already high

nésun čáʔaqi-qal lit. my heart is going up; my heart is pounding

ʔeháwaway pen-čáʔaq-an-qa mélkiš háwawayñi piyk lit. I raise up your words to the white man's words; I translate your words into English

-čáʔaš- v.itr., in periphr. (=-čáʔ-aš with submorph. -aš-, see -čáʔaqi-; AL: -čáʔaqaš [prob. =-čáʔaq-aš]) to lift oneself up a little and go back to the former position (e.g., while sitting; or in dancing)

čáʔaw-ika adv. sideways, to the side

čáʔaw-ŋax from sides

CIT. kélawat kávakiwe čáʔaw-ika the tree is leaning sideways

čáʔča adv., ALLOM. čáʔči quickly, fast

CIT. máas ʔéʔiy ʔita neʔívawen čáʔči ʔenvukpáčaypulu I am stronger than you, so I could throw you down fast

-čáʔkav- v.itr. with -če- to lift oneself a little

SYN. -čáʔaqaš-

če- prefix to pronoun, adverb, verb just

CIT. če-ʔípa nehíwqal I am/live just here

ʔét če-péʔ pe that is the same

-čéki- v.itr. to stick in

-čéškem- distrib. to stick in (many subj.)

-čéki-n- caus. to insert

SYN. -číki-

CIT. nelápiski pen-pe-čéke-n-qal nenáqŋa I stick my pencil by my ear

-čékma- v.itr. to stick out from between

-čékma-n- caus.

CIT. máis čékma-qa a cornear is coming out between (the stalk and leaf)

-čéleley- v.itr., ALLOM. -čélel-, -čéll- in periphr. to shake (of body)

CIT. četáxalqal man čéleley-qal he is cold and he is shaking

nésun čell yáxqal neyúkiqaleve when I am scared, my heart shakes

-čéli- v.itr. with -wen- to be standing in order

-vuk-čéli- to be standing disorderly

CIT. čaqe vuk-čéli-we they stand disorderly (e.g., bottles of different size)

čemewáva PN., plur. -ˀam Chemehuevi Indian

-čemewávaˀ-l̃u- v.itr. to speak Chemehuevi language

-čémi- v.itr., ALLOM. čémn- with -ik to stop (crying, talking): to be quiet

-čémi-ni- caus. to make sbdy stop (crying)

SYN. -téklu- to stop (talking etc.), -qámi- to stop (working, etc.), -wéwen- to stop (running)

CIT. ne-čéme-qal neŋáaŋqaleve I stopped crying

-čénen- v.itr., also with -pe-; v.tr., also with -pe-, -vuk-, ALLOM. -čénn- in periphr. (for a slow motion, otherwise -čénen-) to roll (of sth. circular)

-čénen-an- distrib. to keep rolling

-pe-čénen-an- distrib. to keep rolling (by pushing)

čénen-vel n. wheel

SYN. -mána- to roll (of globular shapes)

-čéŋen- v. ALLOM. -čéŋeʔ in imper. sing. v.itr. to dance; v.tr. to kick Mt.Ca., see -híŋ- Des.Ca.

-čéčeŋ- distrib. to kick many times

čéŋeʔn-at/-il̃ n. dance

čéŋen-vaʔal n. pa ___ dancing place

čéŋen-wet n. dancer

CIT. ne-čéŋen-qa néʔiŋa he kicks me on the leg

čepév adj. true

čepév-kʷal n. truth

CIT. míyaxwen piš pentétiyaxpi čepév-kʷal-i I have to tell the truth

-čéqi- v.itr. (cf. -čéki-) to stick between

-čéqi-n- caus. -čéq- in periphr. to stick between

-čéqi-vi- to put on diapers

čéqi-vel n. diapers

CIT. táxŋa čéq penyáxeqal lit. I am sticking it on myself; I am putting my diapers on

-čéx- v.itr. to die with plur. subj., see -múk-

-čéxi- v.itr. to clear up (sky, water)

-čéxi-n- caus.

CIT. wéwniš yúpiqa yéŋil̃ewpa túkvaš čéxi-qa it gets cloudy, later the sky clears up

čéxi-weʔ kútašʔa his words are clear

CIT. nésun čéxx yáxqal lit. my heart gets cleared up; I feel fine

čéxyaˀam n. the Great Bear (7 stars)

-čéˀeqi- v.itr. (=-čéˀ-eqi- with submorph. -aq-, see -čéˀeš-), ALLOM. -čeˀ-e in periphr. to raise oneself slightly up from the lying position

-čéˀeš- v.itr. (=-čeˀeš- with submorph. -aš-, see -čéˀeqi-), in periphr. to raise oneself slightly up and go back to the lying position

čeˀéˀnil̃ adv., see čaqaˀeíl̃ Mt.Ca. secretly, in a sneaky way

CIT. péˀčeˀéˀnil̃ páxqal kíŋa he sneaked into the house

číčikat n. rattle of the snake

-číkav- v.tr.; also with -če-, -vuk- to pinch (as body parts), to pick a little (flowers)

-číškavan- distrib.

ne-če-číkav-qal némaŋa he pinches me on my hand

-číki- v.itr. with -wen- to stick in, to stand (post,etc.)

-číškim- distrib.

-číki-n- caus. to stick in, to put in (post, pole)

-číškim-i- caus. and distrib.

color term base + číki- v.itr. to stick in in a colored appearance: teviš-číki-wen sth. white is sticking

CIT. ˀékʷašmal číki-we lit. the boy is stuck in; the boy is standing too long

qáwiš číškim-we rocks are sticking out

súwelwe číkk súwelwe číkk hémyaxwen somersault stand somersault stand they are doing (Texts, p. 95)

číki-ma adj., VAR. číkiˀ-ma, thick and heavy (wood, coat,etc.)

číki-wet n. one which is thick

CIT. kélawet číkiˀ-ma the wood is thick and heavy

čikišl̃am n. nettle, cf. BandS, p. 143

-čík^{w}a- v.itr., ALLOM. -číšk^{w}ay- autom. redupl. to walk with a walking stick

čík^{w}a-pi n. a walking stick

-čík^{w}a- v.itr. to get stiff (body, starched clothes)

-čík^{w}al- v.itr. with -pe- to stumble over

ne-pe-čík^{w}al-qal qáwiš peta I stumble over a stone

čílčil sound imitation in periphr. to sound (of the rattle)

-čĩ́lay- v.tr. Des. Ca., see -táš- Mt.Ca., ALLOM. -čišl̃ay- autom. redupl. to shell (nuts, corn, etc.)

SYN. -čál-

CIT. ˀenwéesi pen-čišl̃ay-qal sávaˀi I am shelling walnuts

číma n. branch of a tree

CIT. súpl̃i číˀawen kélawet číma-i peta one (bird) is sitting (perching) on a branch of the tree

-čínˀa n., construct hollow of the knee

-číŋal- v.itr. with -wen-, ALLOM. číŋaliŋa in periphr. to be curly (hairs, etc.)

-číšŋal- distrib.

-číŋay- v.itr., ALLOM. -číšŋay- autom. redupl.
to limp, to hop

-číšŋay-ni- caus.

CIT. héʔi kʷánaŋ číšŋay-qa he is hopping on one leg

číŋaay interj. surprise

číŋaay qíčili peyáwqa wow, he has got money!

číŋil̃ n., plur. -am; construct, sing., plur. -číŋim
vulva

-čípal- v.itr., v.tr., also with -če- to chip, to notch (rock, pots)

-číčip- distrib. in periphr.

CIT. neʔúuyaki ʔáy če-čípal-ʔi my olla chipped

čípatma-l n., plur. -l-em; distrib. čišpatmal, construct -čípatma, with classif. -méxanʔa
open basket for sifting

CIT. péy čípatma-l piš pekétqal he covered it with the flat basket

-čípi- v.itr. to get covered (hole)

-číšpi-m- distrib.

-čípi-n- caus. to cover

-vuk-čípi-n- to cover up; to throw, scatter (sands, pebbles etc.)

-vuk-číšpaan- caus. and distrib.

SYN. -kúy- v.tr. to cover (hole)

CIT. ŋáčiči pen-vuk-čípi-n-qal ʔáwsunika I scattered the sands up in the sky

témal piš pen-vuk-čípi-n-qal lit. I covered him with dirt; I threw dirt on him

-číšxin- v.tr., ALLOM. -číšxiŋ- to tattoo

-číšxin-ˀa n. [construct] tattoo

číšxiŋ-il̃ n. tattooing

CIT. náñišmal̃em meem-číšxin-wen hémpuči they tattooed the girls on their faces

číšxiniš n., plur. číšxinč-em twin

CIT. číšxiniš ˀet he is a twin

čívniš n. yerba mansa, cf. BandS,p. 38

číya-t n., plur. -em, construct -číyˀa, plur. -číya-m bundle of feathers

CIT. číyat-em meman hemčéŋenwe they dance with the bundles of feathers

-číˀ- v.itr., v.tr., ALLOM. -číče-, -číča- autom. redupl. to pick to gather from the ground (e.g. acorns)

číˀat n. what was picked

číˀ-avaˀal n.: pa ___ picking place

číˀ-ivaš/-iwet picker

SYN. -ˀay- to pick from the tree, -yékaw- to gather from the tree

-číˀa- v.itr. to sit (e.g. on a chair), to sit upright (on the ground)

-číčeˀa- distrib.

-číˀa-ne- caus. to make sit, to put on a high place (e.g. on horseback, etc.)

-číčeˀ-an- caus. and distrib.

-číˀa+pis- lit. to sit up and come out; to get over the hump

CIT. neñášqa témaŋa ne-číˀa-we I sat down on the ground and I am sitting upright číˀaš n., plur. číˀač-em   a Mexican

-čúk- v.tr.   to claw (cat, etc.), to stick (bur); to grab a handful of sth.

-čúškan- distrib.

-čúčuk- distrib.   to peck (of bird as fruit)

CIT. gáato ne-čúk-qa man nečesálinqa   the cat claws and scratches me

néмay piš kʷíñili pen-čúk-qa   I grabbed a handful of acorns

čúkal n.   jumping cactus, sticker, cf. BandS, p.96

SYN. čúŋal n., ˀíwyal n.

čúkay- v.tr. with -pe-   to peck (of birds)

-pe-čúškayan- distrib.

CIT. ˀáswet ne-pe-čúkay-qa (hémuy piš) the eagle pecks me (with its beak)

čúkaˀwalla n.   lizard (big with rough body, good to eat)

čúkinapi-š n., construct -čúkinapi   bow, gun

CIT. pečehúlulqal čúkinapič-i   he pulled the gun

-čúkla- v.itr., also with -pe-   to jump and stick (prickle, etc.), to claw (cat with its four paws

CIT. piš/piyik čúkla yáxqal   it sticks to it

-čúmi- v.itr.   to finish

-čúšmum- distrib.

-čúma-law-   to run out, to be gone, to die

-čúmi-n- caus.   to finish, to complete, cf. -sičúmin- to think

-čúšmum-i- caus. and distrib.

-čúmi-l̃ew- caus. (čúmi-n-law-) to finish up completely

ménil̃ tax-čúmi-l̃ew-iš lit. the moon which finished up itself; the full moon

CIT. kil̃e híčeʔa ʔáy ʔúmun čúma-law-qal nothing ran out

húnwet tax-ne-čúmi-n-qal lit. I finish myself as a bear; I change myself into a bear

-čúŋ- v.tr., ALLOM. -čúčuŋ- autom. redupl. to suck (of humming bird)

-čúŋ-in- caus., also with -ke- (more frequent than simplex)

-ke-čúšŋame-/-ke-čúšŋaan- caus. and distrib. to kiss

CIT. túčil̃ pe-čúčuŋ-qa séʔiči a humming bird is sucking a flower

čúŋal n. sticker, thorn; jumping cactus

SYN. čúkal, ʔíwyal

CIT. čúŋal nepečáŋinqal a sticker sticks me

ʔíwyalŋa čúŋal-ŋa máluqa he put his hand on prickles and thorns

čúuŋiš n. liar Mt.Ca.; see tamakéñiš Des.Ca.

-čúuŋiš-l̃ew- v.itr. to tell lies

CIT. piyk ne-čú-ŋiš-l̃ew-qal piš nehíčive píka I told him a lie that I went there

čúp čúp sound imitation in periphr. to chirp (as mocking bird, sparrow)

-čúpaq- v.itr., v.tr. with -pe- to stick in (e.g., in body, mud)

-pe-čúšpaan- distrib.

SYN. -petépiš- v.itr.

CIT. ne-pe-čúpaq-al yúliš pa I have got stuck in the mud

ˀíwyal nemay neqáčinqal pečúpaq-al penhúqinqal a thorn poked my hand, stuck into it, so I pulled it out

-čúpi- v.itr. to dip in the water

-čúpi-n- caus. to dip, to soak; to dye

-čúšpum- distrib.

-čúšpume- caus. and distrib. (many obj./many times)

-čúšpayan- caus. and distrib. (many obj.)

SYN. -ˀúpi- to dive

CIT. tax-hen-čúpi-n-ka lit. I am going to dip myself in the water; I am going to bathe

-čúpul- v.itr. in periphr., also with -pe-, ALLOM. -pe-= čúšpulan- autom. redupl. to bubble up

-čúq- v.tr., ALLOM. -čúčuq- autom. redupl. to pound, to mince (meat)

-čút- v.tr. to burn; to brand (e.g., animals)

-čúštan- distrib. many indiv. obj.

SYN. -kína- v.itr., -ná- v.itr.

CIT. kúˀti peemčexélewen peemčútwen pen náqal ˀúmun kínaqal they struck a match and burned it, it started to burn and burned

némaŋa ne-čút-qa kút I have got burned on my hand by fire

-čúvaqi- v.itr., VAR. -čúˀvaqi-, ALLOM. čúviš (prob. =-čúv-iš- with submorph. -aš-) in periphr. to stoop down, to squat down

-čúvi- v.itr., also with -če-, ALLOM. -čúvul- (=-čúvu-l with submorph. -al-) in periphr. to untie (of string, button, etc.); to come off (of shoes, clothes)

-čúvi-n- caus. to untie, to take off

-čúšvumi-/-čúšvaan- caus. and distrib. (many indiv. obj.)

-če-čúšvum-/-če-čúšvaan- v.itr. distrib.

SYN. -húăs- v.tr. to take off; -tũčin- v.tr. to tie

CIT. tax-ne-čúvi-n-qal ˀúmun nexélay súpuli pa penáminka qáyiweneti I take off my clothes to change them for the clean ones

pásukati pentúčinˀi kélawat piyik yan čikóoti če-čúvi-ˀi čaqa ném I tied the horse to the tree but the string untied and it is loose

čúviwenet n. small change, dime; cf. sélekiš one cent, púunku fifty cents (prob. čúvi-wen-et lit. one which is loosened)

-čúx- v.itr. to disappear, to vanish from sight

-čúx-law- to go over and disappear

-čúx-ne- caus. to make disappear

SYN. -sáwaa v.itr. to disappear, to be out of existence

-čúˀan- v.tr., ALLOM. -čúwayn- distrib. with -ka and (ke)-čúˀi- imper. to spit (saliva)

-čúčux-/-čúuˀan- distrib.

-ke-čúˀan- to spit out (esp. on sbdy)

-ke-čúčux- distrib.

SYN. -qépax- v.tr. to spit out

CIT. kíkitam taxta pem-čúčux-wen the kids are spitting on each other

neta pe-ke-čúˀan-qal háñay he spits his saliva on me

D

-déeve- v.tr. span. to owe sbdy

CIT. ˀe-n-déeve-qal qíčil̃ I owe you money

dióos n. Span. God

SYN. ˀámnaˀa n. great one

domíŋgo n. span. Sunday

dúulsi n. span. candy

E

-ˀékamax- v.tr., ˀékamax-aw imper. obj. 3 pers. plur; obj. pref. does not occur with 3 pers. in imper. to give sbdy (food, drinks; otherwise -máx-)

-ˀékamax-ˀa n. [construct] that which was given by sbdy to sbdy; neem-ˀékamax-ˀa that which they gave me

ˀék^{w}ašmal n., plur. -em boy

ˀék^{w}al (intimate), ˀék^{w}asal̃ (most intimate)

-ˀéla- v.tr. to put on (dress), to wear

-ˀéˀla- distrib.

-ˀéla-ni- caus. to put dress on sbdy

ˀéla-t n., construct -ˀélˀa dress

-ˀéla-vi- v.itr. to put on dress

SYN. -xél̃apeta ne-ˀéla-vi-ve lit. the one on whom I got dressed; my deceased father (by daughter) cf. peta newélve (by son)

CIT. neˀéla-y pen-ˀéla-qa I am wearing my dress

-ˀéle- v.itr., v.tr. to blow (wind or air)

-ˀéli-ne- caus. to make blow (as wind)

ˀéel yàxiš n. breeze

CIT. yáˀi čeme-ˀéle-qal the wind is blowing on us

ˀeléle-ma adj., ALLOM. ˀelél in ˀelél-kʷ-iš/-enet/-imal̃ bad, wrong, not right

ˀeléle interj. by women for surprise, etc., cf. ˀáasia by men

-ˀeléle-kʷ- v.itr. to get bad

-ˀeléle-kʷ-ene- caus. to make bad, to damage

ˀelél-kʷ-enet n. being bad

ˀelél-kʷ-iš n. bad person/thing (not good in any manner or degree)

ˀelél-kʷ-imal̃ n. ugly person

CIT. nésun piš ˀeléle-kʷ-al híčeqalepa lit. my heart gets bad about him when he is gone; I am worried about him

ˀésun ˀelél-kʷ-iš lit. your heart is bad; you are feeling sorry/sad

ˀelél-kʷ-ič-i neyik/neta pekúkulqal he did sth. against me

ˀelél-kʷ-iš neméxanˀa I have got bad luck

-ˀéliš- v.itr. usually in periphr., VAR. -ˀéleš- to look back

CIT. ˀéleeš níyaxˀi pentéhuyk húŋayka I looked back slowly to see behind

ˀélka adj., plur. ˀéˀelkat-em pretty, beautiful, young (girl); cf. pašwéliš handsome young man ˀel̃ka (intimate term: AL's mother, uncle, sister used to call her)

ˀélka-lu- v.itr. to grow up and become womanlike (a girl)

ˀélka ménil̃ girl moon = the moon

-ˀéme- v.itr., VAR. -ˀémi- 1. to feel hot 2. to get burned (body parts)

ˀémi-iš n. one who got burned

Cf. -síw- v.itr. to be hot, -čút- v.tr. to burn

CIT. ad 1. ˀívˀax síwma ˀáčaˀe ne-ˀéme-qal now it is very hot, so I feel hot

ad 2. ne-ˀémi-qa némaŋa kút piš I got burned in my hand with fire = némaŋa nečútqa kút the fire burned me in the hand

-ˀéme- v.itr. (KS dnkn.) to get bent, crooked (of body)

ˀémi-iš n. one who is bent

-ˀémiš- v.itr. to be mistaken (recognizing persons)

SYN. -táˀal- v.itr.

CIT. tu hen-ˀémiš-ka lit. I am just going to be mistaken; if I am not mistaken

ˀénene adj. bitter

ˀénene-kat n. bitter stuff

pal ˀénene-ka lit. bitter water; beer

kélawat ˀénene-ka bitter tree (esp. elephant tree)

ˀesan adv. clitic, ALLOM. san; ˀesánem, ˀesáxnem (usually at the end of the sentence) maybe, probably 1. statement 2. interr. (indirect) I wonder ... 3. conditional

CIT. ad 1. háa pál ˀesánem or maybe it is water

CIT. ad 2. qamík ˀesan táwpaki ˀét how old are youˀ
ad 2. qamíyaxwe san piš wáwkive how big it/he is?
ad 3. táxliswet ˀesán pen ˀaxpáxnem lit. maybe he is an Indian and he will go in; if he is an Indian, he will go in

ˀestúˀiš n., plur. ˀestúˀič-em water melon

SYN. sandíiya span.

ˀeswéerta n. span. good luck (as in playing games)

CIT. nemáxnem ˀeswéerta piš taxhenmúknika taxnenénenqaleve he will give me a good luck so that I can win the hiding game (peon)

ˀét demonstr., ALLOM. ˀévat 2nd/3rd pers. sing.: you, he, it; cf. ˀí for proximity; péˀ for distance

ˀéte interj. ouch!

-ˀétel- v.tr. to push (to make sbdy to fall)

-če-ˀétel- to shove

-pe-ˀétel- to knock down

-vuk-ˀétel- to knock down

-vuk-ˀétalan- distrib.

SYN. -ˀúˀuqan- to push

CIT. ˀétel penyáxeqal kíˀati némay piš I shoved the kid with my hand (to make him fall)

ˀévan adv. way up, high up

CIT. péŋa ˀévan pépih čemñášpuliwen way far there we camped

ˀévat demonstr. see ˀét

-ˀéwi- v.itr. with -pe-, ALLOM. ˀéw in periphr.
to fly, to run with wavelike motion

-pe-ˀéˀwam- distrib. = ˀéw ˀéw in periphr.

-vuk-ˀéwi- to fly over sth. with wavelike motion; to bend backward (of body)

CIT. tékvet pe-ˀéwi-qal témayka a chickenhawk flies down to the ground in a swing

nehúluluy pen-vuk-ˀéwi-n-qal I leaned back

kíˀat peˀívaqal pen ˀéw ˀéw yáxqal the kid runs slowly with wavelike motion

ˀéw-il̃ n., construct -ˀéw blood

-ˀéw-lu- v.itr. to bleed

-ˀew-lu-ni- caus. to do puberty rites for, to initiate girls, subj. and obj. in plur.

-ˀéˀew-lu-ne- caus. and distrib.

ˀéw-lu-vaš/-wet n. that which bleeds all the time (e.g., nose)

-ˀéw-ŋa+muk- lit. to get‿sick in blood; to menstruate = ˀéwil piš -múk-

ˀéw-il̃ penáčiš blood clot

-ˀéx- v.itr. with -ap, -ik to behave in that way

-ˀéx-iči-l̃ew to be leaving, to be on the way

-ˀéx-an- caus. 1. to do sth. like that 2. to do to sbdy. 3. to put away, to remove (as spectacles), cf. -táv- to put on

CIT. páypa hen-ˀéx-ik next time I'll be this way; cf. ad 1. caus. páy pa pen-ˀéx-an-ka next time I'll do like that

me-ˀéx-an-qa miš kúkusqa he does to them like that, viz. he makes fun of them

ˀéxama adv. the other day, some time ago

SYN. yéwi; ˀéxama; ˀívˀax; máwa

ʔéxenuk adv., VAR. ʔéxanuk this/that way

-ʔéyawan- v.tr. to sneak upon (to attack, steal)
CIT. neʔámuqaleve men-ʔéyawan-qa nečéxnapim when I hunt, I stalk my game

ʔéyet n. robber

-ʔéyetu- v.itr., v.tr., VAR. -ʔéytu- to steal, to kidnap
-ʔéyetu-iče- to steal and take off
-ʔéʔyetu- v.tr. to have an affair with sbdy's wife (sneaking into his house)
ʔéyetu-il̃ n. stealing
CIT. tax-hem-ʔéʔyetu-wen they are having affairs

-ʔéyewakʔa n. [construct] chin

ʔéʔexiš n., plur. ʔéʔexič-em one of this kind (sing.); different kinds (plur.)
SYN. téetewkatem different kinds
CIT. ʔúmun ʔéʔexič-em táxliswetem all different Indians

-ʔéʔnan- v.tr. to know, recognize; to learn, to find out
-ʔéʔnan-wen- to be known
ʔéʔnan-il̃ n. knowledge
ʔéʔnan-iš n. one who knows a lot
-ʔéʔnan+pis- lit. to learn - come out; to recognize finally
Cf. -tátvan- v.itr. to recognize; -táʔal-, -ʔémiš- to fail to recognize
CIT. peem-ʔéʔnan-wen piš peemkúlpi néʔati they learn to make a basket

ʔéʔniš-ka(t) adj., plur. -t-em skillful; smart, intelligent
-ʔéʔniš-l̃u- v.itr. to be able to do, to be right at home
ʔéʔniš-ka táxmuwet a good singer

CIT. hen-ʔéʔniš-ka piš neʔámuve   I am skillful in hunting

pen-ʔéʔniš-l̃u-qa piš netáxmuve   I am good at singing

-ʔéʔwa- v.itr.   to sweat

ʔéʔwa-ʔal n., construct -ʔéʔwaʔa   sweat

H

haa conj., VAR. haʔ   1. or 2. in interr.: adds indirect character

CIT. ad 1. ʔáy ʔetwáyikika haa máwa   are you going to eat now or later?

ad 2. híčeʔa haʔ man ŋáaŋqa   what is it that he is crying

háhyut n.   sidewinder, Crotalus cerastes

-háka- v.itr. with -wen-   1. to be roomy (house, etc.)
2. to have openings, to be open (store, etc.)

háka-ma adj.   wide, roomy

háka-n adv.   far away, with a distance

SYN. híl̃ima adj.   wide

CIT. ad 1. ʔí kíš kil̃e háka-wen háxami piš pa túkpi   this house has no room, no one can stay overnight

ad 2. kil̃e mívax háka-wen   there is no opening anywhere

-hákuš- v.   1. v.itr., v.tr. to open (door, window, flower, etc.)
2. v.tr. to take off (hat, cover)

*There are no words in Cahuilla that begin with "F" & "G".

-háhkučam- v.itr. distrib. (many things)

-če-hákuš- v.itr., v.tr. to open clear, way through, suddenly

-hákuč-iče- v.tr. to go away leaving sth. open (as door)

hákuš-vaʔal n. sth. that opens (as door)

piš hákuš-vaʔal n. opener (as key, can opener)

SYN. -ʔáqi- v.itr. to open (especially of clothes, curtain)

CIT. ad 1. ʔívʔax ʔámuil̃ ʔáy hákuš-qal qáxalem míyik the hunting season for quail has already opened now

-hál- v.tr., ALLOM. -háal- autom. redupl. to look for, to search

hálave (gerund) few, scarce (only of food, clothes)

hensunsúnika neméxanʔa hálave I am poor, my belongings are very few

-háalkiši- v.itr., v.tr., with -če- 1. v.itr. to step over, to spread legs over
2. v.tr. to spread (as camera stand)

CIT. ad 1. ne-čeháalkiši-ʔi laméesay peta I stepped over the table spreading my legs

-háman- v. 1. v.itr. to get stage fright
2. v.tr. to avoid sbdy (on account of being ashamed)

-sun+háman- v.itr. to feel ashamed, embarassed variant: -siil+háman-

sun+háman-il̃ n. shame

-sun+háman-iš n. one who is ashamed

CIT. ad 2. ne-sun+háman-qal péʔiš pen-háman-qal I am ashamed, so I avoid him

sun+háman-il̃-ʔi pekúkulqa ʔúmun čemeyk he does a shameful thing to all of us

háni adv. 1. [exhortative] alright, now (often with postpos. -ku, -ta, or particles ʔáy, yan, where the verb is usually in imperative) 2. [in desiderative phrases] (often with particle sáxalu)

CIT. ad 1. háni yan neʔékama kahvée now, give me coffee

ad 2. háni sáxalu kile pehíwñašpi I wish he would not stay (here)

háña-l n. construct -háñʔa saliva, spit

CIT. ne-háñʔa čaqe wáneqa lit. my saliva just flows; the water runs in my mouth

háŋal n. arrowweed

kìš háŋal arrowweed house

-hášla- v.itr. to go to a sweat house

hášlaʔ-il n., construct -hášlaʔ, -hášlaʔ-ki sweat house

hášla-vaʔal n. where one sweats

hátava (gerund) open, clear place

SYN. -čáwi- v.itr. to be clear, open

CIT. ʔí témal hátava this land is open and clear

-háti- v.itr. to shine

-háti-n- caus. to turn on a light; to shine sth.

-háhtem-e- caus. and distrib. to light many times

háti-n-vaʔal n. in piš háti-n-vaʔal sth. to light with (as a flashlight)

háti-wen-et n. brightness, light

color term base + háti- to shine in colored light máviy piš péŋal sel+háti-wen péŋaʔ tákuš at night Takuš shines red over there

Cf. -túk- to go out (light, fire)

hávu-n adv., ALLOM. hávu-n-am Mt.Ca. with plur. subj. quickly, fast

hávu-maniš n., plur. hávu-manič-em one who is quick. fast

SYN. hésun pélewet one who is slow in doing things

CIT. wáqiš hávu-n híči go on, hurry! (sing.), wáqičem hávu-n-am híčyam (plur.) Mt.Ca.

hávumaniš piš wáyikive he is fast at eating

háwa conjunction 1. in conditional 2. but

CIT. ad 1. háwa péqi ʔemúqalepaʔ if you are sick

ad 2. ʔípa kíyaka hawa né he is going to stay here, but not me

-háwaway- v.itr. ALLOM. -háwawaʔ-, with -an-/-ni-/-il̃, háway- with -nik, háwiʔ- with -niš to talk

-háwawaʔ-an- caus. to talk to sbdy

-háhwa- caus. and distrib.

háwaway-at/háwawaʔ-il̃ n., construct -háwaway-a language, word; story

-háwawaʔ-ni n. [construct] language

-háwawaʔ-ni-ŋa adv. in one's language

háwaway-nik/háway-nik n. ceremonial talker

háwiʔ-niš n. ceremonial talker; sth. like a song or story

SYN. -kútaš- to talk

CIT. čemeta hem-háwaway-we lit. they talk upon us; they refuse to give us food/money/ clothes

háwawaʔ-il̃ peyunénmiwet lit. one who takes around the words; one who spreads the gossip

ʔeháwaway penčáʔaqanqal/penpéniičiqal mélkiš háwaway piyk lit. I raise/pass your words to the white man's words; I translate your words into English

-háway- v.itr. to be foggy
 háway-š n. mist, fog
 SYN. múlul-iš mist, fog
 CIT. múlulqa háway-qa paamwénive it is steaming and foggy at the place where they are lying (from a wake-song)

-háawi- v.itr., VAR. -háaw- to cry, mock (of bird)
 CIT. támawet háawi-qal a mocking bird is talking

háaxal̃uš n. crippled person
 SYN. lúumiš

háxʔi pron., plur. háxʔi-m, ALLOM. háxa- who, whose in interr.

 qa-háxʔi in indir. interr.
 háxa-mi(vi), plur. háxa-mivi-m someone
 háxa-teteʔ what is he called? cf. híči-tete? what is it called?

-háy- v.itr. to end, to come to an end
 -háy-l̃ew- to stand still, to come to an end
 háy-va/háy-wen-iva adv. at the edge
  háy-va-x adv. at the edge
 háy-ve adv. at the edge, last, the last time
 háy-iwenet n. the end
 CIT. népuš pexékiqa háy-va-x my glasses got cracked at the edge

-háay- v.itr. to cry (of quail)
 CIT. qáxal háay-qal quail is crying

-háyin- v.tr. to be tired; to exhaust
 -háhyami- distrib. to be really/always tired

háyin-at n. fatigue

-háyin-iš n. tired person; one who can't finish

-sun+háhyam- v.tr. lit. to make heart-tired; to threaten

tax-sun+háyamni-wet n. threatener

CIT. pen-háyin-qa kil̃e míyaxwen piš ˀenhúvanip lit. I exhausted it, but I cannot cure you; I did everything that I could ...

wáyikiwenet me-háyin-qa lit. food exhausted them; they ran out of food

háytaa magic word (?) (used in contrast to húyta, see Texts, p. 83)

-háyu- v.tr. to doubt sbdy

mey-háyu-š PN doubter; challenger

-háayu- v.tr. with recipr. obj. -tax-, ALLOM. -háhyu-/-háxyu- to compete (as of two witches against each other); to bet

tax-háxyu-qalet n. one who is going to be the best witch

CIT. tax-čem-háhyu-wen háxˀi más yáˀik we betted who is the faster runner

-háˀtis- v.itr. to sneeze

-hée- v.itr. to make noise (bird)

hée adv. yes

SYN. kíˀi no

-hékik n., plur. -t-em owner of the house, cf. kiš 'house' (hé-ki+-k suff.)

CIT. néˀ pen-hékik I am the owner of the house

-héli- v.itr. with -wen-, ALLOM. -héla- in caus. to be spread (as of clothes on sth.)

-héhlem- distrib. many places/ many subj.

-héli-n-/-héla-an- caus. to spread

-hehleme- caus. and distrib. many subj.

-vuk-héli- to be spread over sth.

SYN. -híye°an- v.tr. to spread (as acorns)
-pélaan- v.tr. to spread (as fan)

color-term base + héli- to spread in a colored appearance

teviš-héli-wen sth. white is spread

CIT. híče°a pé° man vuk-héli-wen séerka°ay peta what is it that spreads over the fence°

nexẽlay pen-héla°-an-qal wáxakati I spread my clothes to dry them

héma adv. clitic 1. probably 2. if (in indir. question)

CIT. ad 1. ha péqi ča° mey°ékamxik °áča°e héma or maybe he will just give it to them

ad 2. pen°áyawqal penámaynik penk^wáik hema kénma piš míyaxwenive I want to try to eat it (to see) if it is delicious

hémax adv.

hémaŋax therefore, that's why (prob. = hé- 'his', -ma 'hand', -x/ŋax 'from')

CIT. nesunhámanqa nekúlve hémaŋax I am ashamed on account of my doing

-hémi- v.itr. with -če- to collapse crumbling (as of grass house, bush, etc.)

-če-héhmem-/-če-héhmaan- distrib. (many subj.)

-hémi-n- caus., also with -če- to wreck, knock down

-héhmeme- caus. and distrib. (many obj.), also with -če-, VAR. -hémayan- with -°i, also with -če

SYN. -čelápaš- v.itr. to collapse

hému n. end, edge, tip

hému-ŋa/-ʔan adv. at the end of

hému-yka to the end of

tèmal hému-ʔan at the end of the earth

CIT. neʔúuyaki hému-ʔan četáliqal my olla is broken on the neck

héena interj. oh yes! oh my goodness (Mt.Ca.)

hénil n. ribbonwood, cf. BandS, p. 30-31

-héñew- v.itr. to get angry, mad

héñiw-aŋa adv. in anger

čaqe/če-héñiw yáxi-vaš/-wet one who is quick, bad tempered

CIT. neyk héñew-qaʔa yéyan hésun yémiʔi he was mad at me but he got calmed down

-héeñiw- v.itr. to fight

héeñiw-il n. fight, war, battle

héeñiw-vaʔal n. war

piš héeñiw-vaʔal weapon

héeñiw-vaš n. fighter

CIT. niyk héeñiw-qal he fights with me

-hépaak n. with P_2 aunt

hépal n. with classif. -wénʔa soup

-héq- v.itr. to cool off (food, etc.)

-héq-ni- caus. to cool off

SYN. -yučíwi- v.itr. to cool off (weather)

héspe-n adv. very much, hard; fast

-héspe-k^w- v.itr. to harden (as of earth in pottery)

héspe-ma adj. hard (rock, etc.); difficult

Cf. héveve soft; pẽlen slow

CIT. néˀ héspe-n pensičúminqal ˀíyey I was thinking about your mother a lot

-héespekuš n. with če-, plur. če-héespekč-em (cf. héspe-n) that which is stiff, frozen (as ice)

-héti- v.itr. to stretch out (of long slim object; of bird on the nest)

-héhtem- distrib. many indiv. subj.

-héti-n- caus. to stretch out

héti-wenet n. line

color-term base + héti- to stretch out in a colored appearance; sámat tukiš-héti-we a strip of green grass is there

Cf. -péti- v.itr. to stretch out (of long big obj., e.g., log)

CIT. témaŋa séwet héti-wen a snake is stretching out on the ground

hétu adv., VAR. hétum, hémutum at all, what on earth (as surprise, in question); cf. tu

CIT. qahíčeam hémutum ˀétem who are they?

héveve (gerund) soft

héveve-ˀil̃ n. that which is soft (as ground)

Cf. héspema adv. hard

héveveqalet n. big butterfly

-héwaš- v.itr. with -če- to have a cramp (spreading on wide area esp. on the side)

-héx- v.itr., see híyax-

-héw- v. v.itr. to weave (of spider), to trap; v.tr. to trap

-héhwan- caus. and distrib. to trap (as animals), to catch (with net as fish)

héw-ʔa n. web

héwne-vaš n. fisherman

kíyulem piš meem-héhwan-wenive sth. with which they catch fish

-héeʔan- v.tr. 1. to believe sbdy 2. to agree on sth.

-héeʔan-ʔa n., [construct] sth. believed

-héeʔan-vaš/wet n. with recipr. obj. -tax- one who believes people, believer

CIT. ad 1. pečem-héeʔan-wen dióos we believe in God

ad 2. péʔiy peem-héeʔan-wen they agreed on it

híčeʔa pron. interr., VAR. híčʔa/híčaxa what

qa-híčeʔa pron. indef.

ʔámnaʔam qa-híčea-m great beings

CIT. híčeʔa pen ʔíʔ what is this?

híčeʔa súpul what else?

-híči- v.itr. to go (on foot, on horseback, on a vehicle)

-híišče- distrib. to go back and forth, to go often

-híči-n- caus. to make walk

híči-qal-et n.: húyal hémuʔan híče-qal-et lit. that which goes at the point of the arrow; arrow head, cf. sivat híči-wen-et n. that which is going (as road)

-sun+híišče- lit. heart + go often; to wish
piš nesun-híišče-qal lit. around it my heart goes often; I wish/want it badly

CIT. pax híče-ʔi kínaŋaʔay lit. he went from his wife; he left her

péʔpi piš pa híči-pi it is a long way to go

pépi pa híči-wen-et ʔáʔalxiwenet lit. a long way to go a story; a story which takes a long time to tell

meta híči-ʔi lit. he went upon them; he got away from them

-híkus- v.itr. to breathe; to take a rest

hikus+témi- v.itr. lit. to breathe + close; to suffocate

híkusa-l n., construct -híkusʔa soft spot (on the baby's head), fontanel

híl̃e-n adv., ALLOM. -híl̃- wide, widely

híl̃e-ma adj. wide (of clothes, ground, house)

-híl̃-kʷ- v.itr. to be wide

-híl̃-kʷ-ine- caus. to make wide

-híil̃-kʷ-ine- caus. and distrib.

híl̃e-wet n. that which is wide, roomy

CIT. híl̃e-n pewálina dig it wide

qamívi ʔáyaxwen piš híl̃-kʷi-ve I wonder how wide it is

-híŋ- v.itr. to fly, to jump; to kick; to bark Mt.Ca., cf. -wéwex- Des.Ca.

-híiŋ- distrib.

-híŋ-iči- to flee, run away

híŋ-iči-š n. refugee

híŋ-ivaš n.: qíŋiš híŋ-ivaš flying squirrel

híŋ-iwet n. airplane

CIT. piyik hem-híŋ-weʔne they jumped on him / kicked him

peta hen-híŋ-ik sívuyʔli I am going to step on a worm

hem-híŋ-iči-wen súpul témal piyk they fled to another land

-híisaxve n. [construct] belongings (as clothes, etc.)

SYN. méxanat

híšte Mt.Ca., ʔíste Des.Ca. 1. (with ʔáyaxwen) as if ..., it seems that ... but it isn't
2. (in question) do you remember that ...

CIT. ad 1. kúktašqal ʔíste ʔúmun híčemivi peʔéʔnanqal ʔáyaxwen he talks as if he knew everything

ad 2. ʔípaʔ yéwi híšte čempeqá remember that we used to be here

-hívin- v.tr., ALLOM. -hív- in periphr., supplet. with plur. obj., see -kús- for sing. obj. to take, get hold of (objects which are not moving)

-híhveme- distrib. to take one by one, take here and there

-híiven- distrib. to take often

-hívin-ikaw- to get one after another

-hívin-ŋi- to come after

hívin-at n. things which have been taken

hívuu (prob. sound imitation) in periphr. with yáʔi 'wind' as subj. to be a breeze

-híw- v.itr. supplet. with sing. subj. and -qal-, ALLOM. -qál- with plur. subj., -máx- with plur. subj. and suff. [-realized] to sit upright; to live, to stay

-qáqal-ŋi- distrib. with plur. subj. to stay here and there

híw-qal-et n. one who lives, e.g., nemáŋax ___ my neighbor

qál-tem n. plur. those who live

CIT. ʔe-híw-ñaš-na ʔáčakʷe lit. stay good; good bye, cf. híwña

-híwen- v.itr. never with verbal derivative suffixes
to be standing; to be (of live plants)
cf. -qál or -wén (when picked or cut down)

híwen-et n. that which is standing

color term base + híwen- to stand in a colored appearance; tul-híwen sth. black is standing (e.g., shadow)

-híwla- v.itr. in compound with color term base as the first component Des.Ca., -híwya- Mt.Ca., ALLOM. -híwi- with suff. -wen-, -híw- in periphr. to turn into (a certain color slightly)

-híhwem- distrib. (one after another)

-híhwi- distrib. with suff. -wen-

-híwla-qal-et n. that which is slightly colored (more frequent than verb form)

-híw yax-iš n. a little colored one; tes-híw-yax-iš yellowish one

SYN. color term base -yúpi-

híwña interjection (= imper. -híw- 'to live')
goodbye!

SYN. -híwñašna ˀáčakʷe stay good!

híwtiniš n. orphan; one who has no place to go

SYN. léepi orphan (Span.)

-híyax- v.itr. supplet. with suffixes [+realized] and -nem Des. Ca., -híya- Mt.Ca., ALLOM. -héx- with suff. [-realized] except -nem
to say what (in question); to say nothing (with kil̃e 'not')

-qa-híyax- (in indir. question): piš ___-ve

SYN. híčeˀa yáx- what ... say ...? kil̃e híčeˀa yáx- nothing ... say.

CIT. nenáanalqal piš qa-híyax-qaleve he asked me what she said

pen ne-híya-ne kil̃ ne-héx-ap míyaxwe well then, what shall I say? There's nothing for me to say

-híysay- v.tr. with recipr. obj. -tax- to take sandbath (e.g., birds) (prob. = -híy- 'spread' -sáy- 'spread, scatter,' cf. -vuk-sáay-)

CIT. wíkikmal̃em tax-hem-híysay-we témaŋa the birds are taking sandbath on the ground

hóopi PN, plur. -m a person of the Hopi tribe

húat n. iodine bush, cf. BandS p. 36

-húkul- v.tr. in periphr., VAR. húk to pinch, to pick (as flowers)

SYN. -číkav- v.tr. to pinch

-húkum- v.itr. with -če- and -sun 'heart' as first member of verbal group, ALLOM. -če-húhkum- autom. redupl. to sob (after having cried, esp. of child; refers to the motion of sucking)

CIT. hésun če-húhkum-qa he is sobbing

húl n. bow

SYN. húyal bow and arrow, čúkinapiš bow, gun

-húlaqan- v.tr. to peek at sbdy (lifting/sticking one's head)

SYN. -čáyʔaqi- v.itr.

CIT. ne-húlaqan-qal he is peeking over at me

-hulhúla- v.itr., ALLOM. húla- with -wet to be pointed (of mountain, rock)

húla-wet n. that which is rugged: qáwiš húla-wet PlN near La Quinta (qáwiš yúlawet Mt.Ca.)

-húlin- v.tr. with -če-, ALLOM. -húl- in periphr. to pull out (the whole thing out of sth.)

SYN. -húlul-, -wípis-

húlul n., VAR. húlulu back (of the body)

húlulu-ŋa adv. in/on the back

húlul puksapúksawet hunchback

-húlul- v.tr., also with -če-, -vuk- to pull sth. (out of a hole, water; out of the roller, like toilet paper)

-húhlume- distrib. to pull out one after another

húlul-at n. that which was pulled out

SYN. -čehúlin- v.tr., -wípis- v.tr.

CIT. káviwenet pax pen-húlul-qaˀle kíˀati I pulled a kid out of a hole

húulvel n. California sagebrush (a tea made of the boiled plant is given to the girls to drink at the initiation), cf. BandS p. 43

-húm- v.itr. to cast off skin (of snake, etc.)

-húm-in- caus. to skin off, to butcher, to dress (as animal)

-húhmum-e- caus. and distrib. many indiv. obj.

-húmay- v.tr. to smear, to paint (on face, house, etc.)

-húhmay- distrib. to smear many times (more frequent than simplex)

húmay-at n. that which is painted, smeared

húmay-vaʔal n.: piš ta-húmay-vaʔal paint, cream

CIT. pen-húhmay-qal tíŋaypiš piš neséqay I smear my shoulder with medecine

tax-hem-húhmay-wen piš taxwíčinvaʔali piš they smear themselves with some spray; they put on perfume

-húmsan- v.tr. to put feathers (e.g., at the end of an arrow)

CIT. húyay piš pe-húmsan-qal he puts feathers around the arrow

-húmulku- v.tr. to wrap around

CIT. kíʔati pen-húmulku-qal xél̃ay piš I wrapped the baby in the blanket (rolling up)

húnal n., plur. húnl-am badger

-húneke- v.itr. to take an Indian bath

húnkat n. elderberry, elder; cf. BandS p. 138

húnuvat n. yucca

húnwe-t n. bear

-húnwe-lu- v.itr. to turn into a bear (= húnwe-t taxčúmin-, s.v. -čúmi-)

húnwe-lu-ʔiš/-s n. one who became a bear

húŋa-yka adv., ALLOM. húŋan- with -ax to the back, way back; afterwards

húŋan-ax adv. behind, in the back

SYN. múči in front of

CIT. híwen ʔĩl húŋan-ax he is standing behind the mesquite tree

né? ne-húŋan-ax néken he is coming behind me

-húpaš- v.tr. to take off, to pull off (as clothes, shoes)

-húhpačan- distrib. (many individ. obj.)

-če-húpaš- v.itr. to come off (of shoes, feathers)

SYN. -čúvin- to untie, to take off

-húqin- v.tr., also with -če- to pull out (sth. bigger than thorn: plants, tooth) [KS: obj. is supposed to be rooted, as tree, tooth, etc., but nowadays some people use also for a sticker stuck in body part]

-húhqame-/-húhqan-/-húhq- distrib. (many indiv. obj.)

Cf. -húš- to pull out (as fine thing: thorn)

-lúpin- to pull out (as handful of grass, feathers)

húsi-l̃ n., construct -húsi/-húsi-a bottom part of the back, tail bone's area, hip

CIT. ne-húsi-a sámm yáqa chill runs in my backbone

-húš- v.tr. to pull out (as sticker, thorn) [KS: now people use -húqin- also for sticker]

-húhčan- distrib. (many indiv. obj.)

SYN. -húqin- to pull out (plants)

-húv- v.itr., ALLOM. -húuv- autom.~vowel lengthening; húʔ- with -il to smell

húʔ-il n. anything that smells; tékʷel húʔ-i sac of a skunk húv-vaš n. that which smells strong

CIT. kénma ʔáčaʔe piš húv-ve ʔeséxʔa your cooking smells delicious

-húva- v.itr. to get cured

-húva-ʔani- caus. to cure

húva-š n. one who has got cured

Cf. -máyew- to doctor

CIT. púul nehúpaʔanqal pepúwaanqal nemúkay peta nehúva-qal the witch doctor sucked, blowed over my sickness and I got well

-húvi- v.tr. to smell sth.

-húhvi- distrib.

-húvi-ni- caus. to make sbdy smell

húwiačet n. sweat house (?)

SYN. hášlaʔil̃

-húyaa- v.itr., VAR. -huy-húya- redupl. to be longish, oblong (bow, head, egg, etc.)

huy-húya-wet n. that which is long

-húya- v.itr. with -če- to be dislocated (of muscles)

SYN. -čepúluš-

húya-l n., plur. -l-em, construct -húya, plur. -huya-m arrow; bow and arrow

húya-l hémuʔan híčeqalet the point of arrow

SYN. húl bow; čúkinapiš bow, gun

húyanaxa-t n., construct húyanaxa (prob. compound húya- + náxat) stick, cane

húyta (prob. húy-ta) magic word (?) (used in contrast to háyta, see Texts, p. 83)

I

-ʔi n. construct 1. leg, foot 2. footstep, track

-ʔi tákʔa heel (prob. sth. pasted to the foot, cf. -táki-)

-ʔi lílikawet bow-legged person

káa hé-ʔi lit. the leg of the car; the wheel of the car

-ʔi káwʔa ankle, cf. -ma káwʔa wrist

-ʔi pétuk^{w}iš lit. sth. under the foot; sole

CIT. ad 1. hé-ʔi k^{w}ánaŋ číšŋayqa lit. the half of his legs is hopping; he is hopping

ad 2. hé-ʔi-ŋa nenéken lit. I came in his footstep; I followed him, I came along with him

-ʔík- v.tr. to hold sbdy (by the hand), some animal (with a chain); to hook sth., to fish (by hooking)

-ʔík-iče- to get hold of sbdy. by the hand and take along

-ʔíʔikan- distrib. to catch many fish; to knit

CIT. pen-ʔík-qalʔe táatwali (hémay piš) I held a blind man (by the hand)

ʔí-ka adv. in this direction

-ʔíkya- v.itr., ALLOM. ʔík-with -ʔil̃, ʔíki- with -wet to be bent like a hook (of nose, beak, etc.)

-ʔík-ʔil̃ n.:mu-/hému ___ that which has a hooked beak

ʔik-ʔíki-wet n.: hému ___ one who has a hooked nose

-ʔík-ʔa n. [construct] stick, cane like shepherd's

CIT. néma ʔik-ʔíkya-qal my arm is curved like a hook

-ʔíka- v.itr. Mt.Ca. to get skinny, to lose one's weight, see -yáwi- Des.Ca.

-ʔíka-ne- caus. to make skinny

ʔíka-š n., plur. ʔíʔika-č-em skinny person

SYN. -sámatlu- to get skinny

ʔíka-t n., plur. -t-em, distrib. ʔíikat, construct -ʔíkʔa carrying net

CIT. neʔúʔyaki pentúkqale ʔíkat piš I carried my olla with a carrying net on my back

-ʔík^W- v.tr. to dip (liquid)

-ʔíik^{W}an- distrib. (many indiv. subj.)

CIT. hépali pičem-ʔík^W-wen kávamal pax we are dipping soup out of the pot

ʔíilu n. Span. (hilo) thread

CIT. penʔúʔlanqal ʔevúuʔuxa ʔíilu-y piš I am sewing it with a needle and thread

ʔíl̃ n., with classif. -kíʔiwʔa mesquite, cf. BandS, p. 107

CIT. ʔíl̃ témaš brush under mesquite trees

ʔínis adv., VAR. ʔíniš Mt.Ca. a little; for a little while

ʔínis ʔáyaxwen   lit. it looks a little; a little, a little while

CIT. túlnek ʔínis ʔáyaxwen it is a little black

peemkúlwenʔe más ʔínis wávuwet lit. they made it more a little long; ... very short

ʔíniš-il̃ n., plur. -il̃-em small one

-ʔíniš-l̃u-k- v.itr. to shrink, to get small

ʔíniš-ik-il̃ n.   one who is small (e.g. baby)

-ʔíniš-ik-l̃u- v.itr. to get small

-ʔíniš-ki-l̃u-ni- caus. to make small

ʔíniš-mal n.   small one

ʔíŋ-il̃ n.   salt

-ʔíŋ+yaw- v.tr.   lit. to hold salt; to salt

ʔíŋ-il̃ pa   lit. where the salt (is); PlN Salton Sea

ʔíŋkiš n., plur. ʔíŋkič-em this kind (prob. ʔí-ŋkiš, cf. péŋki-, míŋki-)

če-ʔíŋkič-em n. plur. the same kind

CIT. ʔíŋkiš paʔ káarŋa nehíčeqal in this kind of car I went

ʔíŋkiš n. with če, plur. ʔíʔiŋkič-em, ALLOM. ʔíŋki with sing. pers. pron. 1. sth. empty; desert 2. unmarried person; person without any family

CIT. ad 2. ʔé če ʔet-ʔíŋki you have no family

ʔí-pa adv.   here (proximate), cf. ʔéŋa and péŋa there

ʔí-pa-ƛ   from here, on this side

-ˀis n. construct tear

CIT. ˀé-ˀis síl̃eqal ˀeŋáaŋqalepa when you cry, your tears run out

ˀísal n., plur. -em meadow lark

ˀísi-l̃ n., plur. ˀísta-m coyote

-ˀísi-lu- v.itr. to turn into a coyote

ˀísiwet n., plur. ˀísiˀwet-/ˀíˀisiwet-em stingy person

-ˀíswalu- v.itr. to become delirious, bizarre; to go out of one's mind temporarily (not becoming insane)

ˀíswalu-š n. delirious person

-ˀíswax- v.tr. with plur. subj. and recipr. obj. to sing against each other (women), cf. -wéx- (men)

ˀíswax-at n. women's hateful song

ˀíswet n., plur. -em wolf

ˀíšva n. the left (as hand)

ˀíšva-yka adv. to the left side

ˀíšva-ŋa-x adv. on the left hand side

CIT. néma ˀíšva-ŋa-x nečepúkušqal I get cramps on my left hand

-ˀíva- v.tr. to run

-ˀíva-ŋi- to run off, (with durat. suff.) to run around

-ˀíva-wet n. with pe- one who likes to run

-yu-ʔíva- v.tr. to run carrying; to kidnap

CIT. pax pe-ʔíva-qal kínaŋay he runs away from his wife

hésun pi-ʔíva-qal héspen lit. his heart is running fast; his heart is pounding fast

-ʔíva- v.itr. with -wen- to be strong

-ʔíva-n- caus. to strengthen, to help (with singing)

ʔíva-ʔal n., construct -ʔíva-ʔa biceps, power

ʔíva-kat n., VAR. -ʔíva-k with sing. pron. pref., plur. ʔíva-kt-em strong person

-ʔívil̃u- v.itr. to talk the Cahuilla language (prob. = ʔívi 'this' -lu- suff. 'to turn into'; to become this/ours)

ʔívil̃u-ʔat n. Cahuilla language

ʔívil̃u-qal-et n., plur. ʔívil̃u-wen-et-em Cahuilla speaking person

CIT. níyk ʔívil̃u-qal he talks to me in the Cahuilla language

ʔíviš n. awl (used for basket making)

CIT. ʔíviš piš penénehqal néʔati I make a basket with a needlelike thing

ʔívʔa-x adv. now; right away

ʔívaʔ-nuk adv. right away

ʔíwya-l n., plur. -l-em thorn, sticker

ʔíwya-ka(t) n. that which has a lot of stickers

SYN. čúŋal, čúkal sticker

-ʔíyax- v.itr., ALLOM. -ʔíya- imper. sing. and in periphr. to be that way; to move (with imperative or directional adv.)

-če-ˀíyax-wen- v.itr. to be just that way

CIT. támit píka ˀíyax-qalepa when the sun moved to that point

-ˀíiyem- v.tr. with plur. subj. and recipr. obj., autom. redupl., see -yím-

ˀíˀ demonstr., ALLOM. ˀívˀi, plur. ˀívi-m this (used to indicate a person, thing, idea, state, event as present, proximate)

ˀíˀexi-š n. (usually preceded by ča(qe) or péqi), plur. ˀíˀexič-em 1. nothing, unimportant one; nonsense 2. desert, wilderness

ˀíˀexi-ŋa adv. in the desert, wilderness

ˀíˀexi-ka adv. to the wilderness

CIT. ad 1. péqi hen-ˀíˀexi-š I am worth nothing

ˀíˀihiŋaviš n., plur. ˀíˀihiŋavič-em different animal

-ˀíˀiklu- v.itr. to want, to be fond of

SYN. -ˀáyaw- v.tr. to like, to want

CIT. miš čem-ˀíˀiklu-wen we like/want them

piš čem-ˀíˀiklu-wen piškúlkatem we want to make it (but we don't know how to)

ˀíˀipiš n., plur. ˀíˀipič-em Mt.Ca., málisap-piš for Des.Ca. doll

-ˀíˀismatu- v.tr. to tease, to joke with (one who is in joke relationship, e.g., aunt, niece, sister-in-law)

tax-ˀíˀismatu-vaš n. teaser

-ˀíˀisne- v.itr., v.tr. 1. v.itr. to write (as a letter)
2. v.tr. to put a design, to paint

ˀíˀisne-at n. construct -ˀíˀisne-a painting

SYN. -kʷáˀisne-

CIT. ad 1. ne-ˀíˀisne-qal piyik I write to him

ad 2. pen-ˀíˀisne-qal népuči tésnat piš I paint my face with yellow clay

ˀíˀive (gerund) without

hésun ˀíˀive lit. without his heart; crazy

hépuš ˀíˀive (= táatwal) blind

náq ˀíˀive (= nàq témel) deaf

táma ˀíˀive dumb

kínaŋa ˀíˀive lit. without his wife; bachelor

-ˀíˀk- v.itr., ALLOM. -ˀíˀik- autom. redupl. Mt.Ca., -málisew- Des.Ca. to play (as ball game)

ˀíˀik-ivač-em n. players

ˀíˀk-il̃ n. game

CIT. ne-ˀíˀik-qa ncˀamíwoki pénew I am playing with my friend

K

-káaka n. construct, plur. -m grandmother, patern. (vocative), cf. -qa

-kákape- v.itr., VAR. -qáqape- to yawn

kákapi-il̃ n. yawning

káal n. Des.Ca., pàl vúkivaš Mt.Ca., crane (white or black)

*There are no words in Cahuilla that begin with "J".

káal n. (KS dnkn.) red clay (used for painting)

káalapi n. afterbirth

kalaváas n. Span., plur. -em pumpkin

-kálaw- v.tr. with -če- to refuse sbdy (to lend, to give, to do a favor)

-če-káklawan- distrib. (many indiv. obj.)

SYN. pe-ta̰ -háwaway- v.itr. to refuse to give (food)

CIT. qíčil̃i neté?eqal pé pen-če-kálaw-qal he asked me to lend him money but I turned him down.

penánalqa pišnemámaywap yan ne-če-kálaw-?i I asked him to help me, but he turned me down

káama? n. Span., construct -káama-ki bed

-kámiš- v.tr. to surround

CIT. ?áy peem-kámiš-wen pé?iy kíiči they surrounded that house

-kanávi- v.itr. to play, to have fun noisily

-kanávi-nḛ- caus. to make play, have fun

kanáve-?il̃ n. fun

-kápal- v., also with -če-, -pe-, -vuk-
1. v.itr. to get a hole, an opening
2. v.tr. to make a hole (through)

-kákpalan- distrib. (many indiv. holes)

-kápalapa- distrib. in periphr. (many holes)

kápal-iš n. hole (e.g., in a pipe)

SYN. -kávin- to make a hole (usually round)

-mupáxul- to drill a hole (as tunnel)

CIT. ad 1. newáqˀa če-kápalˀi my shoe got a hole
ad 2. ˀeyúlukuŋa ˀen-če-kápal-qal I make a hole in your head
ad 2. pen-pe-kápal-ˀi páˀli I dug the water

kápatmal n. Mt.Ca. saucepan (bigger than káputmal)

-kapu-kápu- v.itr. to be crooked (of camel's back, tree, etc.)

káput-il n., distrib. kákput-il (KS dnkn.) a small round basket

káput-mal n. round basket; cup Mt.Ca.
káput-ŋa adv. in the basket
-ma+káput-ŋa lit. hand + in a small basket; wrist

káarne n. Span., construct -káarne-ki meat

SYN. wáˀiš n. meat

-kaskási- v.itr. to give a half-smile (showing off the teeth)
kaskási-wet n. person who gives a half-smile

-kávaqi- v.itr., ALLOM. -kávat- in periphr. to lie on one's side: to lean sideways (of trees, etc.)

-kákvaqi- distrib.
-kávaqa-n- caus. to make lie sideways
kávaqi-vaš/-wet n. one who likes to sleep sideways
color term base + kávaqi- to be lying sideways in a colored appearance; tul+kávaki-wen sth. black is lying sideways

Cf. -čáka- to lie sideways, -táč- to lie with face up, -túmkaw- to lie on one's belly

-kávale- v.itr. to twist, to spin slowly

SYN. -súyuy- to spin quickly

-kávay- v.itr., also with -pe- (more frequent than simplex) to go round, to turn around

-káakvay- distrib., also with -pe to turn round many times

-pe-kávay-l̃aw- to go round out of sight

-pe-kávay-ni- caus. to make go round (e.g., to turn the car)

-pe-kávay-ŋi- to go round here and there

pe-kákvay-wen-et n.: pít ___ curved road

kávay-wen-eva n.: pít ___ curve of the road

CIT. pít kávay kávay yáxwe the road is turning around this way and that way (full of curves)

hémax pe-kávay-qa lit. he is going around his side; he is taking sides with him

kaváayu n. Span., plur. -m horse, see pásukat Ca.

kaváayu-ŋa on horseback

kaváayu peta on horseback

kávaˀma-l n., plur. -l-em, distrib. kákvaˀmal(-em) construct -kávaˀma olla, water jar, pot; cup

-kávi- v.itr. with -wen, ALLOM. -káv- in periphr. to have a hole; to be open (of window, etc.)

-kákvam- distrib. to have many holes

-kávi-n- caus. to make a hole (usually round)

-kakvam-e- caus. and distrib., to make many holes

kávi-ve n. hole

kávi-wen-et n. hole kákvam-wen-et distrib. holes

SYN. -kápal- to make a hole (usually round)

-mupáxul- to drill a hole (as tunnel)

CIT. káv káv yáxwen there are small holes

-káviiči- v.itr. with -sun 'heart' as first member of verbal group and with -wen to be surprised

CIT. nèsun káviiči-wen ˀentéhwanuk I was surprised when I saw you

káviñiš PlN Indian Wells

-káwalva- v.itr. often with čaqe also with -pe- (more frequent than simplex), ALLOM. -káwal- in periphr., -káwalava- in periphr. to wiggle, to stagger (mainly of upper part of the body)

-pe-kákwalan- distrib.

SYN. -kívalva- to wiggle (mainly of legs)

CIT. kíkesawiš káwal yáxqal a drunkard staggers

-káwi- v.itr. with -wen to be hitched to be tied

-káwi-n- caus. to hitch, to tie

káwi-ve n. string, cord; wáqˀa ___ shoe string

CIT. néˀaš kaváayui pen-káwi-n-qal keléesay piyk I hitched my horse to the wagon

káwive n., see -káwi- v.itr.

-káwiya- v.tr., VAR. -qáwiya-, ALLOM. káwi- with -ˀa to hire, to employ

káwi-ˀa n. boss, employer

SYN. -ˀámin- to fire (discharge)

CIT. ne-káwiya-qale hentevxákati piyik he hired me to work for him

káwkun-il̃ n. construct -káwkun pocket; bag, purse

penhámin̨qal ne-káwkun-ŋa I lay it in my bag

-káwlaa- v.itr. to be bent, inclined (of body parts as back, legs; of the new moon, tree)

-kákawlaa- distrib.

-kawla-káwlaa- redupl.

SYN. -likalíika- to be crooked Des.Ca.
hé?i likaliikaqal his legs are bow-shaped

CIT. hé?i kákawlaa-qa his legs are bow-shaped

-káwnax n. [construct] bone of the neck

káw?a n., VAR. qáw?a, as 2nd member of nominal group, 1st member: -?i 'foot', -ma 'hand' ankle; wrist

káxat n. piece of mesquite bean cake, cf. BandS p. 110

-káyaa- v.itr., ALLOM. -kaykáya- to dangle (balloon, egg plant, etc.)

-kákya- distrib. many indiv. subj.

-kaykáya-wet n.: tukiš+kaykáya-wet pál lit. dangling blue water (it refers to the whole body of blue water, e.g., of a pond; when man shakes it standing at the edge, it dangles)

color term base + kaykáya-/-káyaa- to be dangling in a colored appearance

-káyaw- v.itr. to swing (on a swing, hanging on a rope)

-kákyaw- distrib. to swing back and forth

-pe-káyaw- to swing over (like Tarzan)

-pe-kákyawan- distrib.

-káyaw-ni- caus. to give a swing (as to a hammock)
káyaw-pi-š n. swing

kaykáyaʔka n. with -ʔi 'leg' calf (of the leg)

-káyma- v.tr. to put one's arm around sbdy's neck

-káyma+piš- with arm around sbdy's neck and arrive
CIT. ʔí náxaluvel peman nehíčeqal pen-káyma-qal I go with this old man putting my arm around his neck

-káytu n. construct, plur. -m rival, competitor (in a game); enemy

tax-káytu-kt-em n. rivals; enemies

-káyvaa- v.itr., VAR. -kayvakáyva- redupl. to incline being curved (new moon, dog's tail)

SYN. -čánaa- to be curved round

káyval n. bluejay with a crest

Cf. čáʔiš n. bluejay without a crest

kéčiš n. big white lizard

-kélaw- v.itr., v.tr. to gather wood

-kélaw-law- to go gather wood
-kélaw-pul- to come gather wood

kélaw-at n. construct -kélaw-ʔa wood; woods; tree

kelawat n. see -kélaw-

kélel n. manzanita, wild apple

kén-ma adj. delicious, tasty

kéñ-iš n. tasty one

Cf. ʔelélema badly tasting

-kéŋi- v.itr., ALLOM. kéŋ in periphr., always repeated to fall off (of leaves; of small, light objects)

-kéŋ-in- caus. to shake and let fall off

kéŋi-iš n. what is fallen off (e.g., leaves, etc.)

color term base + kéŋi to fall down in a colored appearance: sel+kéŋ kéŋ yáxqal sth. red is falling (e.g., embers are falling down)

CIT. (cf. kéʔmet) ʔí ʔísil̃ kéʔmeti čemeta pe-kéŋi-n-qaʔl this coyote is shaking soot on us (Texts, p. 97)

-képi- v.itr., ALLOM. keep in periphr. to float (of birds, fish, etc.); to glide

-képi-ŋi- to float around

color term base + képi- to float in a colored appearance teviš+képi-qal sth. white is floating

híŋiwet híŋqal kéep témayka náška an airplane flies gliding down to land

-kési- v.itr. to get wet

-kési- n. caus. to wet, to water (plants)

kési-š n. that which is wet, damp

Cf. wáxiš dry one

-két- v.tr. to cover (with a basket, a piece of cloth), to roof

-kéktan- distrib.

SYN. -vukʔúmin- to cover up (the whole thing)

CIT. xél̃al piš tax-hem-két-we they cover themselves with clothes

-kéwe- v.itr. to have a fiesta, a party

kéwe-t n. fiesta

híwqalet kéwet-i piyik the man for the fiesta (the same as nét)

CIT. čémeta hem-kéwe-wen ˀišwáyikikatem they give a party for us to eat

-kéwin- v.tr. with -če- to get away from sbdy who holds one (with a rope, chain etc.)

CIT. políis peyáwqal ˀéyeti pé pe-če-kéwin-qal pax peˀívaqal the policeman got hold of a thief, but he got away from him and ran away

-kéye- v.itr. 1. to get sores 2. to dissolve, to melt (fat, chocolate, dirt on body, overripened fruit)

-kékyem- distrib.

kéyi-š n. sore

CIT. ad 1. ne-kéyi-qa némaŋa I got sores on my hand

-kéˀ- v.tr. to bite

-kékˀan- distrib. many times

-kékˀan-ŋi- distrib. to go around and bite a little here and there

-kéˀ-ni- caus. to make bite

-kéˀ-ŋi- to go around and bite a little here and there

kéˀ-al n. bite; wound caused by biting

tax-kéˀ-wet n. one who bites people always (e.g., a dog)

CIT. netíˀi ne-kéˀ-qa lit. my stomach bites me; I have a twisting pain in my stomach (momentary)

kéˀmet n. soot

kíčam-ka adv., VAR. qíčam-ka, ALLOM. kíčan- with suff. -xwan south (toward south)

kíčan-xwan from south, cf. téman-xwan from north)

kíčan-xwan-vičem n. people from south

-kíhma n. construct, plur. -kíkihmañ-em son (father's)

kíhma wíhkwa lit. son both together; father and son

Cf. -méxan son (mother's), -máyl̃uˀa son (father and mother's)

kíhmay-ˀa n. unknown (with indef. pron. qahíčeˀa in indir. question: I wonder what ...)

-kíhmay-l̃u- v.itr. (with indef. verb qamíyax in indir. question: I wonder why ...)

CIT. qahíčea kíhmay-ˀa man ˀeméxanqaˀl I wonder what you did

qamíyax kíhmay-l̃u-qal man kil̃e píšqal I wonder why he doesn't come

kík(t) n., plur. kíkt-em one who lives in the house; inhabitant (prob. ki- 'house', -ik 'one to whom applies ...')

táxweŋax kíkt-em lit. near each other inhabitants; they are neighbors

-máŋax kík (P_1-maŋax) one who lives near; neighbor

-iš kík (P_1-iš) one who lives around; neighbor

PlN-kík(t-em) inhabitant(s) of an area, member(s) of a clan

-kíkesaw- v.itr., VAR. -kíkesew-, -kíksew- to get drunk

-kíksew-lu- v.itr. to become crazy (drinking jimson weed)

-kíkesaw-ne- caus. to make drunk

kíkesaw-al n. intoxicating drink

kíkesew-vaˀal n. Jimsonweed; cf. BandS, p. 60

kíkesew-iš n. one who is drunk

kíkesew-vaš/-wet n. drunkard

kil̃e proclitic. particle not

-kíil̃ew- v.tr. to follow, to go along with

SYN. -kíin- v.tr. to accompany

-kíl̃iw- n. construct, plur. ___-im partner, companion, friend

tax-kíl̃iw-katem n. companions; members of the same clan

SYN. -táxlew n. partner

kíl̃imuˀat n. lizard with a long tail

SYN. páyul

kímu-l n. door of a house

kímuˀan adv. (AL dnkn.) by the doorway (the door is open); openly (without hiding anything)

kímu-yka adv. to the outside

kímu-ŋax adv. outside

kímu-l hémaŋa lit. at the hand of the door; right in front of the door

-kíin- v.tr. to follow, to accompany

SYN. -kíil̃ew-

CIT. netáxmuˀa wíiwi tuháyimaniš pa tax-kíin-qal two of my songs go always together

-kína- v.itr. to burn, to burn down

-kína-ne- caus. to burn

kína-qal-et n. that which is burning; fire

kína-nay-wet n. the fire which is coming towards sbdy

Cf. -ná?- v.itr. to catch fire, -čút- v.tr. to burn, -?émi- to get burned (of body parts)

CIT. kíš náqal kína-qal the house caught fire and burned down

-kínaŋi- v.tr., ALLOM. -kínaŋa with or without nominal suff. -?a [construct] to marry a wife

-kínaŋi-?a, -kínaŋa-?a, -kínaŋa n. construct, plur. -kíknaŋi-ya-m, -kínaŋa-?a-m, -kíknaŋi-ñe-m wife

kínaŋi-l̃ n. marriage; wife, plur. kíknaŋi-l̃-em wives

kínaŋi-š n. married man

kínaŋa ?íive lit. without his wife; bachelor

kínaŋa múkiš lit. his wife is dead; widower

Cf. -wélisew- to take as husband

-wáy- to marry

-kísal- v.itr., in periphr. to flicker, to spark (stars, fireworks, etc.)

kísalisal L-redupl., in periphr.

-pe-kisal-an-, -pe-kíksal-an- autom. redupl.

Cf. -pálaw- to sparkle

kísil̃ n., plur. kísl̃-am chicken hawk (bigger than k^{W}á?al)

kís-iš n. shade

-kís-l̃u- to get shady

kís-ma adj. shady

kís-vaxat n. roof; shade

kí-š n. distrib. kíki-š, kíki-č-em, construct -ki house; distrib. (usually) empty houses

-kí-ŋa in the house

kíš pétuk lit. under the house; inside the house

kíš ʔámnawet big house; Big House (ceremonial)

kíš čáwal PlN lit. house which is jagged; White Water

-kíval- v.itr. in periphr. to wiggle, stagger (mainly legs)

-kívalava- L-redupl., in periphr., otherwise -kívalva-

-če-kíval- v.itr., also with -pe- to stagger (tripping over sth.), v.tr. to tangle, trip (of rope, wire)

-pe-kíkvalan- distrib. to keep staggering

Cf. -káwalva- to wiggle (mainly upper part of the body)

CIT. hičemi ne-če-kíval-qa píka pe ne-kívalva-qa sth. tripped me and I stumbled wiggling

-kívasaw n. arch. [construct] great spirit, god

SYN. ʔámna n. Great One

-kívlu- v.itr. (AL dnkn.) to be stripped off, be naked

CIT. ʔúmun kélawat kívlu-qa támiva all trees are stripped in winter

-kíwaʔan- v.tr. to chase away (animals, sicknesses, people); to herd (cattle)

-kíkwan- distrib.

SYN. -néemi- to chase away

CIT. meem-kíwaʔan-we ʔelélk^{w}iči híčemivi múkweneti they are chasing bad diseases away (púvulam in Big House)

kíwniš n. Des.Ca. wall

-kíya- v.itr. to stay behind

-kíya-law- to be left alone (e.g., sole survivor of the family)

kíya-law-iš n. one who is left alone; leftover (of food, coffee; coffee grounds etc.)

kíya-š n. one who stays behind

CIT. miš kíya-qal he stays behind with them

wáyikiwenet kíya-law-ič-i penpíkinqal I dumped the leftover food

kíyul n., plur. ___-em, construct -kíyul-ki fish

kíyuˀl-i héwnevaš fisherman

-kíyˀul- v.itr. with -če- to become stiff (body parts)

kíˀat n., VAR. kíat, plur. kíkit-am, classif. -méxanˀa baby, child

kíˀi particle, ALLOM. kíˀil̃ in phrase, compound no (as in response to a question, request, etc.)

kíˀil̃ ˀesánem I don't think so

kíˀil̃ ku No! (expressing dissent), cf. háni ku O.K. Go ahead!

-kíˀil̃-uk- v.itr. not to materialize (plans, etc.) čaqa čem-kíˀil-uk-wen we did not make it

-kíˀil̃-ku-ni- caus. not to let materialize; to turn down

CIT. peem-kíˀil̃-ku-ni-weˀ they turned it down

-kíˀiw- v.tr. to wait for, to expect

-kíˀiw-ˀa n. [construct] that which one expects; belonging (especially fruit tree)

CIT. pe-kíˀiw-qal ˀestó-r piš hákuspi he is waiting for the store to open

pičem-kíˀiw-wen páˀli pismúlulukati we're waiting for the water to boil

CIT. ʔí ʔĩl ne-kíʔiw-ʔa lit. this mesquite tree is my expectation; belongs to me (to my people)

-kíiʔnak n. with a color term base as 1st member of compound (cf. -kíin- v.tr., -ak augmentative?) intensifying the darker shade of the color

CIT. tes-kíiʔnak more brownish, cf. teshíwlaqalet yellowish (tésnekiš yellow)

ku clitic [topicalizing]; [intensifying] with péʔ following, ... you know, cf. háni

CIT. ʔé ku henʔáʔiva ʔíyaxqal pen ʔé ku ʔaxʔíyaxnem you said 'I'm the older', so you have to say ...

-kúča- v. itr. to have indigestion

-kúča-ne- caus. to cause sbdy indigestion, heartburn

kúča-ĩl n. indigestion

kúkul n., plur. kúkl-am ground owl

-kúkup- v.itr. to be sleepy

kúkup-il n. sleepyhead

CIT. ne-kúkup-qal man nekákapiqal I am sleepy, so I am yawning

kúkuʔul n. yucca nolina; cf. BandS, p. 94

-kúl- v., ALLOM. -kúku- autom. redupl. v.itr. to cook; v.tr. to make; to cook

-kúl-pi- v.tr. to go over, fix and come back

-kúkul-pe- v.tr. to fix here and there

kúl-ʔat n., construct -kúl-ʔa that which was made, product

kúl-iš n. one who made sth./sbdy

kúl-ŋi-š n. one who went over, fixed sth, and returned

kúl-va?al n.: pa ___ kitchen; híčemi pa kúl-va?al n. where sth. is made (e.g. factory)

kúl-vaš/-wet n. cook

CIT. ?elélek^{w}iči niyik/neta pe-kúkul-qal lit. a bad thing to/upon me he does; he does sth. bad to me.

tax-kúkul-qal tésel lit. it made itself an olla; it was made into an olla

-kúl- v.itr. in periphr. to faint, to quiver (on account of getting weak)

CIT. táxaw kúll yáx?e he fainted

-kúli- v.itr. with -pe- to fall (into a hole), to stick (an arrow into the ground, etc.), to rush in

-pe-kúkulum- distrib. (many subj. here and there)

-pe-kúli-n- caus. to let fall in, to drop

CIT. hépuš pe-kúli-qal his eyes cave in (on account of sickness)

-kum n. construct uncle, i.e. father's elder brother

-kúm-uk n. deceased uncle

kúmal n. (AL: dnkn), distrib. kúkmal spoon (wooden, flat, oblong round shaped)

-kúmu n. construct nephew or niece, i.e. man's younger brother's child

kún-il̃ n., construct -kún sack

kúnvaxmal PN, see Texts

-kúŋlu- v.tr. to propose to marry (of a woman), to have intercourse

CIT. ?í náwišmal ne-kúŋl̦u-qal yeyayan penčekálaw?i piš penwáypi this girl asked me to marry but I refused to marry her kúŋsexwet n., plur. kúŋsext-em bumblebee

-kúp- prob. sound imitation in periphr. to walk (of a horse)

-kúp-ulup- L-redupl. to run (of a horse)

-kúp- v.itr. to sleep

-kúp-law- to go to sleep, to go to bed

-kúp-viču- to be sleepy (in the evening) Mt.Ca., -kúp-ču- Des.Ca.

kúp-vel n. construct -kúpve bed

kúp-vaš/-wet n. sleepy person

-kup+čá?ay- v.itr. to fall asleep; to oversleep

SYN. -kúkup- to be sleepy

kúpanil̃ n., plur. -em woodpecker

kúpaš n., plur. kúpač-em barrel cactus

-kús- v.tr. supplet. with sing. obj., see -hívin- for plur. obj. to take, get hold of (an object which is not moving); for a moving object see -yáw-

-kúkusan- distrib. to take one after another

-kús-ane- caus. only: súnikati ne-kús-ane-qa he gives me a hard time

-kús-iči- to pick up on the way

-kús-ikaw- to pick up here and there Des.Ca., for Mt.Ca. -híhvime-, see -hívin-

-kús-ŋi- to come after; to take back sth. which one has brought

-tám+kus- v.itr. lit. sun (tám-it) + take; to bathe in the sun

CIT. pe-kús-qal táxmu?ay lit. he took his song; he sang his song; kús-iči (?etáxmu?a) lit. pick up (your song) on the way!; sing your song!

CIT. súnikati pe-n-kús-qal lit. I'm taking a hardship; I'm having a hard time, I'm suffering

-kús- v.itr., -kúkus- autom. redupl. to make fun of, to tease

-tax-če-kús- v.tr., -tax-če-kúkus- autom. redupl. to tell a funny story

tax-če-kús-il̃ n. funny story

Cf. -ˀáˀal- to mock, -ˀísmatu- to tease (only among those under the joke relationship)

CIT. tax-če-kús-il̃ netétiyamaxqal he is telling me a funny story

-kusméti- v.itr. to choke (with sth. like a rope tied around one's neck), (-kus- prob. as in -kúspi- 'throat'; -méti- perhaps in méte-wet 'much of it' [VAR. métiwet?])

-kusméti-n- caus. to choke sbdy at the neck

Cf. -kustémi- v.itr. to choke (with sth. stuck in the throat)

kúspi-l̃ n., construct -kúspi throat

kúspi pétuk inside of the throat

SYN. paxwáyvaˀal n. the inside of throat

CIT. kúspi qél̃aka he has a sore throat

-kustémi- v.itr. to choke (with sth. stuck in the throat; getting drowned)(-kus- prob. as in -kúspi- 'throat'; -témi- 'to close')

SYN. -kusméti- to choke (with sth. like a rope tied around the neck)

CIT. páŋa kustémi-qa lit. he gets choked in the water; he gets drowned kú-t n., construct -kuˀ fire

-kú-lu- v.itr. — to distribute fire from one place to another (putting a big stick into the fire, burning it, taking to another pile of wood to burn)

kú-lu-ˀa n. — stick used for the transfer of the fire

-kut+múx- v.itr. — lit. to shoot fire; to start a fire (by friction)

kùt nániwet — fire-like wind; PN some kind of spirit, see -náˀani-

kùt yáyˀal — small whirlwind (coming at night); dust devil (yáyˀal related to yáˀi wind), cf. téneˀawka whirlwind (coming in day time)

-kútaš- v.itr., v.tr., ALLOM. -kúktaš- autom. redupl. to talk, speak

-kútaš/-kúktaš-max- — to talk to sbdy

-kútaš-ŋi- — to come, talk and leave

-kúktaš-ŋi- — to talk around

kútaš-ˀat n. construct -kútaš-ˀa word

kútaš-wet n. — talker; big shot

SYN. -háwaway- v.itr. to talk

CIT. ˀíyk ne-kúktaš-nem I will talk to you

né-qi taxk^{w}e ne-kútaš-qal or né-qi ne-kútaš-qal táxhuyka I am talking to myself

kúvišnil̃ n., plur. -em small ant, cf. ˀánet big ant

-kúy- v.tr. — to bury (sth. in the ground); to fill up (e.g., a hole with dirt, etc.)

-kúkuy- distrib. — to bury here and there

-kúy-iči- — to bury hurriedly and go on

kúy-il̃ n. — funeral

kúy-vaˀal n. — graveyard

-kuy+ˀúmin- v.tr. lit. bury + cover (-ˀúmin- as in -vukˀúmin- to cover up); to cover up (hole)

CIT. tékiči piš-kúy-iktem témal piš we are going to fill up the hole with dirt

-kúˀa- v.itr. to become wormy

kúˀa-š n. mesquite bean that is wormy

kúˀa-l n., plur. -l-em, construct -kúˀa louse

SYN. náwil̃at louse

CIT. kúˀa-l nekéˀqa nesáqaqa a louse bites me and I feel itchy

kúˀut n. plur. -em soft-flag, cat-tail; cf. BandS, p.142

k^wáča-l n., construct -k^wáčˀa cheek

-k^wa-l n.: hé-k^wa-l, construct -k^wa grandfather, i.e., mother's father, cf. -k^wála-k(t) deceased grandfather

SYN. -k^wáal̃i (intimate)

-k^wála n. construct, plur. -m grandchild, i.e., daughter's child

-k^wala-k(t): ney-k^wála-k lit. he is in relationship to me, the grandchild; my deceased grandfather, cf. -k^wa-l mother's father

k^wála wíhk^{w}a lit. grandchild two of them; grandfather and grandchild together

-k^wáliš- in periphr., also with -pe- to take a long step; to step over (sth.)

CIT. ne-pe-k^wáliš-ˀi pa séweti peta there I stepped over a snake

-k^{w}álaʔan- v.tr. with -če-, ALLOM. -k^{w}álaʔa- in imper. sing. to open (mouth, eyes with hands)

-k^{w}álma- v.tr. to hold under the arm; to put one's arm around sbdy's neck

CIT. ʔen-k^{w}álma-qa I put my arm around you to hug

k^{w}ál̃ʔit n. white sap of mesquite tree

k^{w}àn in: k^{w}àn súpl̃e/wíh/páh/wíčiw six/seven/eight/nine

k^{w}ánaŋ adv. half

k^{w}ánaŋ-viš n., distrib. k^{w}ánaŋ-viš that which has become half: ménil ___ half moon, héʔi ___ person with one leg

k^{w}ániva(ʔan) adv. in another, different place

k^{w}ákniva distrib. in different places

CIT. hemqál k^{w}ánivaʔan témal pa they live in different places in this area

-k^{w}ápi- v.itr. to wake up, to stay awake

-k^{w}ápi-ne- caus. to wake sbdy up, to keep awake

-k^{w}ák^{w}api-ne- caus. and distrib. (many indiv. obj.)

-k^{w}ápi-l̃aw- to become awake

k^{w}ápi-qal-et n., plur. -wen-et-em one who is alert, lively; living person
___ táxliswet a living person, cf. múkiš táxliswet dead person

k^{w}ápi-vaš/-wet n.: mutúleka ___ one who wakes up early in the morning; early riser

CIT. ʔí ʔáwal k^{w}ápi-qalet piš penámaanqaleve this dog is alert to feel things (as a watch-dog)

-kʷas n. construct   tail (of birds, animals)

CIT. wíkikmalem míyaxwen hém-kʷas the birds have tails

-kʷás- v.itr.   to ripen (plants):, to be done (of cooking)

-kʷás-ni- caus.   to ripen, to make ripe; to make fruitful (as plants)

kʷás-iš n.   that which is ripened, cooked

páŋiš kʷás-iš   fresh ripened

CIT. ʔáyapiš čemeta kʷás-qal lit. the fruit to be picked ripened upon us: ... got over-ripened (because we missed picking it up at the right time)

kʷasanemčíip n., plur. -em baldheaded bird

kʷásimayka n. arch.: kìat kʷásimayka (PN?) designating a water-baby who is actually a powerful man

-kʷáš- v.itr., v.tr., -kʷákʷaš- autom. redupl. to pick up (finding sth. on the road, or in the big house [when they throw money])

kʷáati n., plur. -m Span. twin

-kʷáaviču- v.tr. Mt.Ca., -téčekʷ- Des.Ca. to take care of

kʷáwawaʔ-il̃ n., VAR. kʷáwawaʔ one who is light; agile, nimble

Cf. čàxčáaka   lively one; pélema heavy, mušʔíval lazy one

CIT. ʔí náxaniš héspen kʷáwawaʔ-il̃ piš tuvxáve this man is very nimble in working

-kʷáwuš- v.tr.   to tear off (eggshell after cutting into half), to take off

Cf. -kʷélel-   to peel off

-k^wáyaye- v.itr. with -pe- to pour out (solids, as sand)

k^wáywil̃ n., VAR. k^wáʔil̃ and k^wáil with piš hunger

 k^wáil̃ piš because of hunger

 CIT. k^wáwil̃ čemeta púliqa lit. hunger fell upon us; we suffer from hunger

  k^wáywil mečéxenqa lit. hunger killed them; they died of hunger

  k^wáil̃ piš nemúkqal lit. I get sick because of hunger; I'm hungry

k^wáyʔanpi-š n., construct -k^wáyʔanpi tail of the arrow

-k^wáʔ- v.tr. to eat

 -k^wá-ače- v.tr. to eat up

 -k^wáʔ-iče- to eat on the way going

 -k^wá-ŋi- v.tr. to come back and eat

 -k^wáʔ-a n. [construct] that which one ate; feces

 k^wáʔa-piš n. sth. eatable

 k^wáʔ-ivaʔal n., construt -k^wáʔ-iva sth. good to eat, favorite food; piš ___ sth. to eat with: spoon, plate, etc.

 k^wáʔ-ivel n., construct -k^wá-ive: ___ (kíyalawiš) sth. left over

 táxliswetem mey-k^wáʔ-iwet one who eats people; man-eater

 kúti k^wá-ivaš/-iwet fire eater

 CIT. támiti/ménil̃i peem-k^wã-wen lit. they are eating the sun/the moon; there is an eclipse of the sun/the moon

k^wáʔal n., plur. -em chicken hawk (smaller than kísil)

k^wáʔil̃, see k^wáywil̃

-k^wáʔil̃e- v.tr. to hate

tax-k^{w}áʔil̃a-ʔal n. hate

-k^{w}áʔil̃e-ʔa n. person whom one hates

k^{w}áʔil̃i-š n. one who always hates sbdy

-k^{w}áʔisne- v.tr. to paint (face), to put design; to write (e.g., letter)

-k^{w}ák^{w}aʔisne- distrib. to paint one after another

k^{w}áʔisne-at n. sign, painting; letter, writing

k^{w}áʔisne-il̃ n. written word, writing

k^{w}áʔisne-qal-et n. person who writes

k^{w}áʔisne-vaʔal n.: pa ___ sth. to write on (e.g. paper), tax-___ camera

k^{w}áʔisne-vaš/-wet n. writer

SYN. -ʔíʔisne- to write

CIT. súweti pa pen-k^{w}áʔisne-qa néʔat pa I am putting the design of stars on the basket

-k^{w}élel- v.tr. to take/peel off (skin, bark)

SYN. -síʔay- to peel (e.g. fruit)

-k^{w}éniš- v.itr. with -pe- and -wen to be long, straight (road)

-k^{w}étel- v.itr., v.tr. 1. v.itr. to stick out, perk up (usually in periphr.) 2. v.tr. to pry open (e.g. a can), to pry out (e.g. sticker)

-k^{w}ékte- v.itr. distrib.

-k^{w}étet- v.itr., v.tr. in periphr., also with -pe- to squirt

-k^{w}éyʔeqi- v.itr. (=-k^{w}éy-ʔeqi- with submorph. -aq-, see -k^{w}éyʔeš-) to stoop down

-če-k^{w}éyʔ-eqe- to stoop way down

(-če)-k^{w}ék^{w}eyaqe- distrib. to stoop repeatedly
k^{w}éyeˀ-em PN (people stooping down)
k^{w}éyˀ-eqi-vaš n. bug

-k^{w}éyˀeš- v.itr. in periphr. (=-k^{w}éy-ˀeš- with submorph. -as-, see -k^{w}éyˀeqi-) to stoop down at an instant; to buck (horse)

-pe-k^{w}ék^{w}eyčan- distrib. to buck

-k^{w}éˀeqe- v.itr., VAR. -k^{w}éˀ- in periphr. to get up, to lift oneself up from the lying to the standing position

-k^{w}éˀeq-an- caus. to make rise, to help rise

-k^{w}íčeˀan- v.tr. Wan.Ca. to wring (as clothes in washing), to wash (as clothes); -mélen- to wring, -pášam- to wash Des. and Mt. Ca.

-k^{w}ĩlĩla- v.itr. Mt.Ca. to scream (out of pain, surprise; when one meets Takuš at night he is supposed to do so)

k^{w}íñil n., construct -k^{w}íñil-ki, with classif. -kíˀiwˀa acorn, Calif. black oak; cf. BandS, p.123

-k^{w}íñˀa n. construct brother-in-law, cf. -télme sister-in law

tax-k^{w}íña-ktem n. those who are brothers-in-law

-k^{w}is-k^{w}íse- v.itr. to be pointed (stick, horn, beak. mountain)

-k^{w}íkse- distrib. (many indiv. subj.)
k^{w}isk^{w}ísi-wet n. sth. pointed

-k^{w}íwi- v.itr. to whistle

L

-lákaa- v.itr. with durat. suff. -qal to be flat (balloon, stomach, etc.)

SYN. -pátiš- to be swollen up

CIT. k^{w}áˀel piš nemúqal netíˀi čaqa lákaa-qal I am hungry, (so) my stomach is flat

-lákaš- v.itr. with -wen (=-láka-š- with submorph. -aš-, see -lákaa-) to get flat (spherical obj.)

-če-lákaš- v.itr., v.tr., also with -pe-, -vuk- to flatten

-če-lálkačan- distrib., also with -pe-

-láki- v.itr. to flatten, to stoop down (body parts)

-láki-n- caus. to flatten (as grass, bush)

laméesa n. Span. table

-lámi- v.itr. with -če- to fold, to wrinkle (clothes, paper, etc.)

-lámi-n- caus., also with -če- to fold (clothes, paper, etc.)

-lálmame- caus. and distrib.

-če-lálmame- caus. and distrib. to fold in a disorderly way

lámsa n. with mùl 'nose' as first member nominal group, construct -muˀ ___ Des.Ca. nostril -muˀkákvamwenet Mt.Ca.

-lápaa- v.itr., VAR. -lap-lápa- redupl. to be flat (nose, head, etc.)

laplápa-wet n. redupl.: hému ___ flat nosed

-lápaš- v., also with -če-, -pe-, -vuk-, periphr. only v.itr. 1. v.itr. to collapse, cave in (house, etc.) 2. v.tr. to cause to collapse (house, etc.), to break down flattened (box, car, etc.)

-lálpačan- v.tr. distrib.

-če-lálpačan- v.itr. distrib., also with -pe-, -vuk-

lápaš-at n. that which has been flattened

-pe-lápaš-vaš n. lit. one who makes broke; peddler

SYN. -hémi- to collapse crumbling, -qápi- to break

CIT. néki neta če-lápaš-ʔi my house collapsed on me

neyúmuve ne-če-lápaš-ʔa my hat which I have flattened (accidentally)

láqačil̃ n. hide, leather, things made of leather (e.g. sandal)

lávalvanet n., plur. ___-em cottonwood tree

-láwin- v.tr. with -pe- to flick with a finger (watermelon, head, etc.)

-pe-lálwame- distrib.

-láyin- v.tr. with -pe- to cause a slight, dull, pain (especially in head), to make feel dizzy

CIT. neyúluka ne-pe-láyin-qa my head causes me a slight headache

lá?la? n., plur. ___-am goose (greyish, with a white long beak)

-lékeš- v.itr. with -če-, v,tr., also with -če- (prob. = -léke-š- with submorph. -aš-, see VAR. -léke-, ALLOM. -lékel-), VAR. -léke- in periphr., ALLOM. -lékel- v.itr., with -wen-, periphr. only v.itr.
1. v.itr. to be tight (as with a belt); to be notched (wood, etc.)
2. v.tr. to tighten; to notch

-lélkečen- v.itr. distrib. with -wen-, to be notched

-lélke- distrib. v.itr. to be tight, to be notched

lekléke-wet/lélke-wet n. constricted, pressed-in one (as the waist of an ant)

SYN. -pe-ŋátaš- to tighten (as screws, etc.)

CIT. ad 1. čaqe hem-lélke-we hemtí?i ?ántem the ants are tightend at the waist

-lémeme- v.itr., ALLOM. -lémm- in periphr. to burn a great deal

-lépeqi- v.itr. (=lépe-qi- with submorph. -aq-, see -lépeš), ALLOM. -lépeš- in periphr.
to kneel down

-lélepeqi- distrib. (many subj.)

-lélepeq-ane- caus. and distrib.

-lépeš- v.itr. in periphr. (=-lépe-š- with submorph. -aš-, see -lépeqi-) to kneel down

-léer- v.itr., v.tr. Span. to read

-lé?aw- v.tr. with recipr. -tax- to transfer a message

tax-lé?aw-iš n. messenger

CIT. tax-ne-lé?aw-qal I am taking a message

-lé?eley- v.itr. to get loose, to wobble (teeth, tree, stick, etc.)

lé?et n., plur. lé?t-em stranger

-lika-líka- v.itr., also with -če-, ALLOM. lílika- with -wet, Des.Ca. to be crooked (trees), to be bowlegged, see -káwlaa- Mt.Ca.
lílika-wet: hé?i ___ lit. his legs are bowlegged; bowlegged person

-limu-límu- v.itr. in periphr. and with -qal- to be bumpy (road)
-lílmumu- distrib. with -wen- (many indiv. subj.)

-líway- v.tr., ALLOM. -lílway- autom. redupl. to clean (the inside of a cylinder or hole with a circular or stirring motion); to gargle (the throat)
CIT. kélawat piš pen- lílway-qa tékiči I'm poking through the hole with a stick whirling it

-líwiwey- v.itr. to sing aloud, to ring out

lóoku n. Span. crazy person
-lóoku-lu- v.itr. to become crazy
-lóoku-lu-ne- caus. to make crazy

-lúčaw- v.itr., VAR. -lúčuw- to be rough (of the surface of solids, face, etc.)
-luč-lúčaw- redupl. to be rough
lúč-wet n.: hépuš ___ his face is rough

-lúku- v.itr. to bend the body forward, to bow
-lúlkum- distrib. (many indiv. subj.)
CIT. náxaniš lúku-qa híčemi peykúsik témaŋa the man bent down to pick up sth. on the ground

-lúmaš- v.tr. to knock down, crumple (as a house)

-če-lúmaš- v.itr., v.tr., also with -pe- to crumple, mash (as paperbox, tin can, etc.)

-če-lúlmačan- v.itr., v.tr. distrib., also with -pe-

lúumiš n. paralyzed, crippled person or animal

-lúmu- v.itr. to have small pox, chicken pox; measles

lúmuʔ-il̃ n. small pox (refers rather to the resulting state of the disease: lumpy face)

lúŋu-lúŋu imitation of rhythm, in periphr. crawling (smooth-surfaced cylinder-shaped object, as snake)

-lúpin- v.tr., ALLOM. lúp in periphr. to pull out handful (weeds, feathers)

-lúlpume- distrib. (many indiv. obj., e.g. chickens)

-lúyuv- v.itr. in periphr. with čaqe, also with -če- to collapse (of legs of a chair, etc.)

CIT. néʔi čaqe lúyuv yáqa my leg collapses

-l̃ákay- v.tr., ALLOM. -l̃ál̃kay- autom. redupl. Des.Ca., -l̃áykay- Mt.Ca. to tickle

SYN. -séwel- to tickle (throat)

CIT. kíʔati pen-l̃ál̃kay-qal héʔiŋa I am tickling the kid on his foot

-l̃ímaa- v.itr. to frown, to contract (of forehead)

-l̃íl̃ʔan- v.tr. with recipr. -tax- and plur. subj. to shoot at a small bundle thrown in the air as a game

M

máča-ma adj., ALLOM. -máš- with -k^{w}-ene- crowded, full (of place, house, etc.)

-máča-k^{w}- v.itr. to gather in large numbers (of people); to press, to be tight (of clothes, shoes)

-máš-k^{w}-ene- caus. to make crowded, to fill up

CIT. máča-ma ʔáčaʔe néki kil̃e míyaxwen piš pa ʔetúkpi my house is too crowded, (so) you cannot stay overnight there

newáqʔa néŋa máča-k^{w}-al lit. my shoes are pressing forward in me; my shoes are too tight

máčil n., plur. máš̃l-am tick; flea

máiswa-t n., construct -máiswa ceremonial bundle

-mák- v.itr. in periphr. to blink (both eyes closed), to wink; cf. -qítaš- to wink (one eye closed)

-ma-l n.: hé-ma-l, construct -maʔ arm; hand; finger

-má-lu- v.itr. put hand (on sth.)

-hé-ma-k n. one who has big hands

-ma-ŋa-x from the hand of

-maʔ ʔámnawet lit. big finger; thumb

péʔ pe hé-ma-ŋa-x/hé-ma-x lit. from its hand; on that account, that's why

kìš hé-maʔ lit. the hand of the house; the front part of the house

kìmul hé-ma-ŋa(-x) lit. at/(from) the hand of the door; in front of the door

qàwal hé-maʔ PlN lit. rat's hand; Indian Wells

-ma káput-ŋa Mt.Ca. lit. hand basket-in; wrist

-ma káwʔa Des.Ca. wrist, cf. -ʔi káwʔa ankle

CIT. né-ma-ŋa-x pekávayqa lit. he goes round from my hand; he is taking sides with me

mála-l n. flat stone to grind, metate, cf. -mal-mála-

-mal-mála- v.itr. redupl. to be flat (a surface of truncated sphere, e.g., grinding stone)

mal-mála-wet n. flat one: qáwiš ___ flat stone, metate

SYN. palpálawet n. flat one (not spherical)

málisa-piš n., plur. málisapč-em construct -málisap Des.Ca. doll, toy (ʔíʔipiš Mt.Ca., cf. -málisew-)

-málisew- v.itr. Des.Ca., ALLOM. -mámlisew- autom. redupl., VAR. -mámisew- to play, cf. -ʔíʔk- Mt.Ca.

-máliswe-ne- caus. to make play

CIT. ne-mámisew-qal nemálisapi piš I am playing with my doll

málmal n. butterfly

-mámayaw- v.tr. to lend a hand, to help (a person)

CIT. pen-mámayaw-qal tuvxáqalepa I helped him when he worked

man conjunction 1. [coordinating] for nouns prefixed with possessive plur. pron.; for clauses, with identical subjects, see pen 2. [topicalizing] it .... that ... (in cleft sentence)

CIT. ad 1. hémna man hémye their father and their mother

ad 1. néqi ne híwqal man menháalqa only I stayed and looked for them

CIT. ad 2. né? man penmékanqa? súka?ti It is I that killed the deer

mánal n. flat cactus, beaver tail

mánet n., VAR. máanet war dance, eagle dance

SYN. púnil̃

-máni- v.itr., ALLOM. mána in periphr. (redupl.) and in caus. (of a globular object) to stumble over, to fall down (rolling), to roll

-máamni- distrib. to keep falling down

-mána?an- caus. to let fall; to roll

máni-wet n. one who always falls down; Sun-Fire PN, in Creation Story (see Ca.Texts)

Cf. -púli- to fall down, -čénen- to roll (of a circular object)

mánisal̃ n., VAR. mánisa scorpion

mániitu unknown; occurs in a song (see Texts, p. 135)

máŋax adv., construct -máŋax on/by the side of, near

ne-máŋax híwqalet/kík my neighbor

kíš máŋax on the other side of the house

pít máŋax the roadside

-máqi- v.itr. to get together, to go to a meeting

-mámqam- distrib. to gather around

-če-máqi- to get close (to sbdy)

-máqi-n- caus., also with -če- to let get together; to gather (money, etc.)

máqi-l̃ n. meeting

-máqˀu- v.itr., also with -če- to draw oneself together, to huddle (shoulders); to clench (hands)

-če-máqˀu-ki- to get huddled

-če-máqˀu-ki-n- caus. to draw (shoulders)

-mas n., construct uncle i.e., father's younger brother; cf. -ku father's elder brother

más adv. Span. more, rather

CIT. néˀ más ˀéiy ˀeta henˀélika I am more beautiful than you

más ˀínis wávuwet lit. more little long; very short

-mátaš- v.tr. with -pe-, VAR. -památaš- to crush, squash

-máti n. construct, plur. -ˀim niece

-máti-l̃uˀa n. niece (deceased)

-mávay- v.tr. to rub

-mámvay- distrib.

-mávay-xa- v.tr. to ask (sbdy) to rub one Mt.Ca.

CIT. némaŋa ne-mámvay-qa hémay piš he rubbed my hand with his hand

-mávi- v.itr. to get dark, to become night/evening

-mávi-l̃ew- v.tr. to befall (of night) on the way, cf. -páy-lew- to befall (of dawn) on the way

-mávi-l̃u- v.tr. to stay overnight

mávi-š n. evening, night

mávi-š/y piš in the evening, at night

ˀáy máxel̃iš máviš piyk midnight

Cf. túkmiyat night

máwa adv. after a while, later

máwa kil̃e not yet

máwul n., plur. -em, VAR. máwl fan palm, date palm; cf. BandS p.145

kìš máwl palm house

-máx- v.itr. to be, to stay, cf. -híw- to lie down, cf. -qál-

-máx- v.itr. (obj. pref. refers to indir. obj.)
1. to give (money, clothes), cf. ʔékamax- to give (food, water)
2. to sell, with recipr. -tax-

-mámxam- distrib. to give (to each of them)

-máx-iči- to give and go off

-máx-ŋi- to bring to give

-máx-ivaneken- to bring to give many times

-máxʔa n. [construct] sth. given

tax-máx-iwet n. one who gives away (anything)

CIT. páʔli ne-máx-qa piš neweláwalipi he gives me water to irrigate, cf. páʔli neʔékamaxqa (... to drink)

tax-ne-máx-ʔi netémay I sold my land, cf. -vendéer-

máxayil̃ n., plur. -em dove

máxayil̃ máyl̃uʔa baby dove

-máxel̃e- v.itr. to be in the middle (the sun)

máxel̃e-ka toward noon

máxel̃i-š n. noontime Mt.Ca., cf. tékluvel Des.Ca.

máxel̃i-š múči before lunch

máxel̃i-š témayka lit. noon time towards the earth; in the afternoon

ʔáy máxel̃i-š máviš piyk midnight

-máay- v.itr. Mt.Ca., -wéš-, wíčixan- Des.Ca. to dèfecate

máy-va n., construct -máy-va rectum, cf. súyaˀal Des.Ca.

-máyew- v.tr. to doctor (of a witch doctor treating with mouth)

-máyl̃u- v itr., v.tr. to give birth, to lay eggs

-mámal̃u- distrib. to have a child all the time

máyl̃u-ˀat n. baby; construct -máyl̃u-ˀa son (of father and mother), cf. -méxan son (of mother)

máyl̃u-š n. one who gave birth, parent

kil̃e máyl̃u-č-em/mámal̃u-č-em married couple without any child

máays n. corn

máyxal n. lizard, white and small; cf. tíˀal lizard, white and big

-máˀni- v.itr., v.tr., ALLOM. -mámaˀne- autom. redupl. to dodge

-máˀuni- v.tr. (-ma 'finger, hand' instrumental pref. [see Grammar] + -ˀuni- 'to show', thus lit. 'to show with hand') to point at

-mámuˀune- distrib.

piš pen-máˀune-qale-ve lit. that with which I point; my index finger

-méa- v.itr. Mt.Ca., ALLOM. -méhˀa n. sing. to become grayhaired

-méhˀa n. [construct] gray/white hair, plur. -méaa-m; míhˀa, plur. míam Des.Ca.

méa-š n. gray haired person

méčewel n. bush with yellow blossoms (used to cure influenza)

-méči- v.itr. to kneel down (as on a person to press down), cf. -lépeqi- v.itr. to kneel down (refers only to kneeling)

-méči-ŋi- to kneel down on

CIT. peta ne-méči-qal I am kneeling on him

-mék-an- see -muk-

-mélan- v.itr. to discuss, to debate, to argue

-mémlan- autom. redupl.

CIT. piyk ne-mémlan-qal núˀinat piš I'm discussing the law with him

-méle- v.tr. with neg. kil̃e to be fond of, to care for (persons, animals)

SYN. -ˀáyaw- to like, want

CIT. kil̃ men-méle-qal pásuktami

-méleka- v.tr. to scrub off (as dirt)

-méli- v.itr. to curve, to turn (of horn, wheel)

-mémlem- v.itr. distrib. to curve many times

-méli-n- caus. to turn (as steering wheel, doorknob) to wind; to wring (as washing)

-mémleme- caus. and distrib.

-če-méli-n- caus. to twist, to wind, to jerk (as one's body)

-če-mémleme- caus. and distrib. to twist many times

-vuk-méli-n- caus., with -ˀí-y 'leg' (obj. case) to cross one's legs

CIT. néˀiy pen-vuk-méli-n-qa I cross my legs

-méli- v.itr. with neg. kil̃e and in periphr. not to be enough (food, clothes, house, land)

Cf. -háyin- to exhaust
CIT. kil̃e méli yáxwen it is not enough

-mélki- v.itr., ALLOM. -mémlek- autom. redupl. to make a noise (rattle, etc.)
-mélki-ni- caus. to play (musical instrument), to cause to make noise
mélki-ni-l̃ n. music
mélki-ni-pi n. musical instrument
mélki-ni-piš n. music
mélki-ni-vaʔal n. sounder
mélki-ni-vaš n. musician
CIT. kímuʔli pe-mélki-ni-qal náxaniš lit. a man is causing the door to make a noise; he is knocking at the door
mík mémlel-qal lit. how many times does it sound?; what time is it?

mélkiš n., plur. mélkič-em white man
-mélkiš-l̃u- v.itr. to talk English
mélkiš-l̃uʔ-vaš n. one who talks English

méme interj. forget (about it)!
SYN. súnwe

-mémxive- v.tr. Mt.Ca. to mimic , to mock, -ʔáʔale- Des.Ca.

-méni- v.itr. with -vuk- to turn over, to roll, to turn around; to turn into (an animal or different color)
-vuk-mémnem- distrib. to turn over, to roll down many times
-vuk-méni-n- caus. to turn over; to make turn into (as an animal)
-vuk-méni-ŋi- to turn around (e.g. making U-turn)

vuk-méni-iš n. — one who turned over; one who turned into; húnwet vuk-méni-iš one who turned into a bear

SYN. -méye- — to turn around, -súy- to spin, -mána- to roll

ménikiš n., with classif. -kíˀiwˀa (before being picked), -ˀáyˀa/-méxanˀa (after being picked) mesquite beans; cf. BandS p.107

ménil̃ n. — the moon; month

ˀélka ménil̃ — the beautiful (lady) moon

ménil̃ paŋiš — new moon

ménil̃ taxčúmilawiš — lit. the moon which has completed itself; the full moon

ménil̃ nánvayaxiš — lit. the moon which has come to the end; the full moon

-ménvax- v.itr., see néken

-méŋkʷa- v.tr. — to swallow

-méŋkʷa-š n. — one who swallowed

CIT. neˀékamaxqal páˀli pen-méŋkʷa-kati netíŋaypi — she gave me water, so I could swallow my medicine

mésaˀa n. — rattle snake

méte-n adv. — much

-méte-kʷ- v.itr. — to multiply (of objects)

-méte-kʷ-ene- caus. — to get many, to increase; to save a lot

méteˀ-ma adj. — enough

méte-wet adj. — many, much (for the uncountable nouns), plur. méte-čem

mét-kʷ-iš n. — that which is enough

CIT. míyaxwe piš méte-k^{w}-ive how much of it (is there)?

-méx- v.itr. (only neg. or interr.) to do sth., to behave; to happen

-méx-an- caus. to do, to do sth. (to sbdy)

-méx-an-ak n. owner

méx-an-at n. (in affirmative sentence) belongings, construct -méx-an-ˀa doings, behavior; belongings (used also as classif.); luck

-mémex-an-ˀa n. distrib. every belonging

méx-an-piš n.: kil̃e ___ míyaxwen there is nothing one can do

méx-an-vik n. owner of lots of things

CIT. kil̃e méx-ap míyaxwen it couldn't be helped

míyaxwen piš ˀe-méx-ive lit. how is your doing; how are youˀ

-méxan n. construct son (of woman), cf. -púlin daughter (of woman)

méxan wíhk^{w}a mother and son both

méxanuk adv. neg. [not] by any means; interr. how

qa-méxanuk adv. how (in indir. question); somehow (indef.)

CIT. qa-méxanuk kil̃e pepíčap sáxalu lit. somehow he won't come; I wish he wouldn't come

-méye- v.itr., also with -če- to turn, curve, to get crooked (body-part, branch of tree etc.), to twist

-mémyem- distrib., also with -če-

-méye-n- caus. to make turn, also with -če-

-če-mémyeme- caus. and distrib.

-pe-méye- to turn suddenly, mistakenly

méyi-iš n., distrib. méyemn-iš sth. crooked (of body part, branch of a tree): e.g., hépuš ___ cross-eyed

méyi-wenet n., distrib. mémyem-wenet sth. curved: e.g., pít ___ curved road

méyenat n. storage basket Mt.Ca. (prob. descriptive term: méye-n-at that which has been turned/twisted around), cf. pénewet for Des.Ca.

míam, see -méaa-

míʔ interr. pron., plur. mívi-m, ALLOM. míʔvi which (person object)

qa-mívi which (also in indir. question)

míví-ka where to

mí-va where; ___ pa somewhere

mí-k how many qa-mík (also in indir. question)

mí-pa (indef. with neg. kil̃e) ever; ___ pa sometime

-míčan- v.tr. Mt.Ca. to criticize

-míimčan- distrib. to criticize intensively

SYN. -náʔmiš- to accuse

CIT. pen-míčan-qa táxmuqalepa I criticized him when he sang

míčawet PN : pàl ___ (prob. -míčan- criticize; pàl míčawet water which criticizes) one of the first creatures

-mínay- v.itr. to rise up spinning (smoke, whirlwind)

mínay-wet, VAR. mínanay-wet n. smoke which rises up spinning

míňča'an interj. so what?

SYN. čáqa-pa

míñik'i indef. pron. someone/something important

héspen míñik'i very important

(kil̃) híče'a míñik'i it/he is nothing, good for nothing

míñik'i n., plur. míñiki-m, VAR. míŋki-m relative

-míŋki-k n.: e.g., ney-míŋki-k I'm his relative; tax-míŋki-kt-em they are relatives

míŋki interr. pron. what kind

mímiŋki what kinds

qa-míŋki (in indir. question)

míŋki-š n.: čaqe ___ pa lit. just in something; in an odd situation (physical or mental, e.g. embarassment), plur. míŋki-č-em any kinds

-míŋkiw- v.itr. to make offering (harvest at the big house)

míŋkiw-at n. sth. offered (to the big house)

-míŋkiw'a n. construct son-in-law

-míŋkiwa-k son-in-law: e.g., ney-míŋkiwa-k my son-in-law

-míisi- v.itr. Span. (misa) to serve Mass, to attend Mass, to pray to God

-míisi-ne- caus. to say prayer, to bless food (of a priest)

míisi-š n. Sunday: míisi-ŋa on Sunday

míisi-va'al n. church

míisi-wet n. churchgoer; priest who comes to the Reservation regularly

-mísi-k n.: ne-y-mísi-k lit. she is in relationship to me, the mother-in-law; my daughter-in-law

-mísva- v.itr. with color term as first element to be slightly of a certain color

CIT. ʔáwal teviš-mísva-qal the dog is whitish, cf. teviš-híwlaqalet

-míš- v.tr., ALLOM. -mímiš- autom. redupl. to chew

-mímič-elaw- to chew on the way going

-miš n. construct hip, thigh

mívaʔ where, see míʔ

-míyax- v.itr. 1. (with an indef. meaning 'somehow', or an interr. 'what, how') to act, to happen; to exist, to find oneself (with -wen)
2. (used impersonally, 3 pers. sing. and -wen) (followed by piš ... pi) it can/should be that ....; (preceded by ...ve) it used to be, that ...., it happened that; (with -e-pa) why?

-mímiyax- distrib. to behave; to exist (here and there)

-mímiyax-ʔa n. construct doings, behavior

qa-míyax- I wonder what/why

míyax-wen pe why? (also followed by piš ...pi)

qa-míyax yáxepa if anything happens

CIT. ad 1. míyax-qal what is the matter?

ad 1. ʔe-míyax-wen how are you?

ad 2. néʔ míyax-wen piš piyik nekútašpi I have to talk to him

ad 2. penʔáyqaleve míyax-we I used to pick it
penʔáyive míyax-we I have picked it before

-mí°- v.itr., ALLOM. -mími- autom. redupl. to emit smoke (in burning)

-mí°-ne- caus. to make smoke

mí°at n. smoke

CIT. mí°at mími-qal smoke is rising up

mĩyel̃ n. Span. honey

mí°-at n. smoke, cf. -mí°-

-mučáwaqi- v.itr., see -čáwaqi-

-múči construct in front of, before, ahead of

-múči-ŋax adv. in front of

múči-ka adv. to the front; further on

CIT. peemnámaanwen ne-múči híčikatem they tried to go ahead of me

híwqaleve múči-ka miš kúkusnašpulu if he were (there), he would make fun of them further on

muhúlil̃ n., plur. -em mosquito

-muhúyaqi- v.itr. to incline forward

-múk- v.itr. supplet. with sing. subj., ALLOM. 1. -čéx- with plur. subj. 2. -mék- in caus., with sing. obj.
1. to get sick, weak (with suff. durat.)
2. to die (with suff. [+realized])

-mék-an- caus. to kill; to beat up, in periphr. lit. to kill a little; to whip

-čex-en- caus. to kill

-mémek-an- caus. and distrib. to whip, beat

-múk-ne- caus. to hurt (body part or sickness as subj.); to beat

múk-iš n. 1. sick person 2. dead person, plur. múk-ič-em

čéx-č-em n. those who are dead

múk-vel n.: pax ___ lit. to which applies: he passed away from her; widow plur. čéx-vel-em: max ___ widows

múk-wenet n. 1. disease 2. death

čaqe múk-ka ... lit. it is just going to die; to barely do: ___ piyk nepíšqaˀle I just barely reached him

CIT. ad 1. kʷáˀil/tákut piš ne-múk-qal lit. I am getting weak because of hunger/ thirst; I am hungry/ thirsty

ad 2. peta múk-vey peemkúkulwen lit. they are making the day on which he died; they're having a wake or an anniversary for a dead person

múkaš n., plur. múkač-em flea (Mt.Ca.: múkaš efers to that of animals and kúˀa to that of people)

-mu-l n.: hé-mu-l plur. -l-em, construct -muˀ nose

-mu ˀikˀíkˀiwet lit. nose which is hooking; hook nose

-muˀ lámsa nostrils Des.Ca.; -muˀ kákvamwenet lit. nose holes; nostrils Mt.Ca.

-mu laplápawet flat nose

-múl- v.tr., -múmul- autom. redupl. to give enema

tax-múl-il̃ n. enema

-múlay- v.tr., also with -če- to stir (as heavy meal)

-múmlay- distrib., also with -če-

-če-múlay-ŋi- to stir up by accident

múmlay-š/-wenet n., plur. múmlay-č-em sth. mixed

SYN. -ŋéw- to stir (coffee or light meal)

CIT. tévišnekiš sélekiš múmlay-wen the white and red are mixed together

-múle- v.itr., ALLOM. muli- with -š to move swiftly (of dust, dirt), to get dusty

múli-š n. dust

SYN. -néy-

-múlu- v.itr. to go ahead

-múluˀ-law- to go ahead first

múluk adv. (prob. -múlu- 'to go ahead', -k), VAR. múluˀku first, at first; for the first time

múluˀ-nuk first, at first; for the first time

múluk-uš n., VAR. múlunuk-uš the first one

múluk-viš n. the first

mùluk ˀáčaˀe first

túku múluk, VAR. tùku múluˀuk the day before yesterday

-múlul- v.itr., also with -če-, -pe- to come out steaming or bubbling; to swarm out (animals in a mass, or objects, as stones)

-pe-múmlulan- distrib.

múlul-iš n. steam

-pis+múlul- lit. to come out and bubble up; to boil (of water, food)

pis+múmlulan- distrib. (many objects)

Cf. -súlul- to go in (of water), to swarm in

CIT. méteče̊m ˀántem hem-múlul-wen témaŋax a lot of ants swarm out of the ground

-múluluy- v.itr. (prob.= -múlul-uy- with submorph. -ay, see -múlul-) to come out steaming

mṹlak n., plur. -em lizard (generic term, see čáxwal, tíˀal, máyxal)

-munávčine- v.tr. to do sth. by accident

CIT. súp̃li kíˀati penqáčinqaleve pen-munávčine-qal when I hit the kid, I did it by accident

múntakʷet name of one of the first creatures, Creation Myth (see Ca.Texts)

-mupáxul- v.tr., see -páxul-

-mupíl̃i- v.itr., see -píl̃i-

-múqi- v.itr. with -pe-, ALLOM. -múqu- in periphr. to blow, blast (smoke, ocean waves)

-pe-múmqum- distrib. (many times)

SYN. -pepúqi- to blow, blast

mušˀíva-l n. lazy person

-mušˀíva-lu- v.itr. to be lazy

Cf. tuvxáik diligent

CIT. ne-mušˀíva-lu-qa piš nehíčipi lit. I'm lazy that I go; I don't want to go

-mut n. construct, plur. -muut-em sister's child

múut n., plur. múht-am, ALLOM. múh(u)- owl

-múh-lu- v.itr. to turn into an owl

múh-lu-š n. one who turned into an owl (talks like a human being, calls the names of those people who are going to die)

mútal n. buckhorn cholla; cf. BandS p. 95

mutámiti adv. early (prob. mu 'still, farther', támit 'time')

CIT. nekúpqaˀle mutámiti péˀiy peta I slept earlier than he

-mutémi- v.itr., see -témi-

-múti- v.itr. Mt.Ca. to be short (of person, body part); to be cut short (of clothes)

-mut-múti- redupl.

-če-múti-n- caus. to cut short

SYN. -tépi- to be cut short (of clothes, body part)

mu-túleka adv., VAR. mu-túlekaˀan (= -mu 'farther', túleka 'tomorrow') towards early morning, early in the morning, see túleka

-múvi- v.itr. to blow the nose, cf. hé-mu-l

-muvi-l̃: hé-muvi-l̃ n., construct -muv mucus, cf. hé-mu-l

múviˀ n., plur. -im little lizard

-múx- v.tr., ALLOM. -mú-, VAR. múh- to shoot; to sting (of ant, etc.)

-múmaan- distrib. (many times/ many objects)

mú-ak n., plur. __-tem good shooter

mú-ivaˀal n. target

tax-mú-iwet n. one who likes to shoot; one who likes to sting, e.g., red ant, bee

-kut+múx- lit. to shoot fire; to make fire by friction

CIT. ne-múh-qalˀe húyal piš némaŋa he shot me in the hand with an arrow

muxáavikat n. Des.Ca. yellowjacket

-múye- v.itr. to flow out, to fill up (of water, fog, smoke)

-múmyum- distrib. (here and there)

-múye-n- caus. to make full

-múmyumi- caus. and distrib. to make full (here and there)

pàl múye-qal-et n. lake

múyi-wen-et n.: pàl ___ lake

Cf. -témin- v.tr. to fill (objects)

CIT. pál paˀ múyi-qal water fills up in it

-múyˀaq- v.itr. in periphr., also with -pe- (=-múy-ˀaq- with submorph. -aq-, see -múy-) to flow out with force (water)

-pe-múmyaqan- distrib., VAR. -pe-múmyaˀaw-

-muyéŋi- v.itr. to become stiff, numb; to stay home

-muyéŋi-n- caus. to make powerless to move (e.g. a snake does it to a rat or a witch doctor to people)

-muyéxe- v.itr. to go down headfirst

-muyéx-en- caus. to put down or shove headfirst

-muyéyxeme- caus. and distrib.

CIT. pen-muyéx-en-qa páŋa I shoved him headfirst into the water

muˀ adv. still, continuously

múˀ-an adv. further, farther on

múˀ-an-viš n. the next one

túleka múˀ-an-viš the day after tomorrow

túku múˀ-an-viš the day before yesterday

-múˀaqi- v.itr. (=-múˀa-qi- with submorph. -aq-, see -múˀa-š-) to pile up (of dirt, earth, etc.)

-múmaʔqi- distrib. (here and there)

-múʔaq-an- caus. to pile up

-múmʔaq-an- caus. and distrib.

-če- múmʔaqi- v.itr. distrib. to pile up (of obj.), to bubble up (of water) in places

color term base + múʔaqi- to pile up in a colored appearance; teviš-múʔaqi-wen a whitish mound is piled up

-múʔaš- v.itr. (=-múʔa-š- with submorph. -aš-, see -múʔa-qi-), usually in periphr.; Des.Ca. -pe-múʔaš- to pile up in a small quantity (of dirt, earth etc.), to rise in a wavelike motion (water)

-pe-múmʔačan- distrib. to move in successive lines (sea waves)

CIT. pál néken múʔaš múʔaš yáxqal the water is coming, waves rising up and down

-muʔíka- v.itr. to lean forward on sth.

SYN. -muʔíva- to lean on

CIT. kélawat peta ne-muʔíka-qal I'm leaning on a stick

muʔíkil̃ n. bird that imitates, mockingbird

-muʔíva- v.itr. to lean forward on sth., to bear down on

SYN. -muʔíka- to lean on

CIT. čúkinapi peta ne-muʔíva-qa I'm leaning on the bow

-muʔívan v.tr., see -ʔíva-n-

muʔmúʔa-wet n., VAR. múmʔa-wet hills

pàl múmʔa-wet ocean

N

-na n. construct father

SYN. peta newélve my father (son refers to his deceased father), cf. -wél-; peta ne$^{?}$élavive (daughter refers to her deceased father), cf. -$^{?}$éla-

-náki- v.itr. 1. to join oneself to, to get together with; to close (mouth, etc.) 2. to fit (clothes), with -wen

-nánkam- distrib. (many objects)

-náki-n- caus. to put together, to join

CIT. ad 1. pé$^{?}$ piyk náke-qal pé$^{?}$iy he gets together with him (like partners)

ad 2. nexél̃$^{?}$a čaqe niyk náki-wen my clothes fit me

nák^{w}et n., VAR. náqwet sumac (sugar **bush**); cf. BandS p.131

-nálaw- v.tr. to befall (of sth. freakish, bad omen)

-námaan- v.tr., ALLOM. -námayn- with inflex. suff. [-realized] 1. to try (to do sth.) 2. to feel, to taste 3. to measure

CIT. ad 1. pen-námaan-qal piš penkúlpi néati, or: pen-námaan-qal penkúlka néati I tried to make a basket

ad 2. pe-námaan-qal wíwiči héma kénma I am tasting acorn mush, if it is delicious

ad 3 kíči pen-námaan-qal qamík piš wávuk^{w}ive I am measuring the house (to find) how long it is

-námi- v.itr. to cross (road, river), to go over

-námi-n- caus. to change (clothes, mind)

-pe-námi- to cross quickly (by mistake)

-vuk-námi- v.itr. to cross over in (another road)

-yu-námi- v.tr. to cross taking sbdy with

námi-wen-et n.: pít ___ road-crossing

námi-wen-eva adv.: (pít) ___ at a road crossing

CIT. pít pa/peta ne-námi-qal I cross the road

ʔí nexẽla míyaxwen súpuli pa piš pen-námi-n-pi I have to change these clothes of mine **for other ones**

ʔáwali peta ne-pe-námi-qal nekáarkiŋa I ran over a dog with my car

nameč́úmi quantif., VAR. nemeč́úmi ten (prob. name- = néma 'my hands', -č́úmi- 'to finish')

nameč́úmi-s ten times

nameč́úmi peta súpl̃e/wíh/ ... lit. ten on top of it one/two/ ...; eleven/twelve/ ...

nameḱʷánaŋ quantif., VAR. nemaḱʷánaŋ five (prob. name- = néma 'my hand', ḱʷánaŋ 'half')

-námik- v.tr. to meet, to come across

námik-wenet n.: pít ___ junction road

CIT. tax-č́em-námik-nem péŋaʔ let's meet there

námki-ka adv. to/on both sides, both ways

námki-ŋax adv. on both sides

CIT. ʔípa míyaxwen námki-ka piš pentéhwap here I have to look to both sides

pič́emwáxinwen č́emqíčikaʔay námki-ŋax we divided our money on both sides (among both of us)

-nánal- v.tr. 1. to ask sbdy a question (with héma 'if', qamíva 'where', etc.) 2. to ask sbdy a favor (with piš ... -pi, ___-ka)

CIT. ad 1. ne-nánal-qa qamívax piš nenékive she asks me where I came from

ad 2. ʔen-nánal-qa piš newélisewpi I am asking you to become my husband

-nánami- v.itr. to run a race

nánami-wet n. racer; pásukat ___ racing horse

CIT. piyk ne-nánami-qal I race with him

-náanme- v.tr., arch. (KS dnkn.) with -sun 'heart' as first member of verbal group to double up (with pain)

CIT. hésun pe-náanme-qal he doubles up in breathing

nánva-nek adj., ALLOM. nánvay- 1. ready (time, person [to do], fruit to be picked) 2. alike; of proper fit (clothes)

-nánva+yax-, VAR. -nánvax- lit. ready + do; to be ready, to be up (time)

-nánva+yax-ni- caus. to decide, to agree on; to plan, to measure; to compare

nánva-yax-iš n.: méniȴ ___ full moon (= méniȴ taxčúmiȴawiš)

CIT. ad 1. nánva-nek piš héeñiwap he is ready to fight

ad 2. wíhkʷa hem-nánva-nek they are both alike

náanxiš n., plur. náanxič-em 1. bachelor, 2. homosexual

SYN. kìnaŋa ʔíʔive bachelor

-naŋ-iȴ: hé-naŋ-iȴ n., construct -naŋ tongue

náq-al n., plur. náq-al-em, construct -náq-ʔa ear

náq-ak n. one who has special (big) ears

naq+témel n., plur. naq+témelem, lit. ear closing; deaf; disobedient

-naq+téme-lu- v.itr. to become deaf, to play disobediently

naq+yúvisal n., construct -naq+yúvisʔa ear wax

-náqʔa yúvisʔa wax in one's ear

náqa ʔíʔive person without ears; deaf

CIT. ne-náqʔa selpákaaqal my ear gets pink colored; I am embarassed

-náqma- v.tr. to hear, listen; to understand

-pe-náqma- to hear accidentally

náqma-ʔil̃ n., construct -náqma-ʔa that which one heard

-náqma-š n.: tax-náqma-š that which was heard; sth. that happened and was known

CIT. nésun ʔelélekʷal pen-náqma-nuk after having heard it, I was sad

ʔe-náqma-qál ʔekúktašqalepa ʔívil̃uŋaʔ does he understand you, when you talk in your own language?

náswet n. smoke tree

-návax- v.itr. to get old (inanimate), cf. -ʔáʔavuk- to get old (animate)

návax-iš n. that which is old

Cf. páŋiš new

návet n., plur. návt-em cactus (generic), tuna cactus; cf. BandS p.49

náaviš n., construct ___-ki poison

-návki- v.itr. to pick the fruit of tuna cactus

návuk imper. of -néken- come!

-náwal̃ construct, plur. -em, VAR. -náwayl̃ younger sister

-náwan- v.tr., ALLOM. -nánawan- autom. redupl. to take away sth. from sbdy

CIT. čemtémay čeme-m-nánawan-weʔn they took our land away from us

-nawaan- v.itr., v.tr., ALLOM. nawayn- to be jealous

náwayn-ivaš n. jealous person

CIT. ne-náwaan-qal ʔí náxaniš this person is jealous of me

-náwas- v.tr. to grab, to fight over sth.

-nánawas- distrib. to keep fighting over sth.

CIT. banáanas pi-čem-náwas-wen we are struggling for bananas

nawaʔél̃ʔel PN. arch. name of a girl in a story (nawa- as in náwʔa 'girl,' -él- as in ʔélka 'pretty')

náwiči v.tr. imperative bring it here!

CIT. čémeyik náwičiʔ bring it to us

náwil̃a-t n., construct -náwil̃ʔa, plur. -m louse, bedbug

SYN. kúʔa-l n. louse

náwišmal n., plur. -em girl. VAR. náwel (intimate), náwisal (most intimate); náwitel (intimate, used for own daughter) Mt.Ca.

náwxa-l n.: ___ paʔ in the middle

náwxa-ŋa in the middle; in town

náwxa-ʔan/-aŋ: tukmiyat ___ at midnight

CIT. maˀ púliˀi hem-náwxa-ŋa lit. among them he fell in their middle; he lay down in the middle of them

náxaluvel n., plur. nánxaluvel-em old man, cf. níšluvel old woman

-náxaluvuk- v.itr. to become old (of man), cf. -níšluvuk- (of woman)

náxaniš n., plur. nánxanič-em, VAR. náxaš (intimate), plur. nánxač-em/naxáač-em man, male

náxaniš súkat male deer

náxa-t n., construct -náxˀa cane, stick

náxa-t-ŋa on the cane

náxa-t peta on the cane

-náxči- v. 1. v.itr. to answer 2. v.tr. to answer, to help

CIT. ad 1. piyik ˀenáxčiqa you answer him (in a letter)

ad 2. pa pen-náxči-ka lit. in it I'm going to help him; I'm going to take his place

-náyax- v.itr., ALLOM. -nánayax- autom. redupl. to argue, to quarrel

-náyx-ane- caus.

nánayax-wenet n. quarrel

SYN. -mémlan- to argue

CIT. péˀiy piyik ne-nánayax-qal I'm arguing with him

hem-nánayax-wen qíčil piš they argued over the money

hem-nánayax-wen qaméxanuk piš peemkúlpi they discuss how they should make it

náyxal n. big lizard (one species of múlak)

-náʔ- v.itr. to catch fire, to burn (object, fire)

ná-qal-et n. fire

SYN. -kína- to burn

CIT. kís ná-qal kínaqal the house caught fire and burned

-náʔani- v.itr., ALLOM. nánʔi- with nominal suff. -wet to make fire

náʔani-vel n. fire place

kùt nánʔi-wet lit. fire maker (prob. < náʔani-wet fire maker); fire-like wind; PN some kind of spirit

-náʔmiš- v.tr. to speculate (about sbdy); to accuse

Cf. -míčan- to criticize

CIT. peem-náʔmiš-wen héma peménkanʔi they accused him that he killed her

náʔqa adv. (second in sentence) probably

CIT. ʔáy náʔqa peemkúyʔi probably they buried him already

SYN. nésunŋax

-néh- v.itr., ALLOM. -néneh- autom. redupl., né- with nominal suff. -at to make a basket

néh-ak n. good basket maker

né-at n. basket

néh-vaš n. basket/doll maker (woman)

-nék-en v.itr. with suff. [+realized], ALLOM. -ménvax- with suff. [-realized], návuk imper. to come

nék-at n. — one who came

nék-ivey-ka — to where one came

nék-ive-ŋax — from where one came

CIT. niyik nék-en — he is coming towards me

-ném- v.itr. never with durat. suff. to walk around

-nénem- distrib. — to wander around

nénem-ˀa n. — wandering around, travel

-yu-ném- v.tr. — to take along

-yu-nénem- distrib. — to take around

-yu-nénmi-wet n.: háwawail̃ pe-___ one who spreads gossip, gossip carrier

ném-et n. — traveler

CIT. piš ném — he is walking around there

-némal- v. with -če- — v.itr. to be dented (face); v.tr. to dent (metal sheet, hat, etc.)

-vuk-némal- v.tr. — to dent

-némi- v.tr. — to chase, to follow (tradition)

-nénmi- distrib. — to chase

-néemi- v.tr. — to chase away

-néenmi- distrib.

-némˀa n. construct — liver

-nénema- v.itr., VAR. -nénama- to hiccup

nénema-ˀil̃ n. — hiccup

-néŋ- v.itr. — to hide

-néŋ-an- caus. — to hide

-néneŋ- v.tr. distrib. with obj. pref. -tax- lit. to hide each other; to play peon game

-nénŋ-il̃ n.: tax-___ peon game

-nénŋ-ivaˀal-em n.: piš tax-___ little things used for peon game

-nénŋ-iwet n.: tax-___ peon player

CIT. táxuŋa pe-néŋ-an-qal lit. he hides it from himself; he avoids facing it

-nes construct aunt, i.e., mother's elder sister

-nési-k(t) ne-y-nési-k lit. she is in relationship to me, the niece; my deceased aunt

-nése construct nephew or niece, i.e., younger sister's child

nét n., plur. néent-em chief of the clan, moderator of a fiesta

-nétan- v.tr., ALLOM. -nétŋ- with suffixes [-realized] and nominal suffixes to ask sbdy for (foods, money, clothes; favor, permission)

-netŋ-iš n. one who's come to ask

SYN. -sé?wi-, -té?i- (-nétan- more polite)

-new adv. subj. pron. inflected with sbdy (active accompaniment)

CIT. né?aš né-new híčika my pet (dog) is going with me

néxiš n. wild squash (indian soap), cf. BandS, p.57

néxiš piš pášamva?al wild squash to wash with, indian soap

néhmal n., plur. -em small rattle

néhwet n., plur. -em pumpkin

SYN. kalaváas Span.

-néy- v.itr. in periphr. (mainly in songs) to move (sand, waves on the beach, or wind on the road)

SYN. -múle-

CIT. yáʔi ʔéleqalepa héspen ŋáčiš néy yáqa píŋa when the wind blows strongly, the sand moves on the road

néʔwet n. generous

Cf. ʔísiwet stingy

-ními- v.itr., also with -če- to bend (limbs of tree, finger)

-ními-n- caus., also with -če-, -vuk-

-če-nínmim- distrib.

-če-nínmime- caus. and distrib., also with -vuk-

níniĩ n., plur. níñĩ-am fruit pod of yucca, wild bananas (baked in ground, cooked sweet); cf. BandS p. 151

nísxiš ash

nísxiš péŋki ash-grey

níšl̃uvel n. old woman

-níšl̃uvuk- v.itr. to become old (of woman), cf. -náxaluvuk- (of man)

níit n., plur. níint-em one who is pregnant

-núk- v.tr. to create

núk-at n., plur. -at-em, construct -núk-ʔa creature, creation

-núk-iš/-wet n.; čemey-núk-iš our creator

pàl núk-at lit. water created; ocean

-núk- v. 1. v.itr. to have a doll fiesta
2. v.tr. to have a doll fiesta for sbdy (doll making for the deceased simulates creation and implies death of creator)

núk-at n., plur. -em doll

núk-il̃ n. doll fiesta

CIT. ad 2. hémnay pey-núk-ik he's going to hold a doll fiesta for their father

-núŋu- v.tr. to carry, take along

-núŋu-max- to carry sth. to sbdy

-núŋu-vaš/-wet n.; kʷáʔisneati pey-___ mailman

CIT. páʔli pen wáyikiweneti ʔen-núŋu-max-ik I'm going to bring you water and food

-nútka- v.tr. to take along as lunch

-nútka-ve n. [construct] lunch

-núʔin- v.tr. 1. to tell to do 2. to send 3. to send for

-núnʔumi- distrib. to send here and there

núʔin-at n. law

núʔin-qal-et n. boss, spokesman, plur. ___-em/núʔin-wen-et-em; tax-núʔin-qal̄-et Indian agent

núʔin-vaš/-wet leader, spokesman

CIT. ad 1. pen-núʔin-qal peytéwikati I tell him to find it

ad 2. pey-núʔin-kat-em páyka lit. they're going to send him to the penitentiary

ad 3. tax-ne-núʔin-qa neʔélay I send sbdy for my dress

-núʔuqan- v.tr. to push

-če-núʔuqan- to push sth. accidentally

-če-núnaqan- distrib.

SYN. -če-ʔétel- to push (with the intention of making fall down)

-sétaʔan- to push (against the ground / the wall)

CIT. pen-núʔuqan-qal húluluŋa I push him on his back

pen-núʔuqan-qal kíʔati keléesakiŋa I push the baby in the baby buggy

Ñ

-ñámin- v.tr. to bend (bow, etc.)

-če-ñámin- to bend quickly, hard

-ñáš- v. VAR. -náš- Mt. Ca. 1. v.itr. to sit down; to settle down (to live or to camp); to set in (a new moon, a young fruit as pumpkin) 2. v.tr. to set for sth./sbdy (to watch)

-ñáñaš- v.itr. distrib. to sit often or habitually (e.g. whenever one goes somewhere, he sits there always)

-ñáñaš-vaʔal favorite place for camping

-ñáš-ni- caus. to put sth. down

-pe-ñáš- v.itr. to push back (e.g. a horse rears on its hind leg); to set in (of blood clot)

pe-ñáč-iš n.: ʔéwel ___ blood clot

ñáč-il̃ n. young fruit which has set in (of pumpkin or the like)

ñáč-iš n.: páŋiš ménil̃ ___ new moon which has set in

ñáš-vel n. chair, seat

CIT. ad 2. métečem távtemi me-ñáš-qal menčéxnik I am setting for many rabbits to kill them

ñíčil̃ n., plur. ñíŋkič-em woman, female
CIT. ñíčil̃ súkat female deer

-ñúčay- v.tr. with -če-, -pe- to squash, squeeze
SYN. -če-síčaq- to squash with foot
CIT. pen-pe-ñúčay-qal wáxačili peta neñášqaleve
I squashed a frog when I sat on it

-ñukˀu n. construct, -héñuku- with -k cousin
-héñuku-k n. cousin: tax-héñuku-kt-em they are cousins
-ñúku-la n. (deceased)
témal ñukˀu n. lit. earth cousins; wild sand-verbena; cf. BandS, p. 28

-ñúš- v. ALLOM. -ñúñuš- autom. redupl.
v.itr./tr. to make / knead dough;
v.tr. to smash sth. juicy (as fresh mesquite bean)
-ñúš-ˀa n. [construct] dough
ñúč-il̃ n. dough

ŋ

ŋáči-š n. sand
ŋáči-wet n. sand hill
ŋàči-š múmawet sand hill

-ŋálaw- v. with -pe- v.itr. to fall in a hole, to make noise by falling into a hole, by swallowing sth.
v.tr. to throw sth. into a hole

pe-ŋálaw-et n.: tékiŋa tax-pe-ŋálaw-et one who traps people in a hole

CIT. tékišpa ne-pe-ŋálaw-qa I fall into a hole

ʔáčakʷe ʔáčaʔe ne-pe-ŋálaw-qa lit. I fell successfully into the hole; I was lucky, cf. neméxanʔa ʔáčaʔe

-ŋáli- v.itr. with -pe- (or VAR. -pa-) to throw a lasso; to get entangled; to be out of place (e.g. of legs)

-ŋáli-n- caus. to hook

-če-ŋáli- v.itr. to get tangled up

-pe-ŋáŋlami- distrib., ALLOM. -ŋálamn-/-pe-ŋálayn- with -ik, etc.

-pe-ŋáli-n- caus., also with -vuk- to rope (cattle, etc.), to trap, -pe-ŋáŋlame- distrib.

pe-ŋáli-n-il̃/pe-ŋálamn-il̃ n. roping of the cows

CIT. pe-ŋále-qal héʔiŋa he gets entangled in his feet

kímuli pen-ŋáli-n-qa I am hooking the door (with a safety chain)

ŋáliva adv. (prob. -ŋáli- + -va) at the opening, between (as rocks, houses)

CIT. qáwiš ŋáliva čempéniičiwe we passed through between rocks

-ŋáŋ- v.itr., ALLOM. -ŋáaŋ- autom. vowel lengthening, to cry

-ŋáŋ-ane caus. to make cry

ŋáŋi-vaʔa n.: piš ŋáŋivaʔa sth. to cry with (a song)

ŋáŋ-ivaš/-iwet n. crier

ŋáaŋʔa n̰. crying

CIT. pélen ŋáaŋ-qal lit. he cries slow, heavily; he weeps

-ŋáŋeyaʔan- v.tr. Des.Ca. to stare at, to look at meanly

-ŋáŋiya- v.tr., VAR. -ŋáŋiyaw- Des.Ca. to cry for sth. (prob. -ŋáŋ- 'to cry' + -yáw- 'to take')

CIT. kíˀat pe-ŋáŋiya-qal híyey the baby cries for its mother

-ŋáqi- v.itr. with -pe- to get stuck

-ŋáqi-n- caus. to put (securing by fastening), to tack; cf. -táv- to put (just laying flat)

CIT. ne-pe-ŋáqi-qal yúliš pa I've got stuck in mud

-ŋátaš- v.itr. in periphr., also with -pe- in combination with -wen- to be too tight (of screws, doorknobs, drawer)

-pe-ŋátaš-ne- caus. to tighten (screws, brakes, etc.); cf. -če-lékeš- to tighten (as belt)

-ŋával- v.tr. with -če- to touch slightly, to tip

-če-ŋáŋvalan- distrib.

SYN. -yáw- (in periphr.)

-ŋávay- v.tr., VAR. -ŋáavay-, ALLOM. -ŋáŋvay- autom. redupl. to sharpen (knife, hoe, etc.), to file

-ŋáya- v.itr. in periphr. redupl. to shake head (saying "No")

SYN. -wéy-, -ŋéye-

ŋáyal n., plur. -em sea-blite, seep-weed (also called laundry soap); cf. BandS p.141

ŋáy-ika adv. way underneath, to the edge

ŋáy-ŋa at the edge

-ŋáˀa construct, plur. -m (remotest) ancestor

 néˀ né-ŋaˀa támyat míam my ancestor is the sun-white hair

ŋáˀ-a n. end (of space)

 ŋáˀ-ika adv. in the corner

 kìš ŋáˀ-ika in the corner of the house

 qàwiš ŋáˀ-ika along the mountains

-ŋélel- v.itr. to go along the edge (of mountains, waters)

 ŋélel-iš n. edge (of the water, etc.): pàl ___ the edge of the water, qáwiš ___ the edge of the mountain

 Cf. támaw, háyva at the edge

 CIT. pàl háyva ne-ŋélel-qa I'm walking on the edge of the water

-ŋélew- v. 1. v.itr. to come right to the shore (waves) 2. v.tr. to edge (as lawn); to stir around the edge (as sth. in a pot)

 -pe-ŋélew- v.itr. to splash at the edge and go back (of the waves)

-ŋéneney- v.itr., ALLOM. -ŋénen-/-ŋénn- in periphr. to make a noise with vibration (of thunder, car, etc.)

 ŋéneney-qal-et n. that which makes thundering noise

-ŋép- v.tr. Des.Ca., ALLOM. -ŋéŋep- autom redupl. to scrub; to scrape; see -ŋépel- Mt.Ca.

 -če-ŋép-in- caus., -če-ŋéŋpeme- distrib. to scrape Des./Mt.Ca.

 -vuk-ŋép-in- caus. to scrape Des./Mt.Ca.

némaŋa ne-če-ŋépin-qa = némai pe-če-ŋépin-qa it scraped my hand

-ŋépel- v.tr. Mt.Ca., ALLOM. -ŋéŋpel- autom. redupl. to scrub (with a brush, sand); see -ŋép- Des.Ca.; cf. -mávay- to rub

CIT. némaŋa tax-ne-ŋéŋpel-qa néqi I scrub myself in my hand

-ŋéwen- v.tr., ALLOM. -ŋéw- in periphr. to stir (coffee or light meal)

Cf. -múlay- to stir (heavy meal)

-ŋéy- v.itr. in periphr., VAR. -ŋéye-, ALLOM. -ŋéŋey- v.tr. in environment other than periphr.
v.itr. to shake (trees, etc.)
v.tr. to shake, to rock (as baby)

-ŋéy-in- caus. to shake

-če-ŋéy-ʔan- caus. to give a little shake or tap to sbdy (to wake him up)

-puš+ŋéy- lit. eyes shake; to feel dizzy, tipsy

SYN. -ŋil̃áa- to shake (generic)

-ŋíi- v.itr., VAR. -ŋíy- to go home, to go away

-ŋíiŋii- to go back and forth; to go home (each one)

-yu-ŋíy- v.tr. to take home

-ŋíy-l̃ew to come home, to come back

ŋíy-iš n. one who went home, left

ŋíy-l̃ew-iš n. one who came home

páyka/páŋax ŋíy-l̃ew-iš lit. one who has returned from the water; one who has returned from the penitentiary, ex-convict

CIT. pen-yu-ŋíy-ka nemáxay I'm going to take home what I've received; cf. penkúsŋika I'm going to take back (what I've brought here)

-ŋiláa- v.itr. to move (body parts, earth, etc.), to shake

-ŋílay- v.tr., also with -če- to scratch (as body part, in a small motion, without leaving marks), ALLOM. -ŋíŋlay- autom. redupl.

Cf. -česálu-, -čexélew- to scratch (leaving marks)

CIT. nesáqaqa pé?iš tax-ne-ŋíŋlay-qa I feel itchy, so I scratch myself

-ŋíñan- v.tr., VAR. -ŋíiñan- 1. to pay sbdy 2. to be expensive

-ŋíŋñan- distrib. to pay many persons

-ŋíñan-xa- to ask sbdy, to pay, to charge sbdy

SYN. -háyuki- v.itr. to be cheap

CIT. ad 1. ?áy pe-n-ŋíñan-?i hékiŋa I paid him for his house

ad 2. mík pe-ŋíñan-qa how much does it cost?

ad 2. ?úumun híčemi pe-ŋíiñan-qal everything is expensive

-ŋísan- v.itr. in periphr. redupl. arch. to move slowly

P

pa inflected clitic adv. localisation (place or time)

mípa? pa sometime

míva? pa somewhere

CIT. mípa? pa ?ax?ečemtéewne sometime we'll see you

súpuli pa penxélaka qáyweneti I'm going to put on clean clothes instead

-pa n. construct aunt, i.e., father's elder sister

*There are no words in Cahuilla that begin with "O".

-pá- v.itr., v.tr. to drink

-pá-ači- v.tr. to drink up, cf. -k^{w}á-ače- to eat up

-pá?-iči- to go and drink

-pá?-ne- caus. to make sbdy drink

pá?-il n. the drink, construct -pa?-a

pá?-va?-al, VAR. pá?-wa-al n. intoxicating drink; any kind of drink

pá?-vas/-wet n. one who is in the habit of drinking too much; drunkard

-páčaaq- v.itr. to scatter (clothes)

-páčaaq-an- caus.

páčawa-l PlN. the upper village in Los Coyotes, where people used to leach acorn (prob. páči-va-l 'place to leach acorns')

-páčay- v.itr., v.tr., also with -pe- (=-páš-ay- with submorph. -ay-, see -páš-) to drop and splatter (wet, soft objects like mud, food, egg etc.)

-pápčam- v.itr. distrib., -pápčame- v.tr. distrib., also with -pe-

-vuk-páčay- v.tr. to throw flat on the ground, -vuk-pápčame- distrib.

CIT. yúliš piš pe-páčay-qa kí?iči he is plastering with mud around the house

ne-páčay-max?-i lit. he dropped and splattered it for me; he served me food (on the plate)

-páči- v.itr. to leach acorns

páadre n. Span. Catholic priest

páh quantif., VAR. páx three

páh-k^w-al the group of three, construct -páh-k^wa a group of three; VAR. me-páh-k^w-al, me-páh-k^wa

páx-ŋa-ˀan adv. in three directions

CIT. mewíh me-páh penˀéˀnanqal I know two three of them (songs)

-pákaa- v.itr. compound with color term base as first element, ALLOM. -pákaq- in caus. (prob. = -páka-q- with submorph. -aq-) to get colored (of body and body parts)

-pákaq-an- caus. to make colored

CIT. nenáqˀa sel-pákaa-qal my ears get pink-colored; I am embarassed

-pákaq- v.itr., v.tr., also with -če- (more frequent than simplex) to rip (clothes, sack, on the seam)

-če-pápkaqan- v.itr. distrib.

če-pákaq-iš n. that which is ripped, če-páki-iš Mt.Ca.

SYN. -čepéki- to rip

CIT. nepáxanive če-pápkaqan-qal my pants are ripping all over

-pákin- v.tr., ALLOM. -pak- in periphr. to tap (as in pottery), to clap hands

-pápak- distrib.

-pe-pákin-, also with -vuk- to slap (face, hand), to clap (hands)

-pe-pápkame- distrib. to slap

pák-piš n. a flat paddle for tapping a pot

CIT. pen-pe-pákin-ka hépuči I am going to slap his face

-pák^we- v.itr. with -pe- to get blister (foot)

-pe-pápk^{w}am- distrib.

-pe-pák^{w}i-n- caus.

CIT. newáqˀa néˀiy pe-pe-pák^{w}i-n-qal my shoes caused my feet to get blistered

pá-l n. water, river

pá-l-(n)ek adj. wet, pál-(n)ek-iš n. wet one

pá-l-uk-lu- v.itr. to get wet, pál-uk-lu-š n. one that has got wet

pá-ˀaqni-wet PN water-dog

pà-l ˀéneneka n. lit. bitter water; beer

pà-l múyeqalet n. lit. water which fills up; lake

pà-l núkat n. lit. water created; ocean = pà-l múumat

pà-l púnive PlN lit. whirling water; Alamo

pà-l pùnive kík, plur. -tem inhabitant of Alamo

pà-l vúkivaš/vúkiš n. lit. one who hits the water; white/black crane

pà-l síwiš n. hot water

pà-l tépawkaš n. frozen water, ice

pà-l téwet PlN lit. one who finds water; Indio

pà-yka/-ŋax ŋíĩlewiš lit. one who has returned to/from the water (sc. from Alcatraz Island); exconvict

CIT. pá-l ˀík^{w}el go get water!

páa-l n., construct -páhˀa, -páa-l-ki wooden mortar

k^{w}íniĩi pentúlaqal páa-l-ŋa páawl piš I'm pounding acorn in the wooden mortar with a stone pestle

-pálaa- v.itr., ALLOM. -palpála- redupl. to be flat (leaf, stone, etc.), cf. -malmálaa-

palpála-wet n. sth. flat (as palm leaf); qáwiš ___ flat stone, mortar

SYN. -malmálaa- to be level (surface of spherical obj.)

pála-t n., plur. -t-em, construct -pála leaf

-pálavla- v.itr., -pálav- in periphr. to flicker (fire); to flash (lightening)

pe-páplavan- distrib. to flash

-pálaw- v.itr. with -wen, ALLOM. -páluw- to be pretty

pálaw-wenet n. that which is beautiful, pretty

-pálaw- v.itr. with -pe- to spark, to go up in flame

-pe-páplawan- distrib. to go up in flame violently

CIT. kút pálaw pálaw yáxqal the fire keeps on burning in a flame

páli-l n., plur. -l-em bat (the animal)

páli-ku-wet bat

páli-sis-mal bat

páli-sis + kʷálma-ika(t), plur. -ikat-em lit. bat which is going to hold under the arm; bat

-pálkiš- v.itr. to straddle

CIT. peta ne-pálkiš-qa I am straddling on it (sitting or standing across)

pálna-t n. salvia carduacea, sage; cf. BandS p.136

pálnekiš n., see pál

pámamal̃ n. blind canyon

-pámuwu- v.itr. to be stubby (as cut short, the end being round), to be thickset or squat

CIT. hé?i pámuwu-qa his leg is cut short (the end being round)

-pánaa- v.itr., ALLOM. -pánu- with -wen- to flare out, to spread out in the full

pánu-wen-ik n. canyon

pánu-wen-et n. canyon way

pána-kʷet n. canyon (where many ridges come down and get together), aurora; PlN Cougar Canyon

CIT. xẽla pánaa-qa her clothes spread out in the full, flare out

pánu?ul n., plur. -em yucca whipplei; cf. BandS, p. 150

páañu n. Span., construct -páañu-ki scarf

-páañu- v.tr. to put a scarf on the head

-páañu-ni- caus. to put a scarf on sbdy

-páañu-vi- v.itr. to put on a scarf

CIT. ne-páañu-vi-wen I've got my scarf on my head

páŋat n., plur. -em reed, tule; cf. BandS, p. 139

-pas n., construct elder brother

pásal n. columbariae, ground wheat, chia

pásivat n. knife, sword

pásnat n. tar, pitch

pásukat n., plur. pásukt-am (prob. pá- ∼ pál 'water' + súkat 'deer'), with classif. -?aš, horse

pásun n. center, heart (of plants), cf. sún 'heart'

-páš- v. v.itr. to drop flat (wet, soft obj.); v.tr. to daub (in painting, plastering); cf. -páčay- to drop splattering

-pápaš- v.tr. distrib.

CIT. páš páš penyáxeqal kí?či penhúhmayqaleve when I paint the house I daub it (the paint)

-pášam- v.itr., v.tr., VAR. -páškam- to wash clothes (sometimes hair), cf. -qáyin- to wash body parts, -yúvušxu- to wash hair

-pápašam- distrib.

piš pášam-va?al n. lit. sth. to wash with; soap
néxiš ___ wild gourd soap

pašwél-iš n., VAR. pušwél-iš, pàš/pùš wél-iš young man, handsome man (prob. paš < páŋiš 'new, young' + wéliš 'grown up')

-pašwél-lu- v.itr. to become/be younger

SYN. páŋiš wéliš young man

páat n., plur. -um duck

patávniva?al n. arrowshaft straightener

-páti- v.itr. to get bloated, to get round (while getting filled with air, food)

páti-š n. that which is swollen up

SYN. -páxan- to swell up

-láqaa- to flatten

CIT. pé? wáxačil̃ čaqa páti-qa the frog got bloated

-pátiš- v.itr. (= -páti-š- with submorph. -aš-, see -páti-) to swell, to bloat

(če-)pátič-iš n. that which is swollen up

-pávas- v.itr. to get wet from rain, dew

pávas-il̃ n. dew, that which is slightly wet

pávas-iš n. that which is wet, damp

CIT. pávas-il̃ peta wén the dew settles down on it

pávu n., plur. -m peacock

-páw- v.itr. to get water

-páw-law- to go after water

-páw-law-ŋi- to go after water and return

páw-at n., construct -páwʔa water that belongs to sbdy

p̮áwiš n. scrub oak; cf. BandS p. 123

páwul n., construct -páwul-ki, with classif. -méxanʔa, VAR. páwal pestle stone

pàwal túʔtu n. worm that grinds

-páx- v.itr. to go in, to enter; to set (the sun)

-pápax- distrib. to go in from house to house, also -pápax-ŋi-

-páx-ane- caus. to make go inside; to invite tax-páx-ani-wet n. one who invites people to the ceremony, cf. net

-páx-iči- to go through

-páx-ikaw- to go in and out

páx-iv-i-ka: támit ___ lit. toward where the sun sets; to the west

páx-iš n. one that is already entered (the sun): tàmit ___ the sun is already set

tam + páx-ika lit. the sun (cf. támit) is going to go in; towards the evening, in the evening

CIT. káviwenepa némaʔi pen-páx-an-ʔi I put my hand in the hole

páxal n. cat's claw; common reed, bamboo, flute made out of it; cf. BandS p. 101

-páxan- v.itr. to swell (body, flesh)

-páapxan- distrib.

páxane-ˀat n.: káarney ___ roasted beef

páxan-iš n. that which is swollen

CIT. néma páxan-iš my hand is swollen

-páxani- v.tr., VAR. -páxni- to put on (pants)

-páxani-vi- v.itr. to put on pants

páxanive-l n. pants

paxáˀ n. ceremonial official, person who calls the guests to the big house (prob. borrowing from Luiseño, see taxpáxaniwet s.v. -páx- for Ca.)

-páxil̃a- v.itr. to foam

páxil̃a-š n., construct -páxil̃a; foam, fog, suds

páxiš fog

SYN. páyiš

-páxul- v.itr. with -pe- to fall down (trousers), to fall through

-mu-páxul- v.tr. to drill through (as tunnel), to shoot through

páxwal̃ n. grinding pestle

paxwáyvaˀa-l n., construct paxwáyvaˀa the inside of the throat (prob. pax 'from there' + wáy-va 'where one calls')

-páay- v., ALLOM. -páy- in caus.
v.itr. to become daybreak
v.tr. to dawn; to sit up all night

-páay-l̃ew- v.tr. to sit up all night through

-páy-ni- caus. to sit up all night

-vuk-páay- to get clear (e.g., when it's foggy)

páay-ika, páay-ve-ka adv. toward the daybreak

páay-iš n. morning, dawn

-páy-ni-vaš n. (súwet) pey-páy-ni-vaš/-wet lit. one which makes it morning; morning star

páy-pa adv. in future, next time

-páye- v.itr. to be foggy; to flow out

páyi-š n. fog

CIT. páyi-š yúpiqal it's getting foggy

páyul n. lizard

páyx^{w}al n. little flat rock to mash plants

pápayx^{w}al n. distrib.

pá?ak^{w}en adv., pá?ak^{w}e Mt.Ca. on top of, on

SYN. peta

CIT. laméesa pá?ak^{w}en métewet there are many things on the table

pá?aqniwet PN. (prob. pa- 'water' + ?aqni 'open') water dog (believed to be living in Palm Springs and feared as bad omen)); water baby (it is said that one could hear his cry at night, but only medicine man could see him)

pá?at n., plur. pa?t-em mountain sheep

pá?aya-l n., construct -pá?ay?a rattle

-pá?aw- v.itr. to put forth buds, to bloom

pá?iwet n. field mouse

SYN. yúul̃

pá?ul n. tule (people used to eat the root, tasted like celery)

pá?uš young

pá?vu?ul n., plur. pápuvul-em witch doctor (more powerful than púul)

CIT. péqi pá?vu?ul míyaxwen piš pe?á?awlupi súkat ?áway
only p. can put on the deer head

-péki- v.itr., with -če-, -pe- to rip, break open (clothes, bag, mainly on the seam)

-vuk-péki- to burst open

-péki-n- caus. to rip open (clothes, skin of animals)

-pépkeme- caus. and distrib.

-če-péki-n caus., also with -pe-, -vuk- to rip open quickly

če-péki-š, also with -pe- that which is ripped

CIT. nepáxanive ?áy če-péki-?i my pants ripped (on the seam)

sú?ičemi men-pépkeme-qa I ripped many jackrabbits (for dressing)

-pélaan- v.tr., ALLOM. -pél- in periphr. to spread open (wings, fan, newspaper -not on the ground-)

SYN. -hélaan- to spread (on the ground)

CIT. wíkikmal pe-pélaan-qa wákay the bird is spreading its wings

-péleley- v.itr. to holler (with hands before mouth)

péle-ma adj., ALLOM. pél-: pél-k^w-iš heavy

-péle-k^w- v.itr. to weigh; to be heavy

-péplemu- distrib., with -tax- to get too heavy

-péle-k^wi-ni- caus. to make heavy; with -tax- to weigh oneself

-péla-ˀa n. [construct] weight

pél-k^w-iš n. one which is heavy

péle-wet n. heavy person

Cf. k^wáwama light

CIT. mík ˀesan péle-k^w-qa how heavy is he?

néˀiy neta péle-k^w-qa wís he weighs twice as much as I

hésun péle-wet piš wáyikive lit. his heart is heavy to eat; he eats slowly

pél̃en adv. slowly; softly (as in sobbing)

CIT. pélema man pél̃en híčeqa he is heavy, so he goes slowly

pe-man adv., object-inflected with it/him (usually carrying, wearing or taking by force), cf. pé-new with him

CIT. nexél̃ai pe-man nehíčeqal lit. my clothes with it I go; I go wearing my clothes

pen conjunction 1. [coordinating] for nouns prefixed with possessive sing. pron., VAR. nen, ˀen (for nouns prefixed with ne- and ˀe- respectively) 2. [topicalizing] in interr.

CIT. ad 1. péŋa hemqálˀe támyat pen ménil̃ pen súˀwet there they were, the sun and the moon and the morning star

ad 2. híčeˀa pen ˀíˀ what is this?

pénev-at n., see -pénew- ~ -pénev-

-pénew- v.itr., v.tr., VAR. -pénev- and pénex- with -at
to make a storage basket, -pénin-
Mt.Ca.

pénew-/pénex-at n. storage basket, cf. méynat Mt.Ca.

pénew-at támive openwork basket

-pénew- v.itr. with -pe- to pass by very quickly, by mistake

CIT. ne-pe-pénew-qal néki piš I passed in front of my house (missing it), cf. -péniči- to pass by

pít pa ne-pe-pénew-qal I passed by the street quickly (or e.g. without stopping by the red light)

pé-new adv. sub./obj.-inflected
with, in accompaniment with,
cf. pe-man with (taking by force)

CIT. héme-new čemtúkʔi we stayed overnight with them

-péniiči- v.itr. to pass by (place, time)

-péepniči- distrib.

-péniiči-ni- caus. to make go through; to translate (as language); treat

-yu-péniiči- v.tr. to take, carry away

-yu-péepniči- distrib.

péniiči-š n. the past time

CIT. ʔelélk^{w}en ne-péniiči-n-ʔi he treated me badly

piš hem-péepniči-wen they passed him

ʔáy páx táwpaxiš péniči-š it's already three years since

ʔeháwaway pen-péniiči-ni-qa mélkiš háwawayňi piyk
I translate your words into English

-pénin- v.itr. with recipr. -tax- Mt.Ca.
to meet each other (two cords in twisting into a rope)

-pénipis- v.itr. to come near; to appear suddenly; to come over (prob. -péni- 'pass by' + -pis- 'come out')

CIT. pénipis yáqa káar the car comes out suddenly (e.g., behind a house, around a corner)

péŋa adv. (often followed by pe) there; then, at that time; in him (obj. pron. inflected)

péŋa-viš n. one who lives there; also péŋa híwqalet

péŋa-x from there

péŋa-x-viči:túleka/páypa ___ the day after tomorrow

múkluk qáyi ʔépuš péŋa pe ʔewáyikinem first wash your face and then you may eat

pé-ŋki-š n., plur. -č-em which is that way, that kind, alike, similar

pépeŋki distrib.

CIT. híčeay pé-ŋki what kind is it?

wíčiw pé-ŋki four times

čepéʔi pé-ŋki-š the same kind of thing

pepéel n. Span. paper; newspaper

pepéel-ŋa adv. in/on the paper

CIT. pepéel-ŋa písqaʔle it came out in the newspaper

pépiy, ALLOM. pépi- with $-k^{w}-$, -ya(-x), -ŋa far

$-pépi-k^{w}-$ v.itr., VAR. -pép- with $-k^{w}-i-$ to be far

pépiy-ika toward the far distance

pépi-ŋa far, in the far place

pépi-ŋa-x from far

CIT. pít $pépi-k^{w}-qal$ lit. the road is far; it is far

míyaxwe piš $pép-k^{w}-ive$ how far is it?

péqi adv., pron. 1. adv. just, only; yet, still
2. pron. (inflected) just it/he alone

péqi ʔíʔexiš — it is nothing, not true, cf. ča(qe) ʔíʔexiš, plur. péqi ʔíʔexičem they are nothing, unimportant

péqi yáxik ... — barely do: péqi yáxik penkʷáqaʔle ʔumun I barely ate all, cf. čaqe múkka

CIT. ad 1. ʔáy máviʔi peqi paʔáyawqal ʔetŋíyka it's evening already, yet you want to go home

ad 2. ʔé-qi ʔehíčiʔí did you go alone?

péesu n. Span. — dollar

-pesyáar- v.itr. Span. — to ride

pe-ta adv. (obj. pron. inflected)
1. on, over; at the cost of 2. for
3. then (in comparative)

CIT. ad 1. ʔáyapiš ne-ta kʷásqal lit. the fruit to be picked ripened over me; the fruit got overripened (e.g. because I couldn't pick it on time)

ad 2. kile pe-ta tuvxáve míyaxwen he didn't work for him

ad 3. kímuŋax más ʔáčaʔe kíš pétuk pe-ta the outside of the house is better than the inside

pétaʔwiš adv. — straight ahead

CIT. pétaʔwiš híčeqal he walks straight ahead

-péti- v.itr. — to lie down stretching (of a long large object)

-péptim- distrib.

-péti-n- caus. — to lay straight

color term base + -péti- to lie stretching in a colored appearance; tul + péti-wen sth. lies stretching in a black appearance

Cf. -héti- v.itr. to stretch out (long slim object as rope)

CIT. peem-péti-n-wen kélawet témaŋa they lay the log on the ground

ʔí man hempéptem-we kúpčem they lie down here sleeping

pe-tuk adv. (subject or object pronoun inflected), VAR. hé-tuk for pé-tuk under; inside

pé-tuk-ŋa adv. inside; under

pé-tuk-wiš n.: héʔi pétuk-wiš lit. one that is under his feet; his sole

kíŋa pé-tuk inside the house (speaker outside), cf. kíŋa (speaker inside)

CIT. témal pétuk-ŋa páxʔi he went in underground

-pévey-, see -péy

-péy- v.itr., v.tr. Mt.Ca., see -túlus- Des.Ca., ALLOM. -pévey- autom. redupl. to pound, grind (acorn, mesquite beans, in the bedrock mortar)

péy-vaʔal n.: piš ___ sth. to pound with (refers to páwl 'pestle' and qáwuvaxal 'mortar')

péy-wet n. one who likes to pound

péyna n. comb; cf. súyaviš arch.

péʔ local-relative pron. distal 3rd pers. sing.: he,she, it (pointing to sth. remote from the speaker); also relativizer

pé-va-t (pé + va [loc.] + t [abs.] ?) that one over there

peʔ/pe clitic pron., ALLOM. pey before consonant and glottals; VAR. pe/pee before stops and non-pause; peʔ before vowels 3rd pers. sing.; also as reinforcement of preceding or following element péʔiš usually with clitic pe that's why, on that account

SYN. hémaŋax/hémax that's why

CIT. ʔívʔax kil̃ pičemʔénanwe péʔiš pe kil̃ pičemkúkulwe we don't know it, that's why we don't do it

hemwésay pekʷásniqaʔle ʔúmun yán púul péʔiš he made all plants ripe but he was a shaman, that's why

pí-ka correlative deictic adv. that way (distant); cf. proximal correspondent ʔí-ka

-píki- v.itr. to get upside down

-pikpíki- redupl.

-piki-n- caus. to turn upside down; to spill (sugar, flour, etc.); to dump, to dispose of

-pípkimi- caus. and distrib.

píki-n-vaʔal n. dump, disposal

naqpíki (nickname) whose ears are curved

CIT. ʔáyil̃ húlul pikpíkiqal the turtle's back is turned upside down (shaped as if it were upside down)

píkl̃am n. strawberry, any kind of berries

-pi-l̃ n.; hé-pi-l̃, construct -pi breast

témal hé-pi lit. the earth's breast; milkweed

hé-piy túʔi her nipple

CIT. hé-pi-y pepísneqal she lets her breast suck; she nurses

hé-pi qáwka her breast is going to get hardened

píi-l̃ n., plur. -m, construct -píh-ʔi, ALLOM. -píh- in construct hair, fur, down (of birds)

CIT. ʔí ʔáwal piyk métewet píhʔi this dog has a lot of fur

-píl̃ay- v.tr. to lick

-pívl̃ay- distrib.

CIT. píl̃ay penyáxeˀi I licked it (once)

-píl̃i- v.itr. to slip, roll in

-píl̃i-n- caus. to slip, to hide in (under the dirt)

-mu-píl̃i- v.itr. to smother in (the dirt)

CIT. múl̃ak píl̃i-qa ŋáčiš pa lizard slipped in the sand

píl̃iˀ-n-am hide it under the dirt! (a game different from peon, women play it)

-pínil̃uˀa n. construct deceased younger brother/sister

píintu adj., plur. -m, Span. striped, spotted

palˀáwalem píintu-m spotted water dogs

-píŋ- v.itr. to get ground, to get pulverized

-píŋ-in- caus.

CIT. pentúlusqal pen píŋ-qal I am grinding it and it gets pulverized

-píipi n. construct mama (intimate)

-pípivis- v.itr. (possibly reduplicated from -pívis- which was formerly in usage in the Chino Canyon) to vomit

pípiviskun kidney (prob. < -pípivis- 'to vomit' + kun-il 'sack')

-pís- v.tr. to suck (the breast)

-pís-ni- caus. to let suck

CIT. kíˀat pe-pís-qal híye hépi the baby is sucking the mother's breast

-pís- v.itr. to urinate

CIT. ˀíš-pís-iktem man čempíswenˀe kímuyka we went out to urinate

-pís- v.itr. to come out

-pípis- distrib. to come out one after another

-pís-ani- caus. to take out

-píips-ani- caus. and distrib.

-pís-alaw- to go out

-pís-iči- to go out quickly

-pís-ikaw- to come out (many subjects)

-pís-ŋi- to go/come out

-pís-puli- to come out

pís-ani-at n. that which has been taken out

pís-iš n. that which has come out, e.g. támit ___ the sun has come out: the sunrise

pís-ŋi-š n. one who went out and came back

-pis+múlul- lit. to come out and steam; to boil (water, food)

tam+pis+páx-vey-ka lit. to where the sun comes and goes in

-číˀa+pis- lit. to sit up and come out; to get over the hump

pemáyewqaleve pe-pís-ani-qa múkweneti he (a medicine man) was curing him and took out the sickness

-pisa- v.itr., ALLOM. pís- with -ˀiš to spoil, to get rotten (foods)

-pisa-ni- caus.

pís-ˀiš n. that which is rotten

písil̃ n. sugar

písil̃-nek, VAR. písil̃-ik adj. sweet

písil̃-nek-iš, VAR. písil̃-ik-iš n. sweet one (sugar, candies, fruits, etc.)

-píš- v. v.itr. to arrive
v.tr. to reach sbdy/somewhere

-píč-ikaw- v.itr. distrib. (many subjects)

-yáw + piš- to bring and arrive

CIT. hemímyaxʔa tax-píč-alaw ʔáyawqa lit. their behaviors almost go and get to each other; their behaviors are similar to each other

p-iš adv. (object inflected) 1. around it/him 2. about it/him 3. with/by means of it/him 4. at/in/on it (as temporal expression) 5. on account of it/him

CIT. ad 1. héqay p-iš hiwqale he lived with his grandmother

ad 2. péʔ netáxmuʔa p-iš qál lit. my song lies around it; my song is about it

ad 3. péʔiy p-iš hemyúlukay pemsústumwene with it they bound their hairs

ad 4. máviy p-iš in the evening, túkmat p-iš at night

ad 5. múkʔi síwiš p-iš he died on account of the fever

péʔiy p-iš ne-kúkusqal I make fun of him

pí-t n. road, way

pí-ŋa adv. on the road

pí-t sámatnekiš the narrow road

pí-ŋaʔ ʔáanzayka híčiwenetpa on the road which goes to Anza

-píitu- v.itr., v.tr., VAR. -pítu-, -píʔtu- to visit

pí?tu-š n. visitor

-píva- v.itr., v.tr. to smoke tobacco, cigarettes

-píva-viču- to feel like smoking

píva-t n. tobacco; smoking

píva-va?al n. smoking

CIT. píva-t-i penqámñik I'm going to quit smoking

neyúliŋa ne-píva-qal lit. I am smoking in my pipe; I am smoking my pipe

píw-il̃ n., plur. -im, construct -píw ancestor; [construct] great-grand-parent (as a euphemism used to designate the bear)

-píiy n., construct nipples, cf. -pi-l̃

píyaxat n., plur. -em 1. rainbow 2. worm with two horns ("they drop from the sky once a year near Fish Traps and the Indians used to cook and eat them")

p-iyk adv. local (obj. inflected) 1. to it/him, there 2. (possession) to it/him 3. for it

p-iyk-^{w}iš n. one who belongs to

wákiweneti p-íyk-wiš lit. one who belongs to the food; food divider

CIT. ad 1. né?iy n-iyk néken he comes to me

ad 2. ?í? qíčil̃ né?iy n-iyk this money belongs to me

ad 3. kil̃e híčey p-íyk ?áča?e lit. nothing to it good; he is good for nothing

píy?x^{W}al n. lizard (little, with blue mark)

-pí?- v.tr., ALLOM. -píy?- to bewitch

-pípa-?an- distrib.

-píy-vaš/-wet n. one who bewitches
-píyˀ-nax n. one who was supposed to bewitch

píˀpiš n. horsefly

-púčaq- v.itr. with -pe- to jump (frog, people in dance)

-pe-púpčaqan- distrib.
-pe-púpčaqan-ŋi- to jump around
púpčaq-vaš/-wet n. one who likes to jump, e.g. púpčaq-vaš návet jumping cactus
CIT. hen-pe-púčaq-ka séerkay pita I'm going to jump over the fence
méteček wáxašlem hem-pe-púpčaqan-wen many frogs are jumping

púči interj. (see húti) expression of anger or resentment for men, cf. wáa for women

púč-il̃ n., construct -púš 1. eye, face 2. seed (absolutive only)

-púš-l̃u-ni- caus. to let have eyes, to put eyes (in the dolls)
-puš-ka one who is the eye(s) in relation to sbdy; ˀe-n-púš-ka I am your (blind person's) eyes
puš-ŋa-viš n. spectacles
-puš + čávay-a [construct] lit. eye-falling; eyelash; he-puš + čávay-al the eyelash
-puš + ŋéy- v.itr., lit. eye-shake; to be dizzy, tipsy
-puš + yúmu-veˀ [construct] lit. eye-hat; eyelid: he-puš + yúmuvel the eyelid
hé-puš ˀíˀive lit. without his eye; he is blind, cf. táatwal
népuš xél̃a lit. my eye clothes; the filth in my eyes
hé-puš tákališ lit. his eye is pasted; he is one-eyed
CIT. čém-puš ŋéy yáqa lit. our eyes shake; we are dizzy

-púču- v.itr. to turn toward, to face

CIT. ne-púču-qal ventáana?i piyik I'm turning toward the window

-púhya- v.itr. to see a witch doctor, see púul

púhya-š n. one who came to see a witch doctor

púuiš n., plur. púhč-em, VAR. púiš road runner (who allegedly sounds like púu)

-púki- v.itr., VAR. -púqi- to bloom (trees, flowers)

-púpkum- distrib. to put forth many buds

-pe-púki- (volcano, hot spring, gun) to shoot up; to blow up

-pe-púpkum-/-pe-púpki- distrib. to shoot up, blow up

pe-púki-vaš/-wet n. that which always blows up (e.g. volcano)

CIT. kélawat púk yáqa the tree puts forth buds

pál pe-púki-qal ?áwsunika the water shoots up into the air

-púksaa- v.itr., ALLOM. -púksa- in redupl., -púksaq-:če-púksaq-iš to be hump-like

-puksa-púksa- to get humped

puksa-púksa-wet n. hunchbacked

če-púksaq-iš n. humped person

CIT. náxaluvel húlul če-púksaq-iš the old man's back is already humped

-púku- v.itr. to root (trees)

-púku-ne- caus. to cause to root

púku-?u n. root (prob. púku?u construct of *púku-?ut)

púkulvaˀa n. brooch

-púkuš- v.itr. with -če- to have a cramp

-če-púkuš-ŋi- to have a slight cramp

-če-púpukuč-an- distrib.

CIT. néma ˀíšvaŋax ne-če-púkuš-qal I've got cramps in my left hand

SYN. -če-súkul- to get a cramp, -če-héwaš- to get a cramp on the side

púul n., plur. púvul-am, ALLOM. -púh- with -lu- witch doctor, medicine man

-púh-lu- to become a púul, to perform the first ceremony

púh-lu-š n. one who has become a medicine man; witch apprentice

púlayiš n. that which has been hatched

-púli- v.itr. with sing. subj., sometimes also with plur. subj., see -čávi- for collect noun and plur. subj. 1. to drop, to fall down; to fall upon (of a bad luck, misfortune, etc.) 2. to be born

-púpli-/-púupli- distrib.

-pe-púli- to fall accidentally

púli-l̃ n. one who was born

púli-vaš/-wet n. one that always falls (e.g. horse)

púli-ve n.: paˀ púli-ve lit. the day on which it fell; birthday

CIT. ad 1. kʷáywil̃ čemeta púli-qa lit. hunger falls upon us; all of us are hungry

ad 1. qíčiˀl̃i peta hem-púli-wen lit. they're falling on the money; they're holding the money; táx(u)ta hem-púli-wen they're stingy

ne-pe-púle-qal káviwenepa I fall into a hole

-púlin n. construct, plur. -púlamñ-am daughter (of a woman), cf. -súŋama (of a man), -méxan son

púlin wíhk^{w}a lit. daughter both; mother and daughter

púlmiš n. nightingale, night hawk; nickname (e.g., an old man at Martinez, who never wore clothes except diapers)

púlmiwet n., plur. -em turkey

-púluš- v.itr. with -če-, -pe- to become dislocated, out of joint (e.g., knee, ankle)

CIT. nepúleqal man néˀi če-púluš-qal I fell and my leg became dislocated

-púm- sound imitation in periphr. sound (by defecating, bumping the head against sth., etc.)

-púmi- v.itr. to have a miscarriage

-púpumi- distrib.

-púmle- v.itr., also with -če-, -pe (=-púm-le- with sub. morph. -al-, see -púmuqe-), ALLOM. -púmlii- with -qal to be round, (spherical), cf. -če-púmuqe- to get round

-púmulumu- in periphr.

-púpumli-ne- caus. and distrib. to make round

-pumlipúmli- redupl.

-če-púmluqe- to get round (=-če-púmulu-qe- with sub. morph. -aq-)

pumli-púmliˀ-wet n. round one

CIT. púmulumu yáxwe there is sth. like a round ball

-púmuqe- v.itr. with -če- (= če-púmu-qe- with submorph.

-aq-, see -púmle-) to become round (like a ball), cf. -púmle- to be round

-púmuqa-n- caus. to roll sth. like a ball

-če-púpumuqe- distrib.

-púpumuqa-n- caus. and distrib., also with -če-, -pe- to make sth. like balls

CIT. némai pen-pe-púpumuqa-n-qa piyik I'm balling up my fist (shaking it at his nose)

-púni- v.itr. to whirl, spin (of water, eagle dancer)

púni-ʔil̃/-ʔat n. eagle dance

púni-vaš/-wet n. eagle dancer

ʔátukul púni-qal-et lit. greasewood which whirls; PlN (name of a rock)

pal + púni-ve PlN lit. water whirling; Alamo

pal + puni-ve-kík one who lives in Alamo, member of a clan in A.

-púnʔa n. construct womb, afterbirth

púuŋku bit (monetary unit)

púpuuŋku distrib.

CIT. wíh púuŋku two bits = one quarter or 25¢

wí wíw púpuuŋku two quarters or 50¢

wíčiw púuŋku four bits; wíwčiw púuŋku many 50¢ pieces

wíwii púpuuŋku many 25¢ pieces

puš, see paš

-púti- v.itr. with -pe- to escape

CIT. hémaŋax ne-pe-púti-qa I escaped from his hand

púti, VAR. húti — well, then (the meaning is not clear; used by men at the beginning of sentence)

púvia-l n., plur. -m, construct -púvia elbow

CIT. ˀenpepúxayqa ne-púvia-y piš I hit you with my elbow

-púvuš- v. — 1. v.tr. to trim the hair 2. v.itr., v.tr. to trim, prune trees

púvuč-at n. — that which is trimmed (e.g. tree)

púvuč-il n.

CIT. kélawati pen-púvuš-qa I trimmed the tree

-púwax- v.itr., VAR. -púuwax- to perform witch dance

púwax-il̃/-at n., construct -púwax-ˀa witch dance

-puwi- v.itr. with -pe-, VAR. -pe-púuwi-/-pe-púy- to split up (a group of people), to scatter, to become clear

CIT. wéwniš pe-púwe-qa the clouds are scattering, it's clearing up

-púx- v.tr., ALLOM. -púpux- autom. redupl. to knock (on the door, on the table, on wooden boxes, etc.) with hand or a stick with a round point

-pe-púx-in- caus. to knock, to hit

CIT. néˀ pen-púpux-qal laméesay némay piš I'm knocking on the table with my hand

-púxay- v.tr. with -pe-, -vuk- (=-pe-púx-ay- with submorph. -ay-, see -púx-) to hit, to bump; to pick (of a bird with its beak)

-pe-púxaan- distrib.

pe-púxay-vaš/-wet n. that which likes to hit (e.g., kúpanil 'woodpecker')

SYN. -če-čúkay- to pick, -pe-téxay- to bump

CIT. pen-pe-púxay-qa laméesay némay piš I knocked the table with my hand

wíkikmal ʔe-pe-púxay-qal a bird picks you

-púxuu- v.itr. to be bald headed

CIT. neyúluka čaqa púxuu-qa my head is bald (see -sáwaa-)

-púy- v.itr. to become full with food

CIT. ne-púy-qal héspen neték^{w}aqal I get stuffed up too much and my stomach gets upset

-púʔan- v.tr., ALLOM. -púwan- to blow the breath out, to blow sth. away

CIT. pen-púwan-qal pívati I puffed the tobacco

yáʔi ʔéleqal pe-púʔan-qal the wind blows and blows it away

-púʔuu- v.itr. with -pe, ALLOM. -púʔu- in -púʔu-ŋi- to be hunchbacked

-púʔu-ŋi to stoop down (like hunchback)

púuʔupul n. weed growing up in the mountains

pyóon n., plur. -em peon stick

Q

qa- pref. (with an interrogative verb, adverb, particle) 1. in indirect question: I wonder how, what, who etc., 2. indef.: somehow, something, somebody, etc.

CIT. ad 1. ʔeenámaynik qa-mík piš ʔehílkʷive ʔetáxaw I am going to measure how wide your body is

ad 2. qamíyax yáxepa if sth. happens

-qáčaw- v.itr. with -pe- (= -pe-qáčaw- with submorph. -aw-, see -qáčin-), VAR. -qáča- in periphr. (with little splash) to hit splashing against (water, waves)

-pe-qáqčawan- distrib., Mt.Ca. -pe-qáqčaw

CIT. pál ŋiláaqal qáčaw qáčaw the water waves and splashes against the ship

-qáčin- v.tr., ALLOM. -qáš- in periphr. to poke (with one's fist, stick, etc.), to hit (with one's fist), to stick in, to stab

-qáqčame- distrib. to poke the same place

-qáqčame-ŋi- distrib. to poke different places

CIT. čúŋal ne-qáčin-i némaŋa a prickle stuck in my hand

čaqa ne-qáčin-qal hémay piš he just hit me with his fist

hésuni pen-qáčin-qale túkvaš piš I stabbed his heart with a knife

-qál- v.itr., supplet., with sing. subj., ALLOM. -wén- with plur. subj. or collect noun (ALLOM. -wéweʔ- with -nem, -wéwn- with -ap ∾ -pi) 1. to be (of objects) 2. to be lying down (of animate beings - refers to the mere existence of an animate being)

wén-et n. sth. that is (there)

CIT. ʔípa ne-qál nepétiwen here I am lying down stretching out

míva qíčil̃ wén where is the money?

-qála n. construct, plur. -m grandchild, son's child

-qála-k(at) n. grandchild (with reference to the deceased grandparent), e.g., ney-qála-k I am his grandchild

qála wíhkʷa grandfather and grandson

-qámi- v.tr., ALLOM. -qámñ- before vowel 1. to leave sbdy (behind), to quit (job, habit), to stop (working, fighting, etc.) 2. to let sbdy do sth.

-qámi-(h)iči- to leave sbdy behind

-tax-qámñ-ani- caus. to fast (=-qámi-wáykiweneti to quit eating)

qámñ-at n. released one (e.g. by the police)

SYN. -téklu-, -wéwen- to stop; -yéŋen- to allow

CIT. ad 1. pen-qámi-ʔi netuvxáʔay I quit my job

pen-qámi-ʔi netuvxáqaleve I stop working (a while)

CIT. ad 2. pen-qámi-ʔi híčikati (=piš híčipi) I let him go

-qáni- v.itr. arch. to become formed (e.g., in mother's womb), to grow

-qáŋ- v.tr. (usually in periphr. redupl.), ALLOM. qáŋa- with -wet to knock (e.g. on the door)

-qáqaŋ- distrib.

qáŋa-wet PlN: qáwiš ___ (télmekiš) rocks hitting against each other (at the entrance of the afterworld)

SYN. -púx- to knock

CIT. kímuli qáŋ qáŋ penyáxeqal I knocked on the door

-qáŋi- v.itr. with -pe- to bump into, to hit against

-pe-qáŋi-n- caus. to bump into, to collide (e.g., persons, cars, etc.)

-pe-qáŋimi-ikaw-, -pe-qáqŋimi-ŋi- distrib. to bump here and there

-pe-qáqŋimi-ŋi-kaw- to bump all around

CIT. kímuli piyik ne-pe-qáŋi-qal I bumped into the door

nekáarki pe-m-pe-qáŋin-we húŋanax they bumped into my car from behind

-qápal- v.itr., also with -če-, v.tr., in periphr. (= -qáp-al with submorph. -al-, see -qápi-) v.itr. to collapse (house); v.tr. to tear down (house), to break (stick, etc.)

-qáqap- v.tr. distrib.

SYN. -čehémi-, -čelápaš- to collapse

CIT. hémki m̦eta qápal yáxʔi their house collapsed upon them

-qápi- v.itr., also with -če- to break (of house, car, bone, etc.)

-qápi-n- caus., also with -če-, -vuk-

-qáqap- v.itr. caus. and distrib., also with -če- (usually) to break into many parts

-qápame- caus. and distrib., also with -če- (usually) to break many objects

qápi-š n. that which is broken

qápi-n-at n. that which is broken

-qás- sound imitation in periphr. redupl. sound (e.g., teeth hitting against each other)

CIT. héspen yúyma nečetáxalqal netáma qás qás yáxqal when it is very cold, I freeze and my teeth chatter

qášil̃ n., plur. qášl-am locoweed, Astragalus; cf. BandS p.44

-qátiw- v.tr. to miss, to fail to find/see

SYN. -ʔaškay-

CIT. paháalʔi yan pa-qátiw-ʔi he looked for it but he missed it

-qáw- sound imitation in periphr. redupl. sound caused by hitting sth. like a box from within

Cf. -púx- to knock

-qáw- v.itr. to harden (of breast), cf. -qáwpi-

qáw-iš n. that which is hardened, cf. qáwiš rock

CIT. néʔ népiʔ qáw-iš my breast has hardened

qáwʔa, see káwʔa

qáwal n., plur. qáwl-am rat

qáwal héma/hémaŋa lit. rat's hand; PlN Indian Wells

-qáwi- v.itr. (cf. -qáw-, -qáwpi-, qáwiš rock) to get tied, hooked (e.g., wagon to a horse)

-qáwi-n- caus. to tie, to harness (e.g. horse to a wagon); (with pref. -tax-) to give oneself up

tax-qáwi-niš n. one who has given himself up

CIT. tax-hem-qáwi-n-wen lit. they hooked themselves; they've given themselves up; they have turned into rocks

qáwi-ka adv. lit. toward the mountain; to/in the west

qáwi-ŋax adv. from the west

qáwi-ŋax-iš, plur. ___-ŋax-č-em PN Morongo Indian

-qawináaw- v.itr., Mt.Ca. -qawináawa- to echo (prob. qáwiš 'rock' + náaw 'to bring')

qawináaw-iš n. echo

CIT. newáwayqalepa héspen pen qawnáaw-qal qáwiš pa when I hollered, it echoed on the rock

qáwisiš n., plur. qawisič-em fox

qáwiš n., plur. qákʷiš rock, mountain

-qáwi-l̃u-, VAR. -qáwi-l̃ax- v.itr. to turn into a rock

qáwi + kut rock fire

tamaʔ + qáwi-š lit. mouth rock; molar

qàwiš sívat arrow-head

qàwiš wéeweliš lit. mountains grown up; mountains outstanding on the horizon (to be seen on a clear day)

qàwiš hulhúlaʔwet, qàwiš yúlaʔwet jagged rocks (hanging down), PlN Coral Reef Ranch

qáwiš piš tésvaʔal stone for rubbing

qàwiš čáwul jagged rocks (sticking out)

qáwiš náawqal (=qawináawqal) lit. the rocks brings; it echoes

qáwive handle, cf. -qawi- to get hooked

-qáwpi- v.itr., ALLOM. -qáqawpi- autom. redupl. to play a ball game; cf. -qáw-, qáwiš rock

qáwpi-at n. ball game

qáwpi-ʔil̃ n. ball, qáqawpi-ʔil̃ distrib.

qáqawpi-vaš/-wet n. (baseball, football) player

qáwuvaxal n. (cf. qáwi-š rock) mortar; mortar and pestle; cf. páwl pestle

qáxal n., plur. -em quail

tis + qáxal brown quail; robin

qàxal tíska, plur. ___ tíska-ʔam lit. brown quail cries tís tís; cf. xaltíska

qáxal piš lit. with quail; with quail feather (= qáxal piš wákay)

qáxalkut n. buffalo gourd

qáxʔa n. seed

SYN. -puš

CIT. ménikiš qáxʔa mesquite bean's seed

-qáyi- v.itr. to get clean, clear (of the ground, body, etc.)

-qáyi-n- 1. to clean 2. to get rid of, to wash, to clear

-qáqyame- caus. and distrib.

qáyi-n-vaʔal: púčil̃ piš qáyi-n-vaʔal soap for washing face; cf. pišpášavaʔal soap for washing clothes

qáyi-wen-et n. one who is clean

CIT. kʷíñil̃ ʔénenekay pen-qáyin-qal I get rid of the bitterness of the acorn

peem-qáyi-n-wen čáaw yáxikati they are clearing it (e.g. the ground, getting rid of brush, trash, etc.) so that it will be clear and level

-qaʔ n. construct, plur. -qa-m paternal grand-parent

-héqa-k n. lit. I am one who is related to her/him the grandparent; I am her/his grandchild

né-qaʔ náxaluvel my grandfather, né-qaʔ nísluvel my grandmother

-qáʔi- v.itr. to speak Luiseño language

qáʔi-qal-et n., plur. qáʔi-wen-et-em Luiseño Indian

-qélek^{W}ene- v.tr. with -če- reflexive Des.Ca., -če-xél̃ek^{W}ene- Mt.Ca. to be proud of

CIT. péleʔey piš tax-če-qélek^{W}ene-qal he is proud of weight

-qél̃a- v.itr. to feel sore

CIT. nehúlul qél̃a-k my back is sore

qél̃ak adj. (cf. -qél̃a-) peppery, pungent, creating a burning sensation

CIT. ʔeséxʔa qél̃ak ʔáčaʔe your cooking is too hot

qél̃a-ka n. cold

CIT. kúspi qél̃a-ka to have a sore throat

qél̃aka nemúkneqal lit. the cold makes me sick; I have a cold

qél̃aka neyáwqal lit. the cold gets hold of me; I have a cold (= yúyat neyáwqal)

-qénxa- v.tr. to have around the neck (as beads)

-qénxa-ne- caus. to put beads on sbdy's neck

-qéqenxa-ne- caus. and distrib. (on necks of many people)

qénxa-t n., plur. -t-em beads (anything that one hangs around the neck)

-qénxa-vi- v.itr. to put on beads

CIT. me-qénxa-qal qénxa-t-mi I have beads around my neck

-qépax- v.tr., also with -če- to spit out (as seeds, blood, etc.)

-qéqpax- distrib. (many objects)

CIT. pen-qéqpaxˀi sandíya hépuš métewet I spat out many seeds of the watermelon

-qépay- v.tr. in periphr., also with -pe- to hit sbdy with a stone or sth. of the sort, round and not long, throwing or not throwing

-pe-qéqpayan- (= -pe-qéqpaan-) distrib.

-pe-qépay-l̃ew- to throw away

-vuk-qépay- to hit (with a stick)

-vuk-qéqpayan- distrib.

-vuk-qépay-ŋi to hit sbdy accidentally

-pe-qépayni-wet n. distrib. one who throws many times; pitcher

CIT. pen-pe-qépay-qal qáwiš piš yúlukŋa lit. I hit him on the head with a rock; I throw a stone at his head

távuti pen-vuk-qépay-qal kélawat piš I hit a cottontail rabbit with a stick

-qépel- v.itr., v.tr., also with -če- to rip on the seam (clothes, etc.)

-qéqpelan-, also with -če-, -qéqpeme- v.itr., v.tr. and distrib.

qépel-nax-(at) n. one who is supposed to rip

qépel-at n., also with -če- that which is ripped

CIT. neyúmuve če-qépel-qa my hat ripped

-qéwi- v.itr. to burp, to belch

-qék^{w}em- distrib. (many times)

-qéx n. construct, plur. -em grandfather's sister

-qéyi- v.itr. to lean against sth.

-qéqyem- distrib.

CIT. kímul piyik ne-qéyi-wen I am leaning against the door

-qéyl̃ekʷene- v.tr., with -če-, VAR. -če-qél̃kʷene- to praise (persons)

kil̃e ___ not to care for, not to bother with

CIT. kil̃e híčey pičem-če-qéyl̃ekʷeni-wen we don't care for anything

qíč-il̃ n., plur. qíšl̃-am; construct -qíš-kiʔa (Des.Ca. -qíč-ika), plur. -kiam money

qíŋiš n., plur. qíŋč-em ground squirrel

-qípi- v.itr., VAR. -qíipi- to be marked (of a line); to float (e.g. fish, bird)

-qípi-n- caus. to mark lines (on the face, on the road); to lay sth. like a string (to measure)

-qíqpeme-, -qíqpaan- distrib., also with -če-

qípi-n-at n. marked line

qíipi-wenet n. line

color term base + qípi- sth. is marked as a line in a colored appearance: teviš + qípi-wen sth. white is marked as a line

SYN. -wíl̃i- to be marked with a line

-qis n. construct, ALLOM. -héqis- with suff. -ka elder sister

-héqis-ka n.: pen-héqis-ka lit. I am in relationship to her, elder sister; my elder sister

-qís-tuʔa deceased elder sister

-qítaš- v.itr., v.tr., in periphr. Des.Ca., also with -pe- Des. and Mt.Ca. to wink

-qíqtaš distrib. Mt.Ca.

-če-qítaš- v.tr. to wink

-če-qíqtačan- v.tr. distrib. (many times)

SYN. -mák- to wink

-qíviš- v., also with -če- 1. v.itr. to be cut and fall down 2. v.tr. to cut off (as tree, body part, clothes)

-qíqvičan- v.tr. distrib., also with -če- (many objects or one object into many pieces)

-vuk-qíviš- v.tr. to cut off with a stroke

qívičat n. that which was cut, qívišn-at distrib. (e.g. chunks of wood)

qívič-iš n., qívišn-iš distrib. also with -če- one which is cut (e.g., tree)

qíviš-vaʔal n.: piš ___ sth. to cut with

qíviš-vaš/-wet n. cutter

CIT. ñúčil̃ čaqe qíviš qíviš yáqa dough breaks up and drops down little by little

hésuni pe-če-qíviš-qal she cut out his heart, cf. pewékqal she sliced it

-qíwiw- v.tr., also with -če-, ALLOM. -qíw- in periphr. to tear (clothes, paper)

-qíqiwen- v.itr., v.tr., distrib., also with -če-

qíwiw-at n. qíwiwn-at distrib., also with -če- that which is torn

wáqat qíwiwn-at torn out shoes

SYN. -čepéki- to rip

CIT. múluku taxéel piš qíviš piyáxnem xélali pen̰ pe-qíwiw-nem first cut the clothes with the scissor a little and then tear it!

yáʔi ʔívakat ʔéleqal pe-qíqiwen-qal néki piš kétvey a strong wind blew and tore the roofing of my house

-qíyne- v.tr. to plow

qíyne-ˀat n. that which is plowed

CIT. témal ˀáy qíyne-ˀat the ground is already plowed

-qúyen- v.tr. to pull out (tree)

-qúquy- distrib. (many trees)

R

ríiku n. Span., plur. -m rich

Cf. sunsúnika poor

CIT. čém más ˀeš-ríiku-m ˀémemi ˀémeta we are richer than you are

S

-sákʷaa- v.itr. to stand shaggy (of hairs), jagged (of rocks)

-če-sákʷaa- v.itr. to be bushy (of hairs)

SYN. -čáŋaa-, -yáŋaa-, -sápaa- to be shaggy

-sákʷay- v.tr. (= -sákʷa-y- with submorph. -áy-, see -sákʷaa-), ALLOM. -sáskʷay- autom. redupl. to mess up (as hairs)

-sálaa- v.itr., also with -pe to be open (of hand with fingers split open), cf. -če-sáli- to tear

-sáslaa-, also with -če-, -sal-sálaa- distrib.

sásla-wet n. distrib. that which is split (e.g. paper)

néma salsála-wet my open hand (with fingers spread out)

-sálaqi- v.itr., also with -če- (= -sála-qi-, with submorph. -aq-, see -sálaa-) to open hands (with fingers spread out), cf. -sálaa- to be open

-sálaq-an- caus., also with -če- to open up, to spread out quickly (hands)

sáalaʔa n., construct -sáala-ki blanket(s)

-sáli- v.itr., with -wen, also with -če- to tear, to rip (clothes, body parts, etc.)

-če-sáslame- distrib.

-sál-in- caus., also with -če-, -vuk- to tear, to rip (e.g. ear-mark of cattle)

-sáslame-, -sásal- caus. and distrib., also with -če-

-če-sáli-vaš/-wet n. that which rips easy (e.g. clothes)

Cf. -čeqíwiw-, -čepéki-, -čepȧki-, qépel- to tear

CIT. ʔaláambri némay peʔíkqal pe-če-sáli-n-qal the wire hooked my hand, ripped it clear down

pepéeli pen-sáslame-qa (= pen-sásal-qa) I am shredding the paper

-sáluk- v.tr., also with -če- to scratch (e.g. body with fingernails, leaving marks)

-sáslukan- distrib., also with -če-

SYN. -ŋíl̃ay- to scratch (without leaving marks)

-čexélew- to scratch

CIT. gáato nečúkqa man ne-če-sáluk-qa the cat clawėd me and scratched me

sálu-l n., construct -sálʔu fingernail

-sámam- v.itr., ALLOM. -sámm- in periphr. 1. to be seized with a chill, to become numb 2. to drizzle (of rain)

SYN. -síi- to feel chill

CIT. táxaw sámam-qa his body is seized with a chill; a chill runs up in the spine

sámat n. brush, herb, grass

sámat-nek adj. slim, skinny; narrow (of a road); sámat-ek (intimate)

sámat-nek-iš adj. slim; sásmat-nek-iš distrib., sásmat-nek-ič-em plur.; sámat-ek-iš (intimate)

Cf. -ʔíka- Mt.Ca., -yáwi- Des.Ca. to get skinny

-sáamsa- v.tr. Mt.Ca., see -ʔúʔuwi- Des.Ca. to buy

sáan-at n. gum

sáan-kat plant which is sticky, Adenostoma sparsifolium

sáanat míšvaʔal chewing gum

sandíya n. Span., plur. -m watermelon

-sáqa- v.itr. to feel itchy

-sásqay- distrib. to feel itchy; caus. and distrib. to itch

-sáqa-ne- caus. to itch

sáqa-ʔil̃ n. the itch

CIT. némaŋa ne-sáqa-qa I feel itchy in the hand

sáqapiš n., plur. sáqapč-em Mt.Ca., see wéwelpiš Des.Ca. mushroom (grows on the cottonwood tree stump); cf. BandS p.106

-sáqin- v.tr., with -pe-, arch. to kill (with power of medicine men: they used to kill each other)

sásaymal̃em n. wild ducks

-sát- v.itr. to strain; to leak

-sát-ni- caus. to strain, to squeeze

sát-ni-at n. sth. sth. that is strained, squeezed (e.g. juice, cheese)

sáva-l n., plur. -em, construct -sávˀa bark, skin (of animals), shell (of eggs, etc.)

CIT. ˀíl̃ sáva-y peemsísipwe they are scraping the bark of the mesquite tree

sáavet n. Mt.Ca., see číˀaš Des.Ca. Mexican

-sáwa- v.itr. in periphr., ALLOM. -sáasway- autom. redupl. to whisper

CIT. sáwa sáwa níyaqa I am whispering

-sáwaa- v.itr., ALLOM. -sáaw- in periphr. to go away, to disappear, to pass away; not to exist

-sáswaa- distrib.

SYN. -čúx- to disappear

CIT. síyaqeˀi píka sáwaa-qal he moved there, he's gone

kahvée sáwaa-qal there was no coffee

-sáw- v.itr., v.tr. to make tortillas

-sásaw- autom. redupl.

sáw-iš n. tortilla

sáw-et n., VAR. sáwaˀ- with -vel raw, green (of plants)

sáw-vel n.: sáw-vel pa Mt.Ca.PlN, lit. where the green, (plants) (are); cf. the modern family name Saubel

sáwaˀ-vel Des.Ca. mesquite which never ripens, evergreen

sáxalu adv. 1. probably, perhaps 2. hopefully, possibly (with háni, qaméxanuk, -pulu)

CIT. ad 1. kil̃ nepeyéŋenpi sáxalu henpívakati (= piš nepívapi) lit. Wi-l you probably not allow me to smoke?; May I smoke?

ad 2. háni sáxalu ˀípa híwqal I wish he were here

ad 2. ˀívˀax sáxalu nehíčipulu I might go today

sáxa-t n. Mt.Ca. willow tree

sáxa-mal n. a species of willow tree

-sáyi- v.itr. with -če- to rip, to snag (clothes, papers, etc., without tearing completely - textiles still hanging)

-če-sáyi-n- caus.

-če-sásyam- v.itr. distrib.

-če-sásyami- caus. and distrib.

če-sáyi-iš n. that which is snagged

-če-sáyi-n-a n. caus., construct that which is ripped

-sáay- v.itr. with -vuk- to scatter, to spread out (of water, sand, etc.)

-vuk-sásaay- distrib.

-pe-sáay- to scatter, to spread out

CIT. páˀli penvukwíčenqal kímuyka ˀúmun vuk-sáay-qal I splashed the water outdoors and it spread out

sáˀi-l̃ n., construct -sáˀi guts

sáˀwal n. louse (of hair)

-sé- v.itr. to bloom

  séˀ-ik n. one which has a lot of blossoms (of plants)

  séˀ-iš n. flower, construct -séˀiš-ki

  sé-l n. blossom

  ˀàswet sé-ˀi PN eagle flower

séken ill, pale

  CIT. yéwi séken-ˀa ˀívˀax ˀáčama he looked ill before, (but) now he is fine

sekʷával n. carrying basket

-sékˀa n. construct, ALLOM. -sék- with -ŋa shoulder

  -sék-ŋa adv. on the shoulder

sel- first member of compounds, cf. sélnek-iš reddish, pink

  sel + híwlaqalet n. pink Des.Ca., sel-híwyaqalet Mt.Ca.

  sel + híwyaxiš n. reddish, pink

  -sel + kéŋey- v.itr., -sel + kéŋ-kéŋ- in periphr. to fall down scattering in reddish appearance (of embers)

seláwa-l̃ n., construct -seláwa the middle part of the back

sélel̃ n. brown weed (for basketery); cf. BandS p.131

sélet n. sumac (basket-weed), rhus trilobata; cf. BandS p.131

sélnek-iš adj., plur. -č-em, VAR. sélek-iš (predicative), sétlek (emphatic) 1. red 2. penny

-sélek-lu- v.itr. to become red

sel̃áxama adj. dirty (of clothes, etc.)

sel̃áxama-niš n. person/thing that is dirty

-sel̃áxmu- v.itr., ALLOM. -sel̃áxmuk- in caus. to become dirty

-sel̃áxmuk-ne- caus. to make dirty

-sel̃híišče- v.itr. to tell a story, a tale

sel̃híiščeʔ-at/-il̃ n. tale

Cf. -ʔáʔalxe- to tell a true story

-sém- v.itr., ALLOM. -sésem- autom. redupl. to laugh

-sém-ne- caus.

-sém-ŋi- to laugh on the way back

-sém-viču- to feel like laughing

-sém + yaw- v.tr. Mt.Ca. lit. laugh + take; to smile at sbdy; -sém-iya- Des.Ca.

sém-ŋi + ʔayaw almost to burst into laughter

piyik ne-sém-ʔi I laughed at him

niš kúkusqal man niš sésem-qal he's making fun of me and laughing at me

CIT. ne-sém-ne-qal netétiyax-maxqaleve yéwi híčemivi sulsímimaniči he made me laugh telling me sth. funny which happened before

semáana n. Span. week

CIT. túku séʔŋaxviš semáana a week before last

-senmúk- v.tr. (originally a compound with -sen-/-sun- 'heart' + múk- 'to get sick', cf.

Seiler 1975:505/6 to become tired of, to become bored, to feel disgusted with

-senmúk-law- to get tired of

CIT. čém pičem-senmúk-wen ʔívi kíʔati ŋáŋqalepa we feel disgusted with this baby when it cries

-séŋi- v.itr. to pull up (of mouth), to grin, to smile

SYN. -sémyaw- to smile

CIT. niyik séŋi-qa he is smiling at me

-séqay- v.tr. with -vuk- 1. to whip 2. to call sbdy over the phone

-vuk-sésqaan- distrib. to whip

-vuk-sésqame- distrib. to spank, to whip

-če-séqay- to switch, to whip a little

-pe-séqay- to whip, to throw (one's power at sbdy to kill him), -pe-sésqaan- distrib.

CIT. ad 1. némay piš pen-vuk-sésqame-qal I am spanking him with my hand

ad 2. piyk pen-vuk-séqay-ʔi piš ŋíylãwap I phoned her to come back

séqnat n., plur. -em long weed (like arrow weed)

sétax adj. salty, sour

sétax-at n. that which is salty

-sétax-lu-ne- v.tr. (sétax-lu- 'to get salty' -ne- caus. suff.) to make salty

Cf. písil̃ek sweet (of sugar), -ʔíŋyaw- to make salty

-sétaʔan- v.tr. (cf. -sétin- to press down), ALLOM. sétaʔn- with -at to press down (with hand or foot)

séta'n-at n. that which is pressed, e.g. sé'iš ___ pressed flower

CIT. peta nenášqal pen-séta'an-qal I sat down on him and pressed him

-sétin- v.tr., ALLOM. sét in periphr. 1. to press, to squeeze sth. into a container (with any instrument) 2. to iron

-sésteme- distrib. to press (many objects)

-če-sétin- to press accidentally

-pe-sétin- to squash, to press accidentally, to step on (as sbdy's foot)

séti-wen-et n. lit. that which is pressed; one hundred dollars, cf. čúviwenet lit. loose one; small change

SYN. -wáwatne- to iron

CIT. pepéeli kahóonŋa pen-sétin-qa I pushed the paper into the box

taxhem-pe-sétin-wen máčama 'áča'e they squashed against each other as it was too crowded

séva' n. autumn

sével n. yucca blossom

séwaxil̃ n., plur. -em 1. mesquite bean which is not ripened and not sweet 2. clan's name in Torres: Levi family

séwel n. bush (for making soap)

-séwel- v.itr., v.tr., ALLOM. -séswel- autom. redupl., -séwelewe- in periphr. to tickle (of the throat)

SYN. -l̃akay- v.tr. to tickle

CIT. nekúspi ne-séswel-qal my throat tickles me

séwet n., plur. séwt-am rattlesnake

séwet háhyut sidewinder

sèwet yúk?a weed which is good for snake-bite (for yúk?a, cf. -yúki 'to be afraid of)

-séx- v.itr., v.tr. to cook (food in water)

séx-?at n. that which was cooked

séx-ŋax-viš PN lit. man from séxey (Palm Springs)

séx-wet n. cook

pàl séxey lit. water cooked; PlN Palm Springs

-séxelxe- sound imitation in periphr. (sound from cooking meat)

sexwálal n. basket for foods

-séy- v.itr. to melt (of lard, butter)

Cf. -čax- to melt (of ice, snow)

séyewet n., plur. -em; Mt.Ca. síyalem (only plur.) baby quail

sé?l̃am n., usually redupl. sè?l̃am sél̃am crickets

-sé?ni- v.tr. (cf. -sé- to bloom) to decorate

sé?ni-?il n. decoration

sé?ŋax adv. later, afterwards, the last; following sbdy, later than

-se?ŋax-lu- v.itr. to be late, to arrive late

sé?ŋax-viš n. the last one, one who is late

Cf. húŋayka later, múluk first

CIT. píšqal sé?ŋax (= sé?ŋax-lu-qal) he arrived the last

hem-sé?ŋax néken he came following them, after them

-sé?we- v.itr., v.tr. to beg, ask (sbdy for food)

-sése?wi- distrib. to beg always

-sé?wi-l̃ew- to go begging

-sé?wi-ŋi- to go around begging

-sé?we-?a n. one that is begged for

sé?wi-š n. one who came to beg, or to borrow

sé?wi-wet n. beggar

SYN. -nánal- to ask (for), -nétaan- to ask for, -té?ya- to ask for money

CIT. ne-sé?we-qa wáyikiweneti yan peta neháwawayqa?a I begged for food, but he turned me down

-síi- v.itr. in periphr. to feel chill (of body)

SYN. -sámam- to feel chill

sí-at n., ALLOM. -síy-?a, -síh-?a in construct, síh- with -ŋa cradle

síh-ŋa adv. in the cradle

-síčaq- v.tr. with -če- to smash, squash (bugs, body parts, etc.)

-síščaqan- distrib. (usually without -če-)

-pe-síčaq- 1. v.itr. to have loose bowels, diarrhea 2. v.tr. to smash accidentally

-pe-síščaqan- v.itr. distrib. to have loose bowels (go to toilet often)

SYN. -peñúčay- to squash (by sitting on)

CIT. ne-če-síčaq-qal né?iŋa lit. he smashed me on my foot; he smashed my foot (= pe-če-síčaq-qal né?i)

-síčúmin- v.tr. to think

-sičúšmeme- distrib. to think over and over

sičúmin-?a n. thought

CIT. pen-sičúmin-qal piš qaneméxive I am thinking about what I did

mu pen-sičúmin-qa lit. I am still thinking (of) it; I remember it

?elélk^{W}iči niyk pe-sičúmin-qa he's thinking a bad thing to me; he's planning a bad thing against me

síkawet n. tree squirrel

-síkik- sound imitation in periphr. (creaking sound, e.g. of a chair when sitting on it)

-síkil- sound imitation in periphr. sound of metals or dishes hitting against each other

-síl̃e- v.itr.,also with -če- to spill, to drip (water, any liquid); cf. -wáne- to flow, to run (water)

-sísl̃em- distrib. to spill here and there

-síl̃i-n- caus. to spill, to pour (water); cf. -píkin- to spill (sugar, etc.)

-sísl̃eme- caus. and distrib.

CIT. hém?is síl̃e-qal their tears are running down

métewet tápamal pax pá?li pen-síl̃emn-ik I am going to spill out water from many pots

-síl̃em- sound imitation in periphr. (sound of cricket)

sil̃em-síl̃em n. cricket

-símm- v.itr. in periphr., with —sun 'heart' as first member of verbal group, ALLOM. -sísmismi- autom. redupl. to get provoked; to feel disgusted

CIT. nèsun símm yáxqal penméknik I feel provoked (I am going to kill him)

símut n., plur. -em salt grass; cf. BandS p.66

sinsímniš adj. attractive, cute

-síŋal̃- in periphr. to make a grim face

CIT. síŋal̃ yáqa niyk he made a grim face at me

-sípi- v.itr. with -če- to scrape, to peel off

-písip-, -síspimi- caus. and distrib.

če-sípi-š n. that which is scraped

CIT. pen-če-sípin-qal némay kélawat piyk I've got my hand scraped against the wood

ʔíl̃ sáv̂ay peem-sísip-wen they're peeling mesquite bark

netámi če-sípi-š qáwiš piyk/pa my knee got scraped against a rock

sísil̃ n., plur. sísl̃-am chipmunk

sískiŋil̃ n. stinkbug

-sív- v.tr., ALLOM. -sísiv- autom. redupl. to shave, to sharpen (e.g. pencil), to scrape

sív-at n. that which is scraped, smoothened; arrow head

tax-sív-vaš/-wet barber

qáwiš sív-at lit. sharpened stone; arrow head

CIT. népuči pen-sísiv-qa, or (népušŋa) tax-ne-sísiv-qa I'm shaving my face

-sívalu- v.itr. to be pointed (of arrow head, etc.), to point (of tree, etc.)

-sívalu-ne- caus. to sharpen, to point

sívalu-wet n. that which is pointed

sívat, see -sív-

sívil̃ n. sycamore, canyon maple; cf. BandS, p.29, 105

sívuy-al n., plur. sívuylam, construct sívuy-a worm

sívuy-iš n. being wormy, having many worms

-síw- v.itr. to become hot, to have fever (with -táxaw 'body' as subj.)

-síw-ne- caus. to heat (water, etc.)

síw-iš n. heat, fever

síw-ma adj. hot

síw-ta-yka lit. hot-on- toward; toward where it is hot

pàl síw-iš hot water

SYN. -ʔéme- to feel hot; to get burned

CIT. netáxaw síw-qal I've got fever

síw-iš neyáwqal lit. fever holds me; I have fever

síw-ič-i pema nehíwqa lit. I am living together with fever; I have fever (=síw-ič-i penyáwqa)

-síyaqi- v.itr., ALLOM. síya in periphr. to move forward, to move out

-sísiyaqi- distrib. to move always

-síyaq-an- caus. to move

síyaqi-š n.: piyk ___ one who moved to it, sísiyaqni-š distrib. one who moved out always

CIT. čem-sísiyaqi-wen tuháyimaniš pa súpul kíš piyk we are always moving out to another house

CIT. súnči ʔáyaxwe síya yáxe come a bit closer!

-síyči- v.itr., v.tr. to milk (as cow, gum plant)

-síʔ- v.itr., ALLOM. -sísi- autom. redupl. to urinate

-síʔal- v.tr., ALLOM. -sísʔal- autom. redupl. to braid (hair, rope with three strands)

-síʔal-ʔa n. [construct] braids

Cf. -wíčiw- v.tr. to twine (with two strings)

-síʔay- v.tr. to peel (fruit, bark of a tree, etc.)

-sísʔay- distrib. to peel

-če-síʔay- v.itr. to peel (of skin)

Cf. -čilay- to shell (nuts), -če-sípi- to scrape

CIT. pen-sísʔay-qa sávay I am peeling the bark

kíʔat púleqal támi če-síʔay-qal the kid fell and his knee peeled

-su n. construct maternal grandmother

súk-at n., plur. -t-am deer

-súk-lu- v.itr. to dance (of Palm Springs Indians, connected with deer)

súk-lu-ʔal n. dance (of Palm Springs Indians)

-súkaa- v.itr. to shrink (body, clothes, etc.), to wrinkle

SYN. -súkul-, -súkuqe- to shrink

CIT. čaqa súkaa-qa nexéla my clothes wrinkled

-súkul- v.itr. with -če- (= -súk-ul- with submorph. -al-; see -súkaa-) to shrink (of body parts)

-če-súkulan- distrib.

SYN. -ʔínišlu- to become small, -súkaa-, -súkuš- to shrink

CIT. néʔi néma ʔúmun če-súsklan-qal all my feet and hands are shrinking

-súkuš- v.itr. with -če- (= -súk-uš- with submorph. -aš-, see -súkaa-) to shrink, to cramp

-če-súskučan- distrib. to shrink constantly

-pe-súkuš- to cramp

SYN. -če-súkul-, -če-súkaa- to shrink, -če-túnuš- to cramp

súul n., plur. -em, construct -ki 1. weed for basketry 2. weed stick for game

-súla n. construct grandchild, i.e., daughter's child

-súla-k(at) n., with obj. pers. pron. deceased matern. grandmother

sulčáamaniš n. feast, dance, merrymaking

CIT. péŋa sulčáamaniš míyaxwen there was some feast

sulsímima adj. (prob. = sun 'heart' + símima) nice, cute; funny, humorous

sulsímima-niš n. sbdy/sth. that is nice, cute, funny or humorous

-súlul- v.itr. with -pe- to swarm into (water, objects, etc.)

-če-súlul- v.tr. to sip, to swallow

-ke-súlul- v.tr. to swallow

-vuk-súlul- v. v.itr. to swarm into; v.tr. to swallow all at once

SYN. -vuksúyuy- to go into (of water), -méŋk^{w}a- to swallow

swallow (solids); -pemúlul- to swarm out

CIT. pál pe-súlul-qal kávika the water goes into a hole quickly

sún-il̃ n., construct -sun, VAR. sil̃-/sel̃- in compound heart

sún-ax-wen-et n. sorrow

-sun-ŋax adv. lit. from one's heart; one thinks

-sun + ʔáʔwuʔwi- v.itr. to be lonesome

sun-ʔáʔwuwi-wen-et n. lonesomeness

-sun + čáy- v.itr. to be happy, to have a good time

sun + čáay-il̃ n. fun

sun + háman- v.itr. lit. heart to avoid (?); to feel ashamed

sun + háman-il̃ n. shame

-sun + háhyam- v.tr. lit. to make heart tired; to threaten

-sun + híšče- v.itr. lit. heart to go often; to wish

-sun + káviiči- v.itr. to be surprised

-sun + táʔatay- v.itr. to hurry up

-sun + táwas- v.itr. lit. heart to lose; to forget

-sun ʔíʔive without one's heart; crazy

-sun -símm- to get provoked, to feel disgusted

-sun -táv- lit. to put heart in place; to relax

-sun -pe-témi- heart to close up; to get disappointed

CIT. né-sun ʔáčama lit. my heart is fine; I am glad, thankful, cf. né-sun ʔáča-ʔe lit. my heart is good; I am a good man

ʔáy hé-sun paʔáminqa lit. he threw out his heart; he sighed

hé-sun yáʔikluqal lit. his heart runs fast; he breathes fast

súnaxwenepa because; that is why

SYN. pé⁹iš (pe)   that's why

CIT. súnaxwenepa pen⁹áyawqal just because I want it

súnči adv.   close, near

súsunči distrib.   close together to each other

CIT. súnči ⁹áyaxwe síya yáxe move/come a bit closer!

súnikat n.   hard time, suffering; sadness

sun + súnikat, plur. -em lit. heart + hard time; poor person

Cf. súne⁹ma   poor; ríiko rich one

CIT. súnikat-i nekúsaneqa lit. he makes me take hard time; he gives me a hard time, he bothers me

súnikat-i penkúsqa I have a hard time

-súnwe- v.tr.   to feel sorry for sbdy

súnwe⁹-ma adj.   sad; poor, VAR. súne⁹-ma poor

sun-sún⁹e-ika(t̰) n. one who is sad, poor

sun-sún⁹e-il̃ n. poverty

tax-súnwe⁹-il̃ n. sadness, sorrow

-súŋama n. construct, plur. -súsŋamañ-em daughter (of a man), cf. -púlin (of a woman)

súŋama wíhkʷa lit. daughter both; father and daughter

-súpaq- v.itr. (= -súp-aq- with submorph. -aq-, see -súpaš-) (of eyes) to close (cf. -túlu-)

-súpaq-an- caus. to close (eyes)

SYN. -súpaš- v.itr. (of eyes) to close

CIT. súpaq-i kil̃e petéhwan close your eyes, don't look!

-súpaš- v.itr. in periphr. (= -súp-aš- with submorph. -aš-, see -súpaq-) to close quickly (of eyes)

CIT. súpaš súpaš yáxqal he is blinking

súpl̃i, VAR. súpl̃e one

súpl̃e-kʷal adv. lit. in one; together (see táxkʷe)

súpl̃i-š adv. once, sometime

súpul, plur. -em other

súspul distrib. each one; súspul-em one by one

súpul-aʔan different

súpul-ika adv. to another way

háxami súpul somebody else

híčeʔa súpul what else

-súti- v.itr. to be tied around

-sústum- v.itr. distrib.

-súti-n- caus. to tie, to bind around

-sústumi- caus. and distrib.

Cf. -túčin- to tie

CIT. kíʔati pe-n-súti-n-qa síaŋa I tie the baby to the cradle

-súval- v.itr. with -pe-, -če-súyal- Mt.Ca., to shrink (e.g., of balloon)

-če-súval- to shrink, to get baggy (of skin)

-súvale- v.itr. to twist, to spin

súval̃e-il̃ n. twist dance

SYN. -súyi- to spin fast

súvi-š n. sth. to clean the mortar with (like a brush?)

-súvuvey- v.itr. to whirl around (KS dnkn.)

suwánawet n., plur. suwánawt-em, VAR. ʔeswánawet wild grape

-súwelu- v.itr., ALLOM. -súwelwe- in periphr. to somersault, to twist

-súww- sound imitation in periphr. (sound of a stone falling from the air, or by the wind hitting a wire, cf. -wéx-)

-súyal- v.itr. with -če- to shrink (of the skin, e.g. when one gets burned on the hand)

súyaviš n. arch. comb

SYN. péyna comb

-súyaʔa n. construct; -máyva Mt.Ca. rectum

súyil̃ n. scorpion

Cf. mánisal̃ little scorpion

-súyiš- v.tr., also with -če- to tighten by screwing or with a belt

Cf. -čelékeš- to tighten; -xál̃aqan- to loosen

CIT. nekáarki čénenvey pen-súyiš-qal I am bolting the wheel of my car

neyúlukay pensútinqal pañuy piš héspen ʔáčaʔe če-súyiš-wen I wrapped a handkerchief around my head, it is too tight

-súyuy- v.itr., ALLOM. -súyy- in periphr. to spin, to whirl (e.g. of water)

-súyuy-ne- caus. to make spin

-če-súyuy-, -vuk-súyuy- to spin fast (e.g. of an eagle-dancer)

-vuk-súyuy-ne- caus. to spin

SYN. -vuk-méni- to turn round

CIT. čikóoti pen-vuk-súyuy-ne-qal ʔáwsunika I am spinning a rope in the air (like a cowboy)

súʔiš n. jack rabbit, rabbit (gener.)

súʔwe-t n., plur. -t-em star

-súʔwe-lu- v.itr. to become a star

T

-táča- v.itr. to lie down on the back, to lie down flat

-táča-ne- caus. to make lie down on the back

-tátača- distrib.

-tátača-ni- caus. to make all lie on the back

color term base + táča- to lie down in a colored appearance; tul-táča-we sth. black is lying down

táča-l n. the bark of tree

táčikal n., plur. táčikul-am, táčikl-am cicada

-tákaa- v.itr. with -puš 'eye' as first member of verbal group to be blind

-tákal- v.itr. (= -táka-l-, with submorph. -al-, see

-tákaa-) to get patched up, pasted (e.g. eye); to be spotted

-tákalaka- distrib. with l- redupl. in periphr.

-puš tákal-iš lit. eye patched up; one-eyed

color term base + tákalaka to be spotted in a colored appearance

SYN. -táki- to be spotted

CIT. qáwiš tùkiš tákalaka yáxwen the mountain is spotted with green (plants or grass)

-táki- v.itr., VAR. -taqi- to be pasted (paper, etc.)

-tátkam- distrib. to be pasted (many objects)

-táki-n- caus. to patch up (as clothes, pots), to paste (as paper on the wall, etc.)

-tátkame- caus. and distrib. to patch up, to make quilts

-pe-táki- v.tr. to stop, to block

táki-š n. sth. pasted

táki-wet n. sth. patched up

color term base + táki- to be spotted in a colored appearance

CIT. hémaˀ ˀúmun taxk^{w}e táki-wen his hands are pasted together

kíˀat híye húluluŋa táki-we lit. the baby is pasted on the back of its mother; it hangs on the back of its mother

tákiš n., plur. tátkiš pestle

tákuš PN one of the spirits feared by people (appears in the creation myth as one of the first creatures)

tákut with piš with/because of thirst

CIT. tákut piš nemúq̣al lit. because of thirst I am sick; I am thirsty

ták'a n. with -ʔi 'foot' as first member of nominal group heel

-tálal- v.itr. to snore

-táli- v.itr., usually with -če- to break into pieces (potteries, glasses, houses made of earth)

-táli-n- caus., also with -če-, -vuk-

-tátal- caus. and distrib., also with -če- to break one by one

-če-tátlame-, -če-tátal- caus. and distrib. to break one by one

táli-š, also with če- that which is broken into pieces

táli-vaš/-wet n. sth. that breaks easily (e.g. glass)

CIT. púleqal ʔáwsuŋax man yúluka če-táli-qal he fell off from above and the head was broken

neʔúuya ʔúmun tátal-ʔi my olla is all smashed

tál̃ki n., plur. -ʔim Indian potato , mariposa lily; cf. BandS p.50

-táma- v.itr. with -wen to be sharp (knife)

táma-k(at) n. sth. sharp

táma-wet n. that which is sharp

táma-l n., plur. -l-em mouth, tooth

-támaʔ-vi- v.itr. to get teeth (on) (natural or artificial)

tama + kéñiš lit. mouth-sweet; liar cf. čúuŋiš

-tama + kékenawk- v.itr. lit. mouth + (prob.) to sweeten (kéñ-iš sweet one); to tell lies, cf. -čúuŋišlew- to tell lies

-tama + qáwiš lit. mouth rock; molar

tàma ʔíʔive lit. without mouth; dumb

tàma méyiš crooked mouth

CIT. ne-táma ʔívawen piš nekútašve lit. my mouth is strong for me to talk; I talk loud tamasésket n. whistler, gopherlike animal

támaš n. with -yùl̃ as first member of nominal group, cf. yúluka 'hair' beard, bearded person

támaw adv. around/at the edge (of water, mountain)

SYN. háyve the edge (of table, etc.)

CIT. nehíčeqale pàl támaw I went around the edge of the water

-támaw- v.tr. to mock

támaw-et n. mockingbird

-támawet-lu- lit. to become a mockingbird; to mock, to sing

támi-ka adv., VAR. tám-ka toward the east, cf. támit

támi-ŋax from the east

támi-kan-viš n. one from the east

támi-l̃ n. knee

CIT. ne-támi-y peta on my knee

támit n. Mt.Ca., támyat Des.Ca., VAR. tam- as first member of compounds the sun; day; time

tam + xálal-ika in the afternoon

-tám + kus- lit. sun + take; to sunbathe

tam + páx-ika lit. the sun is going to enter; in the evening

mu + támit-i lit. still time (-i object marker); early

tàmit písqalevax from where the sun comes out

támiʔt-i túkmaati day and night

páh támit-paʔ on the third day

CIT. mík támit ˀívˀax peyáwqal lit. how many days does it have today; what day is it today ?

ˀáčaˀe támit túleka it is going to be fine tomorrow

támit-i peemkʷáwen lit. they are eating the sun; the solar eclipses; cf. méñili peem-kʷáwen the lunar eclipses

-támituk- v.itr. to make a camp, to stay overnight

támivaˀ adv. winter

-támiˀvax- v.itr. to become winter

támiˀvax-iš n. lit. that has become winter; it's winter already

tánwivel yerba santa (used as tea for cold); cf. BandS p. 71

-táŋ- v.itr., v.tr., ALLOM. -tátaŋ- autom. redupl. to roast the agave in a pit

tápaˀmal n. pot, pottery

tátpaˀmal distrib.

-taqtáqa- v.itr. to be flattened (of button, pig's nose, etc.)

taqtáqa-wet n. flat one (e.g. nose)

-tas n. construct, plur. -em uncle (maternal)

-tás-tuˀa deceased uncle

táspaˀ adv. in the budding season, springtime

-táš- v.tr., see -čĩlay- Des.Ca., ALLOM. -tátaš- autom. redupl. to shell, to crack (as nuts, acorns)

CIT. pen-tátaš-qa tášvaˀali I am cracking nuts

-tášl̃a- v.itr. to gamble (people used to gamble with acorns, cf.-táš-); see -túxpi- Des.Ca.

tášl̃a-ʔil̃ n. gambling game

CIT. píyk ne-tášl̃a-qa I gamble with him

tášvaʔal n. (táš-va-ʔal sth. to crack, see -táš-) nuts

tášʔa n. bark (of tree)

-táata n. construct, with 1st pers. pron. father (vocative)

tátaxil n. (cf. tax-) egoist

-tátaxel̃ew- v.tr. 1. to behave mean, to be jealous; to dislike 2. to sing against each other in fiesta (with recipr. pron. -tax-)

tátaxsil̃ n. little lizard

-táatusne- v.tr. (see -táwas-) to tell lies

CIT. niyk kúkutašqaleve ne-táatusne-qa when talking to me, he lied

SYN. -čúuŋišl̃ew-

táatwal n., plur. -em blind

-táatwal-lu- v.tr. to become blind

SYN. tákališ

-táv- v.tr. with sing. obj. (see wén for plur. obj.) to put sth. in place, to put in order

-táv-alaw- to take sbdy home

-táv-iči- to take/bring sth. along and leave it at a place

-táv-ŋi- to bring sbdy home

-távi-vi- v.itr. to hang in the nose as decoration (e.g. beads)

táv-at n. that which was put in place; creature

táv-iš n. one who puts sth. in place; creator: čemey-táv-iš lit. one who has put us in place, cf. čemeynúkiš, čemeykúliš

CIT. pe-n-táv-ka népuči I'm g. to put on my glasses, cf. pe-n-ˀéxan-ka népuči I'm g. to take off my glasses

ˀésun táv-e lit. put your heart in place; relax

-távan- v.itr., ALLOM. -távni- (with -k, -vaš), -tátvan- (autom. redupl.) to guess at, to come to know

pa-távni-vaš PN lit. one who guesses at it; one who knows everything

CIT. néˀiy néŋa tátvan-qal he is guessing me, he recognizes me

Cf. -ˀéˀnan- to know; -táˀal- to fail to recognize

táviš n. big woodpecker

táviš n. projectile point

táviš-nek adj. straight

táviš-nek-iš n. 1. straight one 2. right

-táviš-lu- v.itr. to get straight

-táviš-nek-lu-ni- v.tr. to straighten out

-táviš-kuni- v.tr. to straighten out

távut n., plur. távt-em cottontail

SYN. súˀiš rabbit

-taw n. construct chest, breast

CIT. yúyat né-taw-ŋa penyáwqa I've got a cold in my chest

-táwas- v.itr., v.tr. 1. to get lost (on the way, in the game) 2. to lose

-táatus- distrib. to get lost often

-táatus-ne- caus. to tell lies, to fool sbdy without keeping words

táwas-iš n., plur. -č-em one who is lost

-sun + táwas- v.itr. lit. heart + lose; to forget

-sun + táatwas- distrib. to forget various things

CIT. hemqáqawpiweˀne pen hem-táwas-ˀi they played the ball game and they lost it

pe-n-táwas-qal nepélaˀay I am losing my weight

Cf. -múk-ne- to win

-táwe- v.tr. to hold sth. in the arm, to hug

CIT. tax-čem-táwe-we we hug each other

kíˀati penkúsqal pe-n-táwe-qal peman wéy wéy níyaxqal I pick up the baby, hold it in my arm and rock it.

-táwi- v.itr. in periphr. or with -wen only to be level, to be clear (of land)

SYN. -čáwi- to get clear, level

-čéxi- to clear up

-tawiš construct (cf. -taw chest, breast) personally (to)

CIT. né-tawiš neˀtétiyamaxap míyaxwe you have to tell me personally

táwpaˀ n. summer

-táwpax- v.itr. to be summer

táwpax-iš n. year

-táwpa-ki n. [construct] age

súp̃le táwpax-iš one year, next year

ˀáy páx táwpax-iš péniičiš three years have passed, it's three years ago

CIT. mík ˀe-táwpa-ki   lit. how many are your ages?
how old are you?

táwva-l n.   thunder

-táwva-lu- v.itr.   to thunder

tàwval téˀayawˀa   lit. thunder power; lightning, electricity

CIT. táwva-l mémlaqal   lit. the thunder is making a noise; it is thundering

tax- pron.   1. reflex. pron. oneself
2. reciproc. pron. each other

tax-k^{w}e   together, among each other

tax-(u)ŋa   in oneself

táx-ŋa-x   from each other

táx-uta   to/upon oneself

táx-wik   to each other

CIT. táx-ŋa-x čemhíčiˀi   lit. we went from ourselves; we got separated, we got divorced (= tax čemwíčaxniˀi)

-táxal- v.itr. with -če-   to feel cold, to be cold

-če-tátxalan- distrib.   to be cold all the while

-če-táxal + pis-   lit. be cold + come out; to be cold always

SYN. táxaw yúyma   his body feels cold

-táxalxa n.[construct] shin

táxat   he, that guy (used by men as an intensifier); brave man (cf. Strong:72)

CIT. ˀét táxat híčeqal   he, that guy, is going

táxaw-il̃ n., construct -táxaw   body

-táxlew construct, VAR. -táxluʔa 1. partner, boss
2. tribe, family

CIT. híyaxwe ʔe-táxlew what is your family name?

SYN. -kíl̃iw partner, káwʔa boss

táxliswet n., plur. -em, VAR. táxlist-, táxst- plur.
1. person 2. Cahuilla Indian

taxmíŋkik n., plur. taxmíŋkikt-em relative

-táxmu- v.itr., v.tr. to sing

-tátaxmu- distrib.

-táxmu-ne- caus. to make sing

táxmu-ʔat n. song

táxmu-vaš/-wet singer

CIT. péʔ netáxmuʔa piš qál my song is about that

pekúsqal táxmuʔa-y lit. he takes up his song; he starts to sing his song

-táxpi- v.itr. to gamble

CIT. hem-táxpi-wen qíčil̃ piš they are gambling with money

-táxʔisl̃u- v.itr. to look toward, to look forward to

CIT. miš táxʔisl̃u-qal lit. around them he looks toward; he looks back to see what they are doing

-táyul- v.itr. to become smooth, slippery

-táyul-ne- caus. to polish

-tátyal- distrib. v.itr., v.tr. to iron

-táyul-k^{w}e-ni- v.tr. to make smooth

-pe-táyul- v.itr. to slip down

-pe-táyulan- distrib. to slip down many times

-pe-táyul-ne- caus. to make slip

-táyul-ki- to slide down

táyul-ˀil̃ n. one which is smooth, slippery

taˀ clitic particle emphatic for a contrast

CIT. péˀem (taˀ) páˀvačem, néˀ taˀ kil̃e páˀvaš they are drunkards, but I am not

ˀívˀax kíˀi yan yéwi ta now no, but before

-táˀal- v.itr. to fail to recognize (esp. persons)

tax-če-táˀal-ne- caus. to pretend

táˀal-a-ŋa lit. in not recognizing; without knowing, without being informed

táˀal-at n. failure to recognize

CIT. néˀiy neŋa táˀal-qal he doesn't recognize me

pa táˀal-qa táxmuˀay he got confused in his song

tax-ne-če-táˀal-ne-qal hentáxliswet I am pretending, as if I were an Indian

-táˀatay- v.itr. with -sun 'heart' as Ist member of verbal group; Mt.Ca. -táˀata- to hurry up; to be anxious

-sun + táˀatay- to hurry up; to be anxious

-sun + táˀata-ni- caus. to hasten sbdy

CIT. ˀésun táˀataˀ yáxˀe hurry up!

ne-sun-táˀata-qa piš penčúminpi netuvxáay I am anxious to finish my work

-táˀin- v.tr. to winnow

-téček^{w}- v.tr. Des.Ca., see -k^{w}áaviču- Mt.Ca., ALLOM. -tešk^{w}- with -ik, -ap, -alu to take care of

CIT. néˀ nénay pen-téček^{w}-al I am taking care of my father

-téeŋ- v.itr., ALLOM. -téhŋ- with -ive, in caus. 1. to appear, to look 2. to emerge, to come about

-téhŋ-ini- caus. to make appear, to show

piš téhŋ-ive his/its appearance

CIT. ad 1. híčeˀa ˀáyaxwen piš téhŋ-ive what is his appearance like? what does he look like?

ad 2. paam-téeŋ-wen qaméxenuk wam how did they get there, I wonder

-ték- v.itr. to settle down (mud in the water)

-ték-ne- caus. to let settle down; to purify (water)

ték-iš n. one which settled down; e.g., pàl ___ the water which settled down

CIT. pál ték-qal pen pál tévelve the water settled down and it's clear

yúliš ték-qal témayka páŋa the mud settled down to the bottom of the water

SYN. -túpa- to settle down

téki-š n. cave, hole

téki-ŋa adv. in the hole

SYN. káviwenet hole

-ték-lu- (ték in periphr.) v.itr., ALLOM. -ték- in periphr. 1. to be quiet, still 2. to stop (of rain, wind, etc.)

-téteklu- distrib.

-téklu-ne- caus. to leave sbdy alone/ in peace

téklu-vaš/-wet one which is quiet; e.g., túkmiyat silent night

CIT. ad 1. kúktašqal pen ték luqal he was talking and became still

ad 2. ˀáy téklu ˀetuvxáqaleve stop working!

SYN. -čémi- to stop (crying, talking)

tékluvel noon, midnight (prob. = -téklu- 'to stop' -vel), see máxeliš noon, Mt.Ca.

téklu vel pa — at noon

tékluvel témayka — lit. noon to the earth; in the afternoon

tékvet n., plur. -em — chicken hawk

SYN. kísil̃ — chicken hawk

-tékʷaxa- v.itr., ALLOM. tékʷax- with nominal suff. -il̃ — to get upset in the stomach

tékʷax-il̃ — upset stomach

CIT. nepúyqal ne-tékʷaxa-qal — I have got stuffed up (and) my stomach gets upset

-tékʷe- v.itr., also with -pe- — to be shaken off/down (leaves, fruit, etc.)

-tékʷe-n- caus. — to shake off

-tétkʷeme- caus. and distrib.

CIT. kʷíñil ʔáy tekʷe-qal — acorns have fallen down (shaken off by wind or person)

pen-tékʷe-n-ʔi nexẽ́lai — I shook my clothes off (to dust off)

tékʷel n., plur. tekʷl-am — skunk

-tékʷel- v.tr., with -pe- (= -pe-tekʷe-l- with submorph. -al-, see -tékʷe-) — to flip off

-vuk-tékʷel- — to blow off

CIT. nexẽ́lay pen-pe-tékʷel-qa némay piš — I flipped off my clothes with the finger

yáʔi pálʔai pe-vuk-tékʷel-qa — the wind blows the leaves off

-télaa- v.itr. — to be baggy, loose (of clothes)

CIT. nexẽ́la čaqe télaa-qal — my clothes are baggy and hanging

-télaš- v.itr. with -če-, -pe- (-če-téla-š- with submorph. -aš-, see -télaa-) to get baggy, to loosen (clothes, the skin of face, etc.)

CIT. nepáxanive čaqe télaš yaqa súnaxwenepa neta ˀámnawet my pants get loose (slipping down), because they are too big for me

télk^{w}aam — storage of food

-télme n. construct — sister-in-law

télmekiš n. — place where dead people live

CIT. téwlavelem hemqál télmekiš pa the spirits live in 'télmekiš'

ˀáy penméknik télmeki-ka I am going to kill you and send you to hell

télmu n. — black sap of mesquite tree

tel̃ˀáˀayamal̃ n. — proud, arrogant

téma-l n. — 1. land, ground 2. dirt, earth 3. world

téma-yka adv. — to the ground, way down

pey-téma-k n. — he is the owner of that land

tékluvel téma-yka — lit. noon toward the earth; in the afternoon; Mt.Ca. máxeliš téma-yka

tèma-l hépi — milkweed

tèma-l ñúkˀu — wild sand-verbena

CIT. téma-yka ˀeemtéewe lit. they are looking at you way down; they are looking down upon you

témam-ka — north, toward the north

CIT. témam-ka púčiwen it is facing to the north

témaš n., classif. -méxanˀa thick underbrush, bush (esp. under the mesquite tree)

ʔíl̃ témaš — brush under mesquite trees

temasésket n. — weasel

témayawet n. — one of the two creators in the creation story, see múkat (prob. = téma-(1) + yáw-wet lit. one who takes the earth)

témayka, see témal

-témi- v.itr., also with -če- — to close (of doors, etc.); to lock up

-tétmem- distrib.

-témi-n- caus. — to close, to lock up

-če-témi-n- caus. — to slam

-pe-témi- with -sun as first member of verbal group: hésun pe-témi-qal lit. his heart shuts up; he gets disappointed, he feels disgusted

-témi-l̃ew- — to close, e.g. with pít 'road': pít témi-l̃ew-en the road is closed

-mu-témi-(l̃ew-) — to get blocked on the way, to be dead-end (street)

témi-ve n. — lid (of the box)

témi-n-vaʔal n. — lit. place to lock up; jail, also tax-témi-n-vaʔal n. jail

-kus + témi- (-kus- cf. híkus) lit. breath-close; to get choked; e.g. páŋa kustémi-qal he gets drowned

-kus + témi-n- caus. — to suffocate

CIT. náqʔa témi-wen lit. his ear is closed; he cannot hear

-témi- v.itr. — to fill (of solids), to crowd in

-témi-i-n- caus. — to fill

-tétmaan- caus. and distrib.

CIT. k^{w}íñili pa pičem-témi-n-we — we are filling acorns in it

SYN. -múy- — to fill (of water)

temtéma?an — not knowing anything, without any purpose (wandering about)

téne?awka n. — whirlwind, tornado

SYN. kùt yáy?al

-téneq- v.tr., VAR. -tének-, ALLOM. -ténq-/-ténk- occurs with -?í, -ik, -?il̃, -at — to roast in a pit

ténq-at n. — pit barbecue, construct -téneq?a
ténq-il̃ n. — pit
Cf. -wáwa- — to roast on an open fire

ténil̃ n., plur. ténl-am — antelope

tépa PlN (cf. -tépaqa-) — a flat rock (pressed against the hill) north of Los Coyotes

tépačewet n. — that which is frozen

-tépaqa- v.tr. — to tighten (as belt)

-tépaqa?-ne- caus. — to let tighten, to use as belt
tépaqa-l n. — belt
-tépaqa?-vi- v.itr., v.tr. — to have a belt on
CIT. pen-tépaqa-qal ne-tépaqa-y — I am tightening my belt

-tépawka- v.itr. — to freeze

tépawka-š — one which is frozen; e.g. pàl ___ frozen water
CIT. ne-tépawka ?áyaw?i — I almost froze

-tépi- v.itr. — to be short (clothes)

-tep-tépi- distrib.

-tépin- v.tr. to track, to follow tracks

-tépin- v.tr. with -če- to trip, to cause to stumble (stone, wood, etc.)

SYN. -čekíval- to trip, to tangle; -petíˀal- to stumble over

-tépeš- v.tr. usually with -pe- to hammer (a nail)

-pe-tétpečan- distrib. to hammer (many nails)

CIT. pen-pe-tétpečan-qal kaláavoy I am hammering many nails

-tépiš- v.itr. to get constipated

-če-tépiš- v.itr., also with -pe- to get stuck (e.g. in the chair sitting too long)

CIT. ne-pe-tépiš-qal neñášvey piyik I have got stuck to my chair (as having sat too long)

SYN. -pečúpu- to get stuck, -peŋáki- to get stuck (between two objects)

-téqan- v.tr., ALLOM. -tétqan- (autom. redupl.), -tétqan-/-tékn- (with -ik, -at) to parch (to make popcorn)

téqn-at n. popcorn

tésax adv. also, too

CIT. neˀáyawˀa kíyul pen tésax káarne I like fish and also meat

tésel n. yellow clay (used for pottery, for painting faces)

teseqáxal n. a kind of quail; see qáxal 'quail'

tésnat n. clay for pottery or painting; pot, olla

tésnek-iš adj. plur. -č-em/tétesnek-č-em, ALLOM. tes- (as first member of compound), tésetnek-iš yellow, brown

-tésnek-lu- v.itr. to turn yellow

-tes + yúpi- to become yellowish: túkvaš tes-yúpi-qal the sky becomes yellowish

-tes + yúpi-n- caus. to make yellowish

tésevel n. cabbagelike plant

tésvaʔal n.: qáwiš piš ___ pumice stone

téetewkat n., plur. -em different kinds of

téetewkat-em táxliswetem different people

tétinat n. butcherbird

-tétiyax- v.itr., v.tr., ALLOM. -tétiya- with deriv. suff. -max- to tell (sbdy sth.)

-tétiya-max- v.tr. to tell sbdy (a story, etc.)

CIT. tax-tétiyax-qal lit. he tells himself; he tells about himself

ʔívʔax ʔen-tétiya-max-ik sel̃híiščeʔati now I am going to tell you a story

tétiyax ʔáčak^{w}en lit. tell well!; tell the truth! (= tétiyax čepévk^{w}al ʔáčaʔe)

čeme-tétiya-max-pu qamíva ʔesan hemqál could you tell us where they are?

-tétvis- v.itr. to become numb

CIT. ʔáy néʔi tétvis-ʔi kil̃e míyaxwen piš nek^{w}éʔeqepi my legs got numb, (so) I cannot get up

-tétxe- v.tr. Des.Ca., see -téxin- Mt.Ca. to store food (acorns, grains, etc.); cf. -tex storage

-tétˀayaw- v.itr.   to dream

-tétˀayaw-ne- caus. lit. to make dream; to dream of
tétˀayaw-niš/-iš n. dreamer
CIT. ne-tétˀayaw-ne-qal caus. lit. he made me dream; I dreamed of him

tévv sound imitation, in periphr. sound with air vibration (e.g. before earthquake)

tévat n. classif. -kíˀiwˀa pine-nut, piñon; cf. BandS 102

tévaxalem n.   hail

CIT. tévaxalem hemčáviwen hail are falling

-téveve- v.itr.   to vibrate (water)

-téveleve- v.itr., L-redupl., in periphr.

tével-tével- distrib. to be checked, to be striped
CIT. túkut téveleve yáxwen the tiger is striped

tévelve (gerund) sparkling clear (water)

CIT. yúliš téqal témayka páŋa pál tévelve the mud settled down to the bottom in the water and the water is clear

-tévelvey- v.itr., ALLOM. téveleveleve L-redupl. in periphr. to shimmer (of heat waves)

tévelvey-š n.   heat waves
CIT. témal síwiš téveleve yáqa píŋa (when) the ground is hot, heat waves shimmer on the road

tévil̃mal̃em n., construct. -tévil̃mal̃em, VAR. tévil̃am, tévinmalem beans, pink beans; cf. BandS p.100

téviŋil̃ n., plur. téviŋil̃-em/tétviŋil̃, construct -téviŋi-ki ALLOM. téviŋimal̃, construct -téviŋima, téviŋimal -méxanˀa small globular basket

tévisiˀwet n. heavy wind with rain (with thunder following)

téviš-nek adj. white

tétviš-nek distrib.

téviš-nek-iš n. white one, plur. ___-em/tétvišnekč-em

-téviš-nek-lu- v.itr. to turn white

-teviš + képi- v.itr. to float in whitish appearance

-teviš + táqi- to be spotted in white

pàl téviš-nek-iš paˀ PlN White Water

-téw- v.tr. to find, discover

-tétwan- distrib. to find (a lot of things)

téw-ap-iš n.: kil̃e ___ one which is not supposed to be found, seen

CIT. ˀí ˀék^{w}ašmali pennúˀinqal piš pe-téw-ap I told this boy to find it

-téew- v.tr., ALLOM. tée (imper. sing.), -tehw- (before vowel) to see, to look at, to watch

-téteew- distrib. to look around

-téew-ŋi- to watch, to stare (with accusing eyes)

-téw-axa- to ask to look after (one's belonging) Mt.Ca., as: pen-téw-axa-qa nékiˀi I asked him to watch my house

-téew-wen to be seen, to be clear to appear

téew-enet n. sth. visible; tax ___ visit, seeing each other (e.g. visiting a sick person or a dead person at a funeral)

-téew-qalet one who looks after, tax ___ Being that is looking at people from above

-téew-ˀa n. construct what one saw

tax-téhw-iwet n. one that likes to stare at people

CIT. ˀí náxaniš ˀáˀavuwet nét kíš ˀámnawet pey-téew-qalet this elderly man, the ceremonial leader, looks after the big house

ˀelélkʷiči piyk pen-téew-qa I see sth. bad about him (referring to the future)

téew yáxe ˀépuš lit. see your eye; open your eyes

téw-al n. construct -tew, cf. -téwan- name

-téwan- v.tr., ALLOM. -tétewan- autom. redupl. 1. to give sbdy a name, to name, to call 2. to count, to tell

téwan-il̃ n. counting

CIT. ad 1. néˀiy ne-tétewan-qal ˀísil̃ tévišnekiš she named me white coyote

ad 2. pen-téwan-ˀi qíčil̃i I counted money

téwiil̃em, construct -téwim testicles

téwka(t) n., plur. téwkat-em deceased person

péqi téwkat-em táxliswetem they are just deceased people (they are always just drinking, dancing and all that together)

téwlavel n., plur. -em spirit of the dead, cf. téwka deceased person

-téwlave + tuk- v.itr. lit. spirit + to stay (overnight?); to go into the underworld of spirits

-téwyaw- v.itr. to have an accident, to suffer misfortune

-tex n. construct only storage; cf. -téxte- to store food

-téx- v.tr., ALLOM. -tétex- autom. redupl. to knock (on the door, the table, etc.), to give a tap

CIT. téx penyáxeʔi I knocked on it (once)

-téx- v.itr., VAR. -téxan-, ALLOM. -tétex- autom. redupl. to grind and make flour

SYN. -pévey- to pound in the hole on a rock (acorns)

-téxay- v.tr., with -pe- = -pe-téx-ay- with submorph. -ay-, see -téx) to bump against/into; to nudge

-pe-tétxaan- distrib.

SYN. -pe-púxay- to bump

CIT. tax-hem-pe-téxay-we they bumped into each other, they collided

téxay penyáxeqal nepúviyay piš I nudged him with my elbow

-téxin- v.tr. Mt.Ca., see -tétxe- Des.Ca. to store (acorns, grains); to fill (sack with food)

-tétxemi- distrib. to store

CIT. máysi pen-tétxmi-qa kúnil̃ pa I am packing corns into sacks

-téyan- v.tr. Mt.Ca. to preserve, to carry on (custom, right)

CIT. ʔáčama piš peem-téyan-pi yéwi hemnémiwenive it is good that they preserve their old tradition

-téyʔa n. construct body odor

CIT. ne-téyʔa húuv-qa my body odor smells, my body smells (badly)

téʔayawa n. power

táwval téʔayawa lit. the power of thunder; the lightning

CIT. té?ayawa-y piš pepesáqinqa he (a medicine man) killed him with his power

-té?e- v.tr., ALLOM. té?- with -iš to borrow, to rent from

-té?e-ne- caus. to lend, to rent to

té?-iš n. borrower

CIT. qíčil̃i ne-té?e-?i (pen-té?e-n-?i) he borrowed money from me (I lent him)

SYN. -lé?i- v.tr. to borrow from

-té?eqe- v.itr. v.tr. to pile up (sand)

CIT. ŋáčiš píka té?eqe-qal the sand piled up there (e.g., the water caused it)

té?i-ĩ n., construct **-té?i** bone, bones for playing

-tíkal- v.itr., in periphr., also with -pe- to flash (of lightning, to sparkle, to twinkle

-pe-títkalan- distrib. to flash many times

SYN. -háti- to shine

CIT. táwval pe-títkalan-qa lit. the thunder (the lightning) is flashing

gáato hépuš tíkal tíkal yáxqal mávipiš the cat's eyes sparkle in the evening (at night)

tíŋ-iš n. warm

tíŋ-ma adj. warm

tíŋ-ta-:tíŋ-ta-ŋa in the warm place, tíŋ-ta-yka toward the warm place

-tíŋ + wax- v.itr. lit. warm + dry; to warm; -tíŋ-wax-ne- caus. to warm

pa? tíŋ-wax-va?al sweat house

CIT. némay pàl tíŋ-išpa pen-tíŋ-wax-ne-qal I am warming my hand in the warm water

-tíŋˀay- v.tr. to cure, to doctor

tíŋˀay-piš n. medicine

tíŋˀay-vaš/-wet doctor

CIT. héˀiy piš piy-tíŋˀay-ka. he is going to cure his foot with it

tax-tíŋˀay cure yourself/people

-típil̃- v.itr., in periph., also with -pe- to drip (water)

-pe-títpil̃an- distrib.

tíwil̃ n., plur. -em small mushroom (growing under trees)

tíwma adj. warm

-tíwmax- v.itr. to get warmer

SYN. tíŋma warm

tíˀal n., plur. -em white lizard

-tíˀal- v. with -pe- 1. v.itr. to stumble over stone, etc.) 2. v.tr. to cause to stumble, to trip

SYN. -četípin-, -čekíval- to trip

CIT. ad 1. ne-pe-tíˀal-qȧl qáwiš peta I stumbled over a stone

ad 2. qawiš ne-pe-tíˀal-qal a stone caused me to stumble

tíˀi-l̃ n., construct -tíˀi belly, stomach, waist

-tíˀi pétuk lit. under one's stomach; inside oneself

tríiwaˀa n. Span. wheat

-tú- v.itr. to bear fruit

-tú°-ne- caus. to cause to bear fruit

tú°-iš n. fruit, berries

tú°-un-iš n. one who caused the harvest

héma tú°-i lit. berries of his hand; his fingers

hé°i tú°-i his toes

hépi tú°-i lit. berries of her breast; nipples of her breast

-túči- v.itr., also with -če-, ALLOM. -túš- in periphr. caus. to have a knot; to get tangled up (of ropes, shoelaces, etc.)

-túči-n- caus., also with -če-, -vuk- to tie, to make a knot

-túščumi- caus. and distrib.

če-túči-iš n. tangled (e.g., a dog with its leash)

túči-ve n. shoelace

CIT. pásukati pen-túčin-°i kélawat piyik yan čikóoti čečúvi°i I tied the horse to the tree, but the rope untied

túčil̃ n., plur. túšl̃-em humming bird

-tuháyin- v.tr. to be sleepy, weary, exhausted; cf. -háyin- to be tired

CIT. pen-tuháyin-qal I am weary

tuháyemaniš all the time, always

tuháyemaniš pa° all the time, forever

-tuk adv. loc. (object pron. inflected), see pé-tuk

-túk- v.tr. to carry sth. on the back

-túk-ne- caus. to load (sbdy with sth.)

-túk-iče- to go carrying on the back; to put on the back

-túk-ŋi- to carry home sth. on the back

-túk-ive- v.itr., v.tr. to carry on the back; to put on one's back

túk-iva?al n. a net for carrying on back, cf. ?íkat

túk-ive n. bundle

CIT. ?en-túk-ni-qal kí?ati I put the baby on your back

ne?ú?yaki pen-túk-qale ?íkat piš I carry my olla on the back with a carrying net

-túk- v.itr. to go to bed, to stay overnight

-túk-law- to go to sleep

túk-va?al n.: pa___ place to stay overnight, camping ground

Cf. -kúp- to be or fall asleep

-tuklákma n. construct palate

túkmiyat n., VAR. túkmaat night

tùkmiyat náwxaŋa at midnight

túkmiyatpa throughout the night

túkmiyat piš in the night

túku adv. yesterday, recently

túku-viš yesterday's (whatever one had yesterday: food, newspaper, etc.)

túku máviš last night

túku múlu?uk the day before yesterday

túku sé?ŋaxviš semáana lit. recent, the last week; the week before last

túkut n., plur. túkt-em wild cat

túkvaš n., VAR. túk^{w}iš, túkiš sky

tùkvaš ?áwsunika way up to the sky

tùkvaš ˀámika high above in the sky

tùkvaš hémiš lit. the leg of the sky; star

túkvaš n., VAR. túk^{W}aš, túkiš iron, knife

túkvaš-nek-iš adj. (attributive and pred.); túkvaš-nek (pred. only), VAR. túk^{W}iš-nek, green, blue (cf. túkvaš 'sky')

túk^{W}iš-nek-lu- v.itr. to become green, blue

tùk^{W}iš + yúpi- lit. blue + get cloudy; to get blue

túkwet n., plur. túkwet-em mountain lion

-túkˀu n. construct flesh; cf. wáˀiš meat

-túla- v.tr. Des.Ca., see -pévey- Mt.Ca., VAR. tuˀ- to pound (acorn, mesquite beans in a mortar), to grind

túˀ-at, túla-ˀat n. one which is pounded

pa túˀ-vaˀal place where one pounds

CIT. k^{W}íñili pičem-túla-wen qáwiš peta páwl piš we're pounding the acorn on the rock with the pestle

túleka adv., túlekaˀan 1. tomorrow 2. in the morning

mu-túleka early in the morning

túleka múˀanviš lit. what is ahead of tomorrow; the day after tomorrow

túleka péŋaxviš lit. what is from tomorrow; the day after tomorrow

túl-nek adj. (cf. túl̃ 'coal'), ALLOM. túl-ek black

túl-nek-iš n. black one, VAR. túl-ek-iš

túl̃-ek-iš n. negro

-túl-ek-lu- v.itr. to become black

-tul + híwyax-iš n. blackish one

-tul + sáwe- lit. black + disappear; to become dark

-tul + sáwaqi- (= -sáwa-qi-, with submorph. -aq-) v.itr. to get dark

tul + sáwi-š n. darkness

tul + sáw-yax-iš n. darkish

-tul + yúpi- v.itr. lit. black + get cloudy; to turn black, dark

-tulsáwe- v.itr., see túl-nek

-túlu- v.itr. Mt.Ca. (see -súpaq-) to close eyes (cf. túlnek 'black')

CIT. ne-túlu-qa I am closing the eyes

túlu túlu yáqa he is blinking

-túlus- v.itr., v.tr., VAR. -tús- to grind (acorn, etc.)

-túlus-ŋi-	to come back and grind
-tús-xa- v.tr.	see below
-tus n. construct	see below
túlus-at n.	that which is ground: máys túlus-at ground corn
túlus-vaʔal n.	place to grind: qáwiš piš ___ a rock to grind with
túlus-vaš/-wet n.	one who usually grinds; máaysi túlus-vaš corn chopper

túl̃ n.	coal

-túmaw- v.tr.	to attack (vulture, its game from above), to raid, to attack in surprise
túmaw-law-et n.	ready to attack
túmaw-iš n.	person who is going to pick a fight with sbdy

-túmaw- v.itr. only with -wen to be steep, precipitous (mountain, road; hazardous to climb)

túmaw-iš n.; 1. steep one 2. cliff
túutmawi-š distrib.

qáwiš túmaw-iš steep mountain

-túmawan- v.tr. not to know how to do (as to dance, etc.); not to recognize persons, things

CIT. pen-túmawan-qal piš nečéŋenpi I don't know how to dance

-túmkaw- v.itr. to lie down on belly, with face down

-tútumkaw- distrib.

-túmkaw-ne- caus. to make lie down on belly

color term base + túmkaw- to lie down on belly in colored appearance

CIT. híče⁹a man tul-túmkaw-en what is that black thing lying down on its belly?

-túnuš- v.itr., in periphr., also with -če- Mt.Ca., -pe- Des.Ca. 1. to have a cramp 2. to shrink (of clothes) Mt.Ca.

-če-tútnučan- distrib.

SYN. česúkuš-

CIT. ad 1. né⁹i čaqe túnuš yáqa my leg has got a little cramp

ad 2. nepáxanive pe-túnuš-qal my pants have shrunk

-túpa- v.itr., ALLOM. -túp- in caus. to settle down (mud in the water, etc.)

túp⁹a n. what's left in straining; kahvée ___ coffee ground

-túp-in- caus. to strain

SYN. -ték- to settle down

CIT. pàl yúliš túpa-qa čéxiqa muddy water settles down and it gets clear

-túpiš- v.itr. — to get hardened (of oil)

túpič-iš n. — lard

-túq- v.itr. — to go out (of fire, light)

-tútuq-an- caus. (redupl.) to extinguish

CIT. tútuq-an penyáxeʔi I dimmed it (the light)

-túqi- v.itr. — to be short (of clothes, a tail, etc.)

CIT. ʔáwal hékʷaš túqi-qa the dog's tail is short

SYN. -múti- to be cut short

-tús- v.tr. — to grind

-tús-xa- v.tr. — to ask sbdy to grind

-tus n. construct — that which is ground

tútumiš n., plur. tútumič-em, VAR. tútmiš bug, stinking bug

tútumič-em yúlam strings made of stinking bugs (as beads)

-túutu n. construct — grandmother (maternal), cf. -káaka (paternal)

tútuš n. Mt.Ca. — horsefly

tútut n. — mormon tea, miner's tea; cf. BandS p. 70

SYN. čáh — tea

túv sound imitation, in periphr. big noise, cf. tév

túva PlN: ___ (múaʔniš) Oasis, Agua Dulce

-túvave n. construct — filth, dirt

túvave(k) n. filthy, dirty (body, clothes, etc.)
-túvavek-ne- v.tr. caus. to dirty
SYN. seláxma dirty

-tuvxáˀ- v.itr. to work

tuvxáˀ-at n. work
tuvxáˀil̃ n. work, job
tuvxáˀ-iš n. work; hard time
tuvxáˀ-vik(at) n. plur. tuvxávikt-em (diligent, industrious) worker
CIT. peta netuvxáˀqa I am working for him
neténkluˀi ne-tuvxá-qaleve I stopped working (for a while), I made a pause during my work
ˀáy penqámiˀi ne-tuvxáˀ-ay I quit my work
ˀí nemáxqal hespen tuvxáˀ-ič-i he gives me a time

-túxpi- v.itr. Des.Ca. to play a game of chance, to gamble; see -tášla- Mt.Ca.

túxpi-ˀil̃ n. the gambling game
túxpi-š player
túxpi-vaš n. player
piš túxpi- vaˀal n. things you play with (as cards, domino)

-túyva- v.itr., ALLOM. -túyvaa- with -qal to be circular, round (of a flat object, hole, etc.), cf. -púmlee- to be round (of a spherical object)
-tuyva-túyva- redupl. to be round
-túyva-ne- caus. to make round (e.g. by cutting a sheet of paper into a circular form)
tuyvatúyvaˀ-wet n. round one; ménil̃ ___ full moon

-túyvaqe- v.itr., also with -če- (= -túyva-qe- with submorphemic -qe- ~ -aq-, see -túyva-) to get round

-túyvaq-an- caus., also with -če- to make round (by rolling up, as a sheet of paper)

túyvaq-iš n. that which has just got round

túʔ, VAR. tum, tun, tuwen only, just

tu mípa pa lit. just sometime; any time

tu míva pa lit. just somewhere; anywhere

tu méxenanuk lit. just somehow; necessarily

ʔét/péʔ/hémem + tum lit. you/he/they + just; so, it's just you/he/they

CIT. kiĩ híčeʔa pa wén tun wáyismaʔli petéwqal there was nothing he saw, only one dish

túʔat n., see -túla- flour, meal (bean, acorn)

SYN. túlaʔat, túlusʔat ground stuff (acorn, bean)

U

-ʔul n.: hé-ʔul, construct -ʔuʔ navel

-ʔúlan- v.tr., ALLOM. -ʔúʔlan- autom. redupl. to sew

ʔúlan-iĩ n. sewing

ʔúlan-at n. that which is sewed

ʔúlan-vaʔal n.: piš ___ sth. to sew with

ʔúlan-vaš n.: wàqay ___ shoemaker; a kind of fly or bug with wings

ʔúuliʔ n. rubber

ʔúmun, VAR. ʔúmu all, all over

ʔúʔmun distrib.

CIT. ʔúmun táxliswetem all the people

-ˀúmin- v.tr. with -vuk- to cover up completely

-vuk-ˀúmi- v.itr. with -wen- to be covered

SYN. -két- to cover

CIT. xél̃ay piš peem-vukˀúmin-wen they covered it up with a blanket

-ˀúne- v.tr. to show (sbdy) sth.

-ˀúˀune- distrib. to show around; to teach

tax-ˀúˀune-vaš n. teacher

CIT. ne-ˀúne míva híwqal show me where he is

me-ˀuˀúne-qal̀ néati piykúlkatem she is teaching them to make baskets

-ˀúpi- v.itr., also with -pe- to dive

SYN. -čúpi- to dip

CIT. páŋa hem-ˀúpi-wen they go underwater

-ˀúx- v.tr., VAR. -ˀúˀ- to wash away (of flood, as people), to drown

-ˀúˀan- distrib., -ˀúˀyan- Mt.Ca.

CIT. wániš pe-ˀúx-qa ˀúmun híčemivi peyáwičiˀi the flood washed everything off and carried it away

-ˀúxvey- v.itr. to be messy, sloppy

CIT. néma ˀúxvey-qa my hands are messy

ˀúuyaˀ n. construct -ˀúuya-ki, span. olla

-ˀúˀ- v.tr. to put sth. on the head; to carry

ˀúˀ-iš (plur. ˀúˀč-em) n. person who carries sth. on the head

CIT. ˀúˀ peemyáxeˀi they put it on the head

CIT. yéwi hemyúlukay peta peem-ʔúʔ-ve míyaxwe in the old days they used to carry on the head

-ʔúʔuhu- v.itr. to cough

ʔúʔuhu-ʔil̃ n. cough

-ʔúʔuhu-ʔa n. [construct] cough

CIT. qél̃aka neyáwqal ne-ʔúʔuhu-qal I have a cold and I am coughing

ʔúʔut n., plur. -em chamise, greasewood, adenostoma fasciculatum; cf. BandS p.29

-ʔúʔuwe- v.tr. Des.Ca., -sáamsa- M.Ca. to buy

héki niyk pevendéerqal pen-ʔúʔuwe-qal he sold his house to me, I bought it

V

váakaʔ n. Span. cow

váani PlN. Banning

váani-ŋa-xviš n. one that is from Banning

-véley- v. ALLOM. -vévley- autom. redupl. v.itr. to wave, to flutter (flags, clothes etc.); v.tr. (hands)

CIT. némay pen-vévley-qal piš netéhwap I waved my hand so that he would see me

véley véley yáqa pášmat wíwaywet yáʔi ʔéleqalepa the hanging wash flutters when the wind blows

-vendéer- v.tr. Span. to sell

CIT. héki niyk pe-vendéer-qal he sold his house to me

-véni- v.itr. to coil (of a snake, etc.)

-véni-n- caus. to coil (as a rope)

-vúk- v.tr. 1. to hit (sbdy) with a stick, to throw a stick (at sbdy) 2. to hoe

-vúvan- syncopated form of *-vúvkan- distrib. -vúv- occurs with -alaw-, -ap to hit many times

-vúk-alaw- 1. to go over and hit 2. to throw away; -vúv-alaw- distrib.

vúk-ivaš/-wet n. that which hits all the time, pàl vúk-ivaš lit. that which hits water; crane-like bird

vúv-ap-iš n. lit. that which is supposed to hit repeatedly; a kind of bug that bites

CIT. ad 1. neyúlukay ne-vúk-qal (kélawat piš) he hit me on the head with a stick, he threw a stick at me on the head

ad 2. pen-vúk-qal sámati I am hoeing up weeds

yáʔi ʔéleqal pe-vúk-alaw-qal neyúmuve the wind blows, and blows my hat away

vúvapiš n., see -vúk-

W

wáa interj. (used to attract attention) hey, hallo

CIT. mívika wáa ʔehíčeqal hey, where are you going?

-wáči- v.itr. to be side by side

CIT. ʔípaʔ nemaŋax híwen čem-wáči-wen here he is standing by me, we are both standing together

-wákal- v.itr., with -wen and -iš, also with -če- 1. to break open (of side of the ditch); as a result of it) to run over dyke (of water) 2. to come off (of a tooth)

wákal-iš n. tàma ___ tooth which is gone (refers to the place where it stood); pàl če-___ water which ran off

CIT. ad 1. pál če-wákal-qa the water is running over (dyke, by splitting it)

ad 2. netáma če-wákal-qa my tooth is coming off

wáka-t n., plur. -m, construct -wákˀa wing; cf. wíkil̃ feather

wáka-k n. one which has big wings, hen-wáka-k I have big wings

-wákaˀ-ni- v.tr. to put wings on

CIT. wíkikmal ˀínišil̃ wákˀa pél pél yáqa the wings of a small bird are fluttering (the bird is trying to fly)

-wákaˀan- v.tr. 1. to sweep, to clean 2. to comb; to rake

-wáwakaˀan- distrib.

CIT. ad 1. yúyati pen-wákaˀan-qal penqáyenqal píti I sweep the snow and clean the road

ad 2. pen-wákaˀan-qal neyúlukay I am combing my hair

wák^{W}ay-kiktem PN Torro family

-wála- v.itr. to send out roots and begin to grow

wálˀa n. trunk, stump; ˀíl̃ ___ the trunk of a mesquite

wála-yka adv. to the bottom (e.g., of water)

wála-ŋa adv. at the trunk (of a tree), under a tree

wála-ŋa-x from the beginning

SYN. -púku- to root

CIT. kélawat wála-qa the tree is rooting

-wálin- v.tr., ALLOM. -wáli- with -wen to dig, to dig up (as a trunk)

-wáwlame- distrib. to dig (many objects)

wálin-at n. lit. what is dug; a ditch, hole

CIT. pen-wálin-qal káviweneti I am digging a hole

wáltun PlN. Mecca

wám postp. modal expression of speaker: I guess

Cf. yal postp. I hear

wáma v.itr. in periphr., redupl. to wiggle (the word occurs in a song of medicine-man, pávuʔul, describing how he wiggles with a deer head in deer-hunting, to make him look like a deer)

wámkiš n. ceremonial enclosure (with a fence)

Cf. yáŋiš fence as wind-break

wámax PlN lit. lower part of an enclosed place; in Los Coyotes

wánal n. ropelike thing

-wáne- v.itr. to flow

-wáwne- distrib. to flow all over, to flood

wáni-š n. running water, river

pàl wáne-qal-et water which flows, running water

wáni-š yáwʔa PN lit. river which was caught; river catcher (a family name) wáŋam adj. deep (water, ditch, etc.)

-wáŋam-kʷe- v.itr. to be deep Des.Ca.

-wáŋma-lu- v.itr. to be deep Mt.Ca.

wáŋam-iš n. that which is deep

CIT. pál túkišnekiš pen wáŋam the water is blue and deep

wáqa-t n., plur. -t-em, construct -wáqʔa shoes, cf. -wáqča- to put on shoes

wáqa-y ʔúlanvaš shoe sewer, shoemaker

wáqʔa káwive shoestring

-wáqča- v.tr. to put on, to wear (as shoes, sandals); cf. wáqat shoes

-wáqča-ne- caus. to put (as shoes) on sbdy

-wáqča-vi- v.itr. to put on shoes

-wáqi- v.itr. to be split (of hoofs of a cow, deer, etc.; of a tree)

-če-wáqi- v.itr. to split, to rip (e.g. of branches of a tree, getting overburdened with fruit or being hit by a storm)

-če-wáq-i-n- caus. to tear apart

wáqi-š n., also with -če- one that has torn by itself (e.g. a rim, which has fallen)

wáqi-n-at n., also with -če- one that was torn apart

CIT. héʔiy pe-n-če-wáqi-n-qa I am tearing his legs apart

wáqiš interj. for sing., plur. wáqičem Go! Go on! (used as an exclamation to urge a person to go)

CIT. wáqiš pemámayawan Go and help him!

wáqvaʔal n. place to roast agave

-wási- v.itr., also with -če-, -pe- to stretch (of rubber, or any elastic objects)

-wási-n- caus., also with -če- to stretch

wási-wet n. that which is stretched

-wátin- v.tr., also with -če- ALLOM. -wáti- with -wen, and in imperative to dig out (as pit barbecue, any buried objects)

CIT. pen-wátin-qa nekúyaˀi qíčil̃i I am digging out my buried money

penténeqal pen-wátin-qal I roasted it (in the pit) and I am digging it out

wávu-ma adj. long, tall

wávu-n adv. long

-wávu-k- v.itr., also with -če- to get tall, long

-wávu-k-law- v.itr. to get longer

-wávu-k-ni- caus. to make longer

wávuˀ-wet adj., plur. wáavuˀ-čem long, tall

CIT. peqívišqal wávu-n he cuts it long

néˀ hen-wávuˀ-wet ˀéˀiy ˀeta lit. I am tall on you; I am taller than you

wáw sound imitation, in periphr. sound of a barking (dog, coyote)

-wáwatne- v. 1. v.itr. to iron 2. v.tr. to stretch, to iron

SYN. -táyulne- to smooth, to iron; -sétaˀan- to press, to iron

CIT. pen-wáwatne-qal nexél̃ay I am ironing my clothes

tax-ne-wáwatne-qal I stretch myself out (e.g. waking up in the morning)

wáx sound imitation, in periphr. sound of the wind

-wáx- v.itr. to become dry

-wáx-ne- caus. to make dry

wáx-iš n. that which is dry

pàl wáx-iŋi/ikaw-qalet lit. water which dries up here and there; drought

Cf. -qési- to get wet

CIT. penhíya⁹anqal kʷíñili wáx-ak-at-i I am spreading acorns to let them dry

wáxačil̃ n., plur. wáxašĩ-em frog

-wáxal̃ n. construct, plur. -em younger sister

-wáxal̃-tu⁹a deceased younger sister

-wáxi- v.itr. to separate (persons)

-wáxi-n- caus. to divide (food, money, etc.)

-wáwxam- v.itr. distrib. (of many people)

-wáwxami- caus. and distrib.

wáxi-čem n. separated persons

wáxi-n-vaš/-wet n. food divider

CIT. pax ne-wáxi-qal I have got separated from him

nekínaŋa wíhkʷa čem-wáxe-⁹i lit. we separated, both my wife (and I); we got divorced

kʷánaŋ pi-čem-wáxi-n-wen we divided it into half

-wáy- v.itr., ALLOM. -wáway- autom. redupl. to holler, to make noise (e.g., of a train)

-wáy-ni- caus. to call sbdy; to invite

-wáway-ne- caus. and distrib.

-wáaway-ŋi to holler here and there

wáy-ni-wet n. one that calls the people to eat

pax wáy-va⁹a lit. where one hollers from; throat

CIT. wáway-qal piš peemnámkap he is hollering so that they would meet him

-wáy- v.tr., ALLOM. -wáway- autom. redupl. to take as wife, to marry, to propose marriage

SYN. -kínaŋi v.tr. to take as wife

CIT. tax-ˀiš-wáy-ikatem we are going to marry

ˀí náwišmali pen-wáway-qalˀe I married this girl

-wáye- v.itr. to flap (of wings in flying, of arms in swimming), to fly

CIT. wáy wáy yáxqal wíkikmal a bird is flying

páŋa wáye-qal lit. in the water he is flapping; he is swimming

wáyisma-l n., construct -wáyisma, VAR. wáyeˀma-l plate, dish

-wáyiki- v.itr. to eat, to take a meal

-wáyiki-ni- caus. to feed

wáyiki-ˀat n. food, construct -wáyiki-ˀa

-wáyiki-vaˀa n. construct: piš ___ sth. to eat with (as fork, spoon)

wáyiki-vaš/wet n. gourmand

wáyiki-wenet n. food

CIT. wáyiki-wenet-i píyik^{w}iš lit. person who is to food; person who takes care of food

-wáˀ- v.tr. to roast (as meat)

-wáwa- autom. redupl.

pa wáˀ-vaˀal n. place to roast

wáˀ-at n. roast meat

SYN. -téneq- to roast in a pit

-wáˀaqe- v.itr. (= -wáˀ-aqe, with submorph. -aq-, see -wáˀaš) to open one's mouth

-wáˀaq-an- caus. to make sbdy's mouth open

-če-wá'aqe- to open quickly

-wá'aš (< -wá'-aš [submorpheme]) only in periphr. to open one's mouth

SYN. -'áqi-, -hákuš to open (as a door, etc.)

CIT. pen-wá'aq-an-qal kí'at támay (némay piš) I opened the kid's mouth (with my hand)

-wá'aš- v.itr., v.tr., with -pe- to scatter (seeds, sands, pebbles etc.) Mt.Ca.

wá'iš n. Mt.Ca; káarne Span. Des.Ca. meat; cf. wá'at roast meat

súkat wá'iš deer meat

-wék- v.tr. to cut, to slice; to plow

-wéwkan- distrib. to cut many times

wék-at n. that which is cut; slice(s)

SYN. -qíviš- to cut off

CIT. métewet páani wék wék penyáxeqal I sliced many loaves of bread

héma wék-we his hand is cut; hémaŋa wék-we he is cut on his hand

pen-wék-qal témali I am plowing the ground

-wél- v.itr. to grow, to rise up high (of waves, etc.)

-wéewel- distrib. to rise up (e.g. waves), to appear (of a mirage)

-wél-ne- caus. to make grow, to raise

wél-iš n. that which grew up

wél-vaš/-wet n. that which grows really high; 'í máwul ___ this palm grows really high

páŋiš wél-iš young man

peta ne-wél-ve lit. one upon whom I grew up; my deceased father [referred by the son] qáwiš wéewel-iš lit. mountain which is really high; mountain which is seen outstandingly high in the clear morning on the horizon: pál wéewel-iš refers to Salton Sea in the same situation

SYN. -wávuk- to become tall, -ʔáʔavuk- to grow

CIT. ʔí kíʔat ʔámnakʷal, ʔáʔavuqal, wél-qal this boy is getting bigger, advancing in age, growing up

-weláwali- v.itr., v.tr. Mt.Ca. to water, to sprinkle with water (as plants), to irrigate; cf. -wíčin- to sprinkle with water Des.Ca.

CIT. pen-weláwali-ʔi newésay I irrigated my plants

wélnet n., plur. wéwelnet-em, VAR. wélet mean, bad tempered

CIT. ʔí ʔáwal wélet ʔáčaʔe taxkéʔwet this dog is mean, he likes to bite people

-wélʔisew- v.tr. to marry a man

wélʔisew-il̃ n. marriage, plur. wélʔisewl-/wéwelisewel-em

-wélʔisew n. construct, plur. -wéwelisew-em husband

wélisew-iš n. married woman

Cf . -kínaŋi- to take as wife, -wáy- to marry

-wén- v.tr. with plur., or sing. obj. of uncountables (see -táv- for sing.) to put in place/ order

-wén-alaw- to put away; to take people back (home)

-wén-ikaw- to put in place, to put together; to put away

-wén-ʔa n. [construct] prepared meal, stored food: ne-wén-ʔa hépal my soup

čéxčemi pa meem-wén-wen-ive place where they put dead people, mortuary

CIT. ʔíŋil̃i pa pen-wén-ʔi tésax I put salt in it too

-wépin- v.tr., ALLOM. wép in periphr. to winnow, to blow (as husks) away from grain, to sift

wépin-il̃ n. winnowing

piš tax-ne-wépin-va lit. sth. to blow oneself with; fan

SYN. -tá?in- to winnow

CIT. wép wép penyáqa yá?i piyk I am winnowing it in the wind

-wéqaš- v.itr., ALLOM. -wéwqaš- autom. redupl. to jerk (as in sleep)

CIT. wéqaš yáqa né?i my leg jerked

-wés- v.itr., v.tr. to plant

wés-at n., construct -wés-?a that which is planted, vegetable

CIT. penwálinqal témali pa pen-wés-ik sé?iči I am digging the ground to plant flowers there

wésanwet n., plur. -em chickenhawklike bird; cf. tékvet chickenhawk

-wéš- v.itr. Des.Ca., ALLOM. -wéweš- autom. redupl. to defecate; see -máy- Mt.Ca.

wéevu? n., plur. wéevu-m, VAR. wéevu-?um, Span. egg

wéwa?, ALLOM. wéwa?ay- with -ka having a downward spot (of a road)

wéewa? bumpy (of a road)

wéwa?a-yka adv. downward, way down

Cf. ?áwsun way up

CIT. pit wéewa? the road is bumpy

netáyukiqa wéwa?ay-ka I slid down (the hill)

-wéwču- v.itr. to stretch the legs

SYN. -wáwatne- to stretch

wéwelpiš n., plur. wéwelpič-em, Deṣ.Ca. 1. mushroom 2. dwarf; see sáqapiš mushroom Mt.Ca.

CIT. ʔí níčil̃ wéwelpiš kil̃e wélqal this lady is a dwarf, she does not grow

-wéwen- v.itr., ALLOM. -wéwni- 1. to stand up, cf. -híwen to be standing 2. to stop (walking, working), to stand still

-wéwne-ne- caus. to make stand up, to stop

-wéwen-ŋi- to stand around

wéwen-qalet n. person who stops here and there

SYN. -téklu- to stop (e.g., working)

CIT. ad 2. ne-wéwen-ʔi ʔáy piyik nehéeñiwqaleve I stopped fighting with him

ad 2. ʔáy wéwe ʔetevxáqaleve Stop working!

-wéwen- v.itr., v.tr., ALLOM. -wéwn- with -ik 1. v.itr. to rain 2. v.tr. to rain on sbdy

-wéwni-ni- caus. to cause to rain

wéwn-iš n. rain; clouds

CIT. ad 2. čeme-wéwen-qal we had a rain

wéwn-iš paʔ témiwen clouds are full there, it is cloudy

wéwni-š sámamqal it is drizzling

wéwn-iš yúpiqa it is getting cloudy

-wéwex- v.itr. to bark Des.Ca.; see -híŋ- Mt.Ca.

-wéx- v.itr. to sing hateful songs

-wéx-law- to sing hateful songs

-wéx-law-ni- caus. lit. to make go over and sing hateful songs; to initiate (boys), to teach hateful songs wéx-at n. hateful song (of men)

CIT. tax-hem-wéx-wen they (men) are singing against each other

wéx sound imitation in periphr. sound by sth. thrown up in the air

wéxet n. pine; cf. BandS p.102

-wéy- v.tr., ALLOM. -wéwey- autom. redupl. to pump (water) (prob. related to -wéyi- to sway back and forth, thus referring to the motion)

-wéyi- v.itr. to incline, to nod, to sway back and forth

-če-wéy- to hang sideways; -če-wéwyam- distrib.

wéyi-ˀa n. inclination: hésun wéyi-ˀa ˀelélk^{w}iš lit. his heart's inclination is bad; his way of thinking is bad

CIT. kíˀati pentáwiqal peman wéy wéy níyaxqal lit. I am holding the baby in my arms, with it I am swaying back and forth; ...., I am rocking it

nečíˀawenive nekúpqal nenášveŋa ne-če-wéyi-wen témayka while I was sitting I slept, on the chair I hung sideways downwards

ˀáy hésun wéyi-qal híčika lit. his heart inclines to go; he wants to go

-wéˀi n. construct, plur. -m, VAR. wíˀil̃ penis

-wíčay- v.itr. to give offering (at the big house)

-wíwčay- distrib. (of many persons)

-wíči- v.itr., with -pe-, ALLOM. wíš in periphr. to splash, spring up

-pe-wíči-n- caus. to wet by dashing water

-wíči-n- caus. to water (e.g. plants)

-wíwčumi- caus. and distrib. to splash or water here and there (e.g. plants), -wíwčumi-ŋi-kaw- to water all over

-wíči-n-ŋi-kaw- caus. to water all over (e.g., plants)

-vuk-wíči-n- caus. to splash accidentally

wíči-n-ˀat caus. n. that which is watered

wíči-n-vaˀal n. piš tax-wíči-n-vaˀal, lit. sth. to sprinkle with ; perfume

CIT. pál neta pe-wíči-qal water splashed on me

pál piš wíš wíš penyáxeqal I sprinkled it with water

wíčiw quantif. four, fourth, four times

wíčiw-ka n., plur. wíčiw-kat-em: hépuš wíčiw-ka that which is provided with four eyes, wíwčiw-ka distrib.

wíčiw-k^{w}al-pa on the fourth day, on Thursday

-wíčiw- v.tr. to braid (as rope, thread)

wíčiw-at n. rope, thread, braiding

SYN. -síˀal- to braid

-wíčixan v.itr., v.tr., ALLOM. wíčix in periphr. 1. v.itr. to defecate Des.Ca., see -máay- Mt.Ca. 2. v.tr. to throw (away), to dump (many objects), to desert (family members)

-wíwčixan- distrib. 1. v.itr. to make offering (at big house or at mourning) 2. v.tr. to throw all around

-wíčixan-iwet person who throws away: máyl̃uami mey-wíčixan-iwet person who throws his children away

SYN. -ˀámin- to throw (single obj.)

CIT. tax-čem-wíčixanˀi lit. we threw ourselves away; we separated ourselves by divorce

wíh quantif. two

wíwi distrib. (always) two

wí-s twice

wíh-k^{W}a adv. two together

wíh-k^{W}al n., plur. wíh-k^{W}al-em 1. having two 2. two of them

wí-s namečúmi lit. twice ten; twenty

yúlukˀa wíh-k^{W}al one having two heads

CIT. nekínaŋa wíh-k^{W}a čemhíčiˀi my wife (and I) both went

-wík- v.tr. to carry with the hand

wíkikmal n., plur. -em, VAR. wíkitmal bird

-wíkikma-l̃u- v.itr. to try to be a bird, to play as birds

wíkil̃ n. feather

wí-l̃ n., construct -wí grease, fat

-wí-l̃u- v.itr. to get fat, to gain weight

-wí-l̃u-ne- caus. to fatten

wí-k n. person who is fat

wí-l̃u-š n. person who has become fat

Cf. ˀíkaš Mt.Ca., yáwiš Des.Ca. skinny

CIT. ˀí ˀék^{W}ašmal ˀámnawet wí-k this boy is big and fat

wíl̃al̃ n. badger

-wíil̃ax- v.itr., with -wen to be narrow and long (road)

wíil̃ax-wenet n., pít ___pa on a road which is narrow and long; on a trail

-wíl̃i- v.itr., with -wen to be marked with a line; to be lined up; to spread

-pe-wíl̃i- to run in a line (of lightning, etc.)
-wíwl̃em- distrib. to have stripes
-pe-wíwl̃em- distrib. to run in a line back and forth
-wíl̃a-an- caus. to mark with a line
-wíwl̃a-an- caus. and distrib. to draw stripes
-wíwl̃eme- caus. and distrib. to draw stripes
wíl̃a-ˀa n. straight line
wíl̃a-n-at n. one that is marked with lines
color term base + wíl̃- to have a colored line on; to run in a colored line
CIT. témal wíil yáxwe the earth is marked with a line
píti peem-wíl̃a-ˀan-wen tésnekiš they are drawing a yellow line on the road

-wípis- v.tr. also with -če- to pull, to drag

-wíwpisan- distrib. to pull many objects
-wípis-iče- to pull away
-wípis-iči-l̃ew- to pull along
-wípis-xa- to ask to pull oneself
piš wípis-vaˀal sth. to pull with (e.g., a tractor)
SYN. -húlul-
CIT. pen-wípis-qal ˀáwsunika taxpélemuqalepa I pulled him up, as he was too heavy (to lift himself up)

-wíiru- v.itr. Span. (güiro) to flute

wíiru-piš n., construct -wíiru-pi, VAR. -wíiru-ki flute
CIT. ne-wíiru-pi pa ne-wíiru-qal I am playing my flute

-wíw- v.itr., v.tr. to make acorn mush

wíw-iš n. acorn mush

-wíway- v.tr. to hang, to hang up

-wíiway- distrib. to hang (many objects)

-wíway-kaw- to hang in different places

wíway-vaš/-piš n., pa ___ coat hanger

color term base + wíway-wen to be hanging in a colored appearance; teviš-wíwaywen sth. is hanging in a white appearance

CIT. pen-wíway-qal kélawet peta I hanged it on a tree

čikóoti piš meem-wíway-wenive míyaxwen yéwi ˀéyetem they used to hang up the robbers with a rope in the old days

wíy ˀístam PN clan of Rockhouse and Coyote Canyon

wíyal n. pencil cactus; cf. BandS p.97

wìyal ˀámuyka PlN Torres Peak

-wíyavi- v.itr., v.tr. to put on an apron, a skirt

wíyave-l n., plur. -l-em apron, skirt

CIT. pen-wíyave ne-wíyave-y I am putting on my skirt

wiyelélek n., plur. -em butcherbird

-wíyˀi n., construct forehead

-wíwiyˀi distrib.

-wíyˀi-ŋa adv. on the forehead

CIT. ne-wíyˀi l̃ímaaqa my forehead is contracting, I am frowning

wíˀasil̃ coast live oak (quercus agrifolia); cf. BandS p.123

wíˀasil̃ hél̃iqat/héliwenet PlN lit. oak tree, which is spreading out

wíˀat canyon/maul oak (quercus chrysolepis); cf. BandS p.123

wí°it n., plur. -em 1. grass hopper 2. plur. PN (of a clan)

X

xáča xáča sound imitation, in periphr. swishing sound (e.g., produced by liquid in a can hitting the wall of the container); cf. qáčaw

xáhilũš n. person who was born deformed

xála xála sound imitation, in periphr. sound (e.g., by turning the doorknob)

-xálal- v.itr., also with -pe- to go down slowly (of the level of water, the sun, etc.)

-xálal-ne- caus. to lower, to bring down (e.g., a window)

tàmit xálal-eyka, VAR. tam-xálal-eyka lit. the sun is going down; in the afternoon

-tam + xálal- (támit 'the sun' + xálal 'go down') of the sun to set, used as VAR. of the form: tàmit xálal-qal

CIT. pál xálal-qa témayka the water is sinking down to the bottom

-xálaš- v.tr., with -če- to burst(as basket, chair made of straw)

xaltíska n., KS: qaxaltíska, see qáxal brown bird

-xál°aqe- v.itr. to loosen (of screw, belt)

-xál̃°aqa-n- caus. to loosen

Cf. -xúyiš- to tighten (belt, wheels, etc.)

CIT. netépaqˀa héspen ˀáčaˀe česúyišwen pen-xál̃ˀaqa-n-ˀi
my belt was too tight, (so) I loosened it

xanemúu n., plur. -ˀum chicken

-xáš- v.itr. to thaw, to soak out (of water, out of wet ground)

xáč-iš n. that which has thawed
SYN. -čáx- to melt
CIT. témal xáš-wen the ground is watery

xáw sound imitation, in periphr., cf. xét sound produced by eating crispy objects (as cornchips)

xáwet n., plur. -em mountain quail

-xáyuqi- v.itr. (= -xáyu-qi-, with submorph. -aq-, see -xáyuš-), ALLOM. -xáyu- in periphr.
1. to slide down 2. to become cheap

-xáxyuqi- distrib. (of many objects)
-xáyuqa-n- caus. to lower, to bring down
Cf. -ŋíiñan- v.tr. to be expensive
CIT. ad 1. ne-xáyuqi-qal témayka I have slid down to the ground (as from a tree)
ad 2. xáyuqi-wen súpul peta it is cheaper than the other

-xáyuš- v.itr. (= -xáyu-š-, with submorph. -aš-; see -xáyuqi-), in periphr.
to slide down (as from a tree)

CIT. xáyuš níyaxqal témayka kélawat pax I slid down the tree to the ground

-xéki- v.itr., with -pe- to crack (of glass, stone, etc.)

-pe-xéxkem- distrib. to crack in many spots
-pe-xéki-n- caus. to crack

CIT. népuš púleqa yan kil̃e četáli pe-xéki-qa my pair of glasses (=eyes) fell, but they didn't break into pieces, just cracked

-xékin- v.tr. Mt.Ca. to spit or cough up (as blood)

SYN. -pípivis- to vomit, -(ke)-čúˀan- to spit out

-xélew- v.tr., also with -če- (more frequently than simplex) to scratch

-xéxlewan- distrib. to scratch many times

SYN. -česáluk- to scratch

CIT. pen-če-xélew-qa kúˀti penčútka lit. I struck a match to burn it; I struck a light

-xelyúla construct, arch. clothes

-xél̃a- v.tr. to wear (as clothes)

-xél̃aˀ-ne- caus. to put clothes on sbdy, to dress

-xéxl̃aˀ-ne- caus. and distrib.

-xél̃aˀ-vi- v.itr., v.tr. to put on clothes

-xéxl̃aˀ-vi- distrib.

xél̃a-l n., plur. xél̃a-l-em, construct -xél̃ˀa clothes

-puš xél̃ˀa lit. eyes' clothes; eye secretion

SYN. -ˀéla-

CIT. néˀaš pásukati pen-xél̃aˀ-ne-qal I put harness on my horse

-xémay- v.itr., v.tr., also with -če-,in periphr. with čaqe to crush (brush, fence, or flimsy objects)

CIT. pásukat peta híŋqa séwel man pe-če-xémay-qa a horse steps on a brush and crushes it

penčexélewqalepa kúˀti čaqe xémay yáqa when I struck a match it broke (because it is flimsy) xét sound imitation, in periphr. sound produced by eating crispy objects, or scratching a wooden wall

xúul̃ n., plur. -em, construct -ki bean; cf. BandS p.100

xúum(un) Des.Ca., see ˀáyaqa pév Mt.Ca. very soon, just about

CIT. xúum henhíčika péˀepišqal I was ready to go, then you came

X^W

x^Wálx^Wal n. spider

CIT. x^Wálx^Wal héwqal a spider is weaving

Y

-yáči- v.itr. to get sifted (of ground acorns, etc.)

-yáči-n- caus. to sift

yáči-n-at n. one which is sifted already

yáči-n-vaˀal n. sieve

CIT. pen-yáči-n-qal k^Wíñil túlay I sift the ground acorn

yamesével PlN Mission Creek

yámil̃ n. leaves

yámu in periphr. Mt.Ca. to move (of the surface of the earth, as in the earthquake)

CIT. témal yámu yámu yáqa the ground is shaking and moving

yan conjunction, VAR. yape, yeyan but

-yáŋa- v.itr. to eat (meat and wíwiš together)

CIT. ne-yáŋa-qal káarneˀi wíwiš peman I am eating meat with wíwiš

-yáŋaa- v.itr. to be shaggy, bushy (of hairs, fence)

SYN. -sákʷaa-, -čáŋaa-

-yáŋi- v.tr. to build an encircling fence or a roofless shed for gathering of people or keeping animals

yáŋi-ˀat n., construct -yáŋi-ˀa encircling fence, roofless shed as windbreak

yáŋi-š n. = yáŋi-ˀat

SYN. wámkiš enclosure

yáŋvaˀ n., plur. -am black lizard (living under the bark of a tree)

yávayva n. lung, liver

SYN. -némˀa liver

CIT. ˀenqáčinqa túkvay piš ˀe-yávayva-ŋa ˀenméknik I stuck you in the liver with a knife to kill you

-yáw- v.tr., ALLOM. -yáwne- with suffix -max- 1. to catch, get hold of (sing. object in motion); to touch (especially with the use of periphr.) 2. to have, hold, take care of (with durative suffix)

-yáw-iči- to take along; kʷáˀisneˀati pe-yáw-iči-wet lit. one who takes along the letter; mailman

-yáwne-max- to bring sth. for sbdy

-yáywan- distrib. to (try to) catch, touch (repeatedly or many obj.)

yáw-at n., construct -yáwˀa that which is caught; wàniš yáw-ˀa lit. river, which he has caught; river catcher PN

-yáw + neken- lit. to hold and come; to bring

-yáw + piš- lit. to hold and arrive; to bring

-sém + yaw- v.tr. lit. laugh and hold; to smile to sbdy

CIT. ad 1. túku wáxačili pen-yáw-ʔi yesterday I caught a frog

ad 2. péʔiš ʔívʔax pen-yáw-qal that's why I have it (frog) now

wíkikmal súpl̃i pen-yáw-ik, yáw penyáxeʔi yan kil̃e pen-yáw I was going to catch a bird, and I touched it but I did not catch it

yúyat/síwiš ne-yáw-qal lit. cold/fever holds me; I have a cold/fever

mík táwpaxiš ʔe-yáw-qa lit. how many years hold you?; how old are you?

súpl̃i ʔócra čeme-yáw-iči-qa piš čemhíčipi píka lit. one hour took us along that we went there; it took us an hour to go there

-yáwan- v.tr., ALLOM. -yáywan- autom. redupl. to make smooth (as arrow shaft)

yáwna-piš n. arrow shaft straightener (made of sth. like clay, but hard; good to scratch off blisters of babies, too)

yáwaywet n. canyon

SYN. pánaay

-yáwi- v.tr. Des.Ca., -ʔíka- Mt.Ca. to get skinny, thin

-yáyawi- distrib. (plur. subj.)

-yáwi-n- caus. to make sbdy skinny

yáwi-š n. skinny one

Cf. sámatnekiš slim , wíl̃uš fat

CIT. ʔí ʔáwal múqal yáwi-qal this dog is sick, it is getting skinny

-yáx- v. itr., VAR. -ya- (Mt.Ca.), "unstressed verb root"
-yax- (see Grammar, pp. 39,187) with stress placement on the personal (subject) P, prefix, quotative: to be so
to be so, to say

CIT. ʔémiyk ní-yax-qaʔl-e — I said (it) to you

ʔenhúmsanmaxaluʔ yáx-qal — 'I could make them for you' she said

sérrrrr yáx-qal — it makes (or says) 'serrrrr'

-yax- v.tr./itr., VAR. -yáxe- before durative suffix and inflective suffixes (the vowel of the object prefix appears as /i/), in complete or partially achieved process:
a little, some of it (so-called periphrase, see Grammar, p. 223 ff.)

CIT. kús pi-yáxe-qal — he takes it (some)

kús pi-yáx-ŋi-qal — he takes some, one by one

kús-ŋi pi-yáxe-qal — id.

yáyʔal (prob. yáʔi 'wind' redupl.): kùt ___ lit. fire-wind; small whirlwind, dust devil

yáʔexiš n., plur. yáʔexičem important person, leader

SYN. ˀéˀexiš different one, ˀíˀexiš unimportant one

CIT. ˀúmun yáˀexič-em heemáqiwen kíš ˀámnawet piyik peynánvayaxniktem all the big shots got together at the big house to negotiate

yáˀi n., plur. -m wind, air

yáˀi héˀaš lit. wind its pet; thistle, little cactus; cf. BandS p.55

CIT. yáˀi ˀéleqal the wind is blowing

yáˀik n., plur. yáˀik-tem/yáyˀik-tem runner, good runner

-yáˀik-lu- v.itr. to run fast

SYN. -ˀíva- to run

CIT. hésun yáˀik-lu-qal lit. his heart runs fast; he is breathing fast

-ye n. construct (accentuated in vocative: -yéˀ) mother

-yékaw- v.itr., v.tr. to pick, gather (e.g., acorns from trees, potatoes, watermelons)

-yékaw-ˀa [construct] gathering

yékaw-vaš n. picker

-yékaw-max-iš n. [construct] deceased mother (of both son and daughter)

SYN. -číˀ-, -ˀáy-

-yémi- v.itr. to calm down (an anger, ache)

CIT. piyk nehéñiwqal ˀáy nésun yémi-ˀi lit. I was mad at him, already my heart calmed down; ..., (but soon) I calmed down

neyúluka/netíˀi yémi-wen my head/stomach is calmed down (pain is gone)

-yéŋ- v.itr., in periphr. except in combination with suff. -law- to pass just a while (of time);

to stay a while

-yéŋ-ĩlew- to pass a long while (of time); to stay too long

-yéŋ-iñi- distrib. 1. v.itr. to pass a long while
2. (like adv.) too long, often, always

-yéŋ-ĩlew-vaš n. person who stays too long

CIT. yéŋ yáx peʔpíšqal he came right back

yéŋ-iñi ʔehíčive míyaxwen piyk you used to go there often

-yéŋin- v.tr. to allow sbdy to do sth., to give permission to

CIT. men-yéŋin-qaʔle (=taxne-yéŋin-qaʔle) piš pa hemñášpi I let them stay there

kĩl ne-pe-yéŋin-pi sáxalu, henpívakati (=piš nepívapi) lit. won't you probably allow me to smoke? may I smoke?

kĩle míyaxwen piš tax-yéŋin-pi he won't give himself up

-yes n. construct mother's younger sister; stepmother

yét n. female (for animals)

súkat yét female deer

yéwi adv. long time ago, before

yéwi-viš n. old one, old-timer; nexéla ___ my dress, which I used to wear in the old days, cf. nexéla návaxiš my old dress

SYN. návaxiš old

CIT. ʔí yéwi kíš ʔámnawetʔah this used to be a big house

yéyax conjunction but

-yím- v.itr., -ʔíiyem- autom. redupl., with plur. subj. and recipr. obj. to have intercourse

CIT. tax-hem-ʔíiyem-wen they are having intercourse

-yučíwi- v.itr. to be cold, to feel cold

-yučíwi-n- caus. to make cool

yučíwi-va/-ve cold season, autumn

SYN. -héq- to cool off (of food)

CIT. yučíw yáxqal it is getting a little cool

héspen síwma míyaxwen piš pen-yučíwi-n-pi kíˀči it is very hot, (so) I have to make the house cool

-yúki- v.itr., v.tr. to get scared, be afraid

-yúyuki- distrib., -yúyukn-, -yúkn- with nominalizing suffix

-yúki-wen to be scary, to be causing fright or alarm, be dangerous

-yúki-ne- caus., also with -če- to scare

yúki-ˀat that which one is scared of

yúki-wet scary one

yúkn-iš n. one who got scared

yúyukn-il̃ n. coward, plur. ___em

yúkn-ivaš/-iwet n. coward

séwet yúki-ˀa lit. that which snake is scared of; plant which is good for a snake bite

CIT. hem-yúki-wen ˀalawá míyaxwen peˀ ˀelélkʷeˀn piš taxhemkúlpi they feared they (the other medicine-men) might harm them [texts p. 65]

-yúl- v.itr., v.tr. to build (as house)

-yúylan- distrib. to build (many houses)

-yúl-ˀa n. [construct] that which is built

yúl-wet n.: kíˀči pe-___ carpenter

yúl-wenet n. building, house

CIT. yéwi kíš yúylan-wen máwulpiš houses used to be built with palm leaves

-yúl- v.tr. to string, to thread

yúl-ʔa n. that which has got a string

CIT. me-yúl-qal ʔíiluŋa he is stringing them with a thread (e.g., necklace)

-yúlaa- v.itr. to hang, to sway (as a cluster, bunch of strings)

-yulyúlaa- to hang more raggedly

yúla-wet in qáwiš ___ lit. mountain which is hanging down; rugged mountain; PN for a mountain behind La Quinta which is also called qáwiš húlawet

base color term + yúlaa- to hang down in a colored appearance: tèviš-yúlaa-qal it is hanging down in a white appearance

SYN. -káyaa- to dangle, -wíway- to hang

CIT. máwul pálʔa yulyúlaa-qal the palm leaves are hanging

yúlal n. mushroom (growing on the oak); cf. BandS p. 106-107

SYN. sáqapiš mushroom (growing on the cottonwood)

yúlil incense cedar; cf. BandS p. 85

yúlil̃ n., construct -yúli pipe

yú(u)liš n., plur. yú(u)lič-em clay, mud

CIT. yúliš tékqal tèmayka páŋa the mud settled down to the bottom of the water

yúluka-l n. plur. -l-em, construct -yúlukʔa hair; head

yúluk-ŋa on the head

CIT. ne-yúlukʔa nepeláyinqa lit. my head causes me a slight headache; I have a slight headache yulsével n., plur. -em, construct -yulsévʔe eyebrow (prob. < yul apocope of yúluka 'hair' + sével [unknown]); cf. yultámaš

-yultáma- v.itr. to have a mustache or beard (prob. < yul apocope of yúluka 'hair' + táma 'mouth')

-yultáma-ne- caus. to put a mustache or beard on sbdy

-yultáma-vi- v.itr. to begin to have a beard (e.g., of a young man)

yultáma-š n. bearded person, beard

yultáma-l n., plur. -l-em, construct -yultámʔa whisker, beard

-yúul̃ n. construct, plur. -em younger brother

-yúul̃-ka(t), plur. -kat-em being brother to sbdy: neʔeme-yúul̃-kat-em you are brothers to me, tax-yúul-kat-em they are brothers to each other

yúul n., plur. yúhlam little rat, field mouse

SYN. páʔiwet field mouse

-yuméxan- v.tr., ALLOM. -yuméemxan- autom. redupl. to dress up, to fix (oneself, bed, etc.)

CIT. taxne-yuméemxan-qa I am fixing myself

yúumu n., plur. yúumum Yuman

yúumu-ŋa in Yuma

-yúmuʔ- v.tr. to put on the head (hat, scarf, etc.)

-yúmu-ne- caus. to put a hat on sbdy

-yúmuʔ-vi- v.itr. to put the hat on

yúmuʔ-vel n. yúymu-vel distrib. hat

-puš + yúmu-veʔ construct lit. eye-hat; eyelid;

he-puš + yúmuvel   the eyelid

CIT. kil̃ peemʔáyawen piš peem-yúmuʔ-pi   they didn't want to put it (the hat) on

yúŋaviš n., plur. yúŋavič-em   turkey buzzard

yúŋaviwet n.   eagle with white circular stripes on the wings; cf. ʔáswet eagle

-yúpi- v.itr.   to be overcast (of the sky), to become cloudy

-yúpi-n- caus.   to cause to be overcast (e.g., by a medicine-man)

color term base + yúpi-   to turn into a colored appearance: neyúlukʔa teviš-yúpi-qal my hair is turning white

color term base + yúpi-n-qal   to make turn into a colored appearance

yúvisʔa n.   earwax

-yúvušxu- v.itr.   to wash one's hair

-yúvušxu-ne- caus.   to wash sbdy's hair

SYN. -pášam-, -qáyin-   to wash

CIT. ʔen-yúvušxu-ne-ka   I am going to wash your hair

-yúy- v.itr., v.tr.   1. v.itr. to snow   2. v.tr. to snow on sbdy

-yúy-ni- caus.   to cause to snow

yúy-at n.   snow

yúy-ni-vaš n., plur. yúy-ni-vač-em   snowbird

CIT. ad 1. čemeta yúy-qal   it is snowing on us

ad 2. čeme-yúy-qal lit.   it is snowing us; the snow is falling on us

CIT. yúy-at čáviqal   the snow is falling, it is snowing

-yúyi- v.itr. to quiver (legs, e.g., when climbing down a steep road)

yúyil̃ n. California juniper; cf. BandS p. 81-2

yúyivaš pines with long needles; cf. tévat, pines with short needles

yúy-ma cold, cool (the weather, water, etc.)

-yúy-uk- v.itr. to get cold, ALLOM. -yúy-kʷ-

-yúy-kʷ-eni- caus. to cause to get cold

yúy-kʷ-iš one who has become cold; ʔáy ___ ʔáy múkiš he is cold already, he is dead

yúy-at n. cold

SYN. -četáxal- to feel cold

CIT. yúy-ma nečetáxalqal netáxaw yúy-ma it is cold, (so) I feel cold, (and) my body is cold

yúy-at ne-yáw-qal lit. the cold got hold of me; I have caught a cold

-yúʔaqi- v.itr., ALLOM. -yúʔa- in periphr. to reach for

-yúʔaq-an- caus. lit. to make reach for; to aim (arrow, gun, etc.)

CIT. némay penwáwutneqa píyk ne-yúʔaqi-qa pepéeli penkúsik I stretched my arm and reached for the paper to get it

yúʔayl̃ n., plur. -em small turtle

-yúʔi- v.itr. to trot

-yúʔi-ŋi to trot around

CIT. pásukat yúʔi-qa a horse is trotting around

yúʔxušxa-l n., construct -yúʔxušxa brain

*There are no words in Cahuilla that begin with "Z".

PART II.

ENGLISH-CAHUILLA INDEX

Note: Cahuilla words beginning with the unaccented prefixes -če-, -pe-, and -vuk- (e.g. -če-télaš- 'to be baggy') can be found in the Cahuilla-English section under the stem which follows these prefixes (e.g. -télaš-).

ENGLISH-CAHUILLA INDEX

A

about it/him p-iš
above ʔáwsun
accident, to have -téwyaw-
accompany, to -kíin-
accuse, to -náʔmiš-
acorn k^{w}íñil
acorn mush, to make -wíw-
acorns, to leach -páči-
act, to -míyax-
afraid, to be -yúki-
after a while máwa
afterbirth káalapi, -púnʔa
afterwards húŋa-yka, séʔŋax
agave ʔámul
age -táwpa-ki
aged person ʔáʔavuʔwet
agile k^{w}áwawaʔ-il̃
agree on, to -héeʔan-,
  -nánva-yax-ni-
ahead of -múči
aim, to -yúʔaq-an-
air yáʔi
alert k^{w}ápi-qal-et
alike nánva-net, péŋki-š
alike, to be -ʔáyax-
all ʔúmun
all over ʔúmun
allow, to -yéŋin-
almost ʔayqapév
already ʔáy, ʔáy-ax
also tésax
always tuháyemaniš
ancestor -ŋáʔa, píw-il̃
and man, pen
angry, to get -héñew-
animal, different ʔíʔihiŋaviš
ankle -ʔi káwʔa (s.v. -ʔi)
answer, to -náxči-
ant ʔánet, kúvišnil̃
antelope ténil̃
anxious, to be -táʔatay-
appear, to -téeŋ-, -téew-en
appear suddenly, to -pénipis-
apple, wild kélel
apron, to put on -wíyavi-
argue, to -mélan-, -náyax-
arm -ma-l
around it/him p-iš
arrive, to -píš-
arrogant tel̃ʔáʔayamal̃
arrow húya-l
arrowhead sív-at
arrowweed háŋal
as if híšte
ascend, to (of road) -čáwa-
ash nísxiš
ashamed, to feel -sun-háman-
ask favor, to -nánal-
ask for, to -nétan-, séʔwe-
ask question, to -nánal-
asleep, to fall -kup-čáʔay-
at all hétu
attack, to -túmaw-

attend mass, to -míisa-
attractive sinsímniš
aunt -hépaak, -nes, -pa
autumn sévaʔ, yučíwi-va
avoid sbdy, to -háman-
awake, to stay -k^{W}ápi-

B

baby kíʔat, máyl̃u-ʔat
bachelor náanxiš
back (of body) húlul, seláwa-l̃
bad ʔeléle-ma
bad tempered wélnet
badger spp. húnal, wíl̃al̃
bag káwkun-il̃
baggy, to be -télaa-
baggy, to get -če-télaš-
bald-headed, to be -púxuu-
ball qáwpi-ʔil̃
ball game, to play -qáwpi-
bamboo páxal
bananas, wild nínil̃
baptism ʔás-ne-ʔil̃
barber tax-sív-vaš (s.v. -sív-)
bark (of tree) sáva-l, táča-l, tášʔa
bark, to -híŋ-, -wésex-
basket, types of čípatma-l, káput-il, káput-mal, né-at, sek^{W}ával, sexwálal, téviŋil̃
basket, to make -néh-
bat (animal) páli-l
bathe, to -ʔáʔas-
bathe in the sun, to -tám-kus-
battle héeñiw-il
be, to -híwen-, -máx-, -qál-
be around, to -méle-
bean tévil̃mal̃em (pink beans), xúul̃
bear húnwe-t
bear down on, to -muʔíva-
bear fruit, to -tú-
beard támaš, yultáma-š
beat up, to -mék-an- (s.v. -múk-)
beautiful (woman) ʔélka
beavertail mánal
because súnaxwenepa
bed káamaʔ, kúp-vel
bedbug náwil̃a-t
befall, to (bad omen) -nálaw-
before -múči, yéwi
beg, to -séʔwe-
behave, to -méx-
belch, to -qéwi-
believe, to -héeʔan-
belly téʔi-l̃
belongings híisaxve, méx-an-at
belt tépaqa-l
bend, to -ñámin-, -ními-
bend backward (of body), to -vuk-ʔéwi-
bend forward (of body), to -lúku-

bent, to get -ʔéme-,
  -ʔíkya-, -káwlaa-
berries píkl̃am, túʔ-iš
bet, to -háayu-
between ŋáliva
bewitch, to -píʔ-
biceps ʔíva-ʔal
big one ʔámna-ʔa
bigger, to get -wél-
bird wíkikmal
bird spp. kʷasanemčíip,
  muʔíkil̃
birthday púli-ve
bit (monetary unit)
  púuŋku
bite, to -kéʔ-
bitter ʔénene
bizarre, to become -ʔíswalu-
black túl-nek
blanket sáalaʔa
blast, to -pe-múqi-
bleed, to -ʔéw-lu-
blind hépuš ʔíʔive, táatwal
blink, to -mák-
blister, to get -pe-pákʷe-
bloat, to -pátiš-
block, to -pe-táki-
blood ʔéw-il̃
bloom, to -páʔaw-, -púki-,
  -sé-
blossom sé-l
blow, to -pe-múqi-, -púʔan-
blow, (wind) to -ʔéle-

blow away, to -púʔan-,
  -wépin-
blow off, to -vuk-tékʷel-
blow one's nose, to -múvi-
blow up, to -pe-púki-
blue túkvaš-nek-iš
bluejay káyval
body táxaw-il̃
boil, to -pis-múlul-
bone téʔi-l̃
bone (neck) -káwnax
bored, to become -senmúk-
born, to be -púli-
borrow, to -téʔe-
boss káwi-ʔa, núʔin-qal-et,
  -táxlew
both sides námki-ka
bow čúkinapiš, húl
bow and arrow húya-l
bowlegged, to be -lika-kíka-
boy ʔékʷašmal
braid, to -síʔal-, -wíčiw-
brain yúʔxušxa-l
branch číma
brand, to -čút-
brave táxat
break, to -qápal-, -qápi-
break down, to -lápaš-
break into pieces, to -táli-
break open, to -če-péki-,
  -wákal-
breast -pi-l̃, -táw
breathe, to -híkus-

breeze, to -hívuu-
brightness háti-wen-et
bring down, to -ʔámi-n-
bring it here! náwiči
brooch púkulvaʔa
brother, elder -pas
brother, younger -yúul̃
brother/sister, deceased
  younger -pínil̃uʔa
brown tésnek-iš
brown bird xaltíska
brush súvi-š
brush, dense sámat
bubble, to -múlul-
bubble up, to -čúpul-
buck, to -k^{W}éyʔeš-
buckhorn cholla mútal
budding season táspaʔ
buds, to put forth -páʔaw-
bug, stinking tútumiš
build house, to -yúl-
bumblebee kúŋsexwet
bump, to -pe-púxay-
bump into, to -pe-qáŋi-,
  -pe-téxay-
bumpy, to be -limu-límu-
bundle of feathers číya-t
bundle túk-ive
burn, to -čút-, -kína-,
  -lémeme-, -náʔ-
burned, to get -ʔéme-
burp, to -qéwi-
burrow, to -mu-píl̃e-
burst open, to -vuk-péki-
bury, to -kúy-
burst, to -če-xálaš-
bush, dense témaš
bush, spp.méčewel, séwel
bushy, to be -yáŋaa-
but háwa, yan, yéyax
butcherbird tétinat,
  wiyelélek
butterfly héveveqalet, málmal
buy, to -sámsa-, -ʔúʔuwe-
buzzard yúŋaviš
by any means méxanuk
by means of it p-iš

C

cabbagelike plant tésevel
cactus spp. ʔámul, ʔávusil̃,
  čúŋal, kúpaš, mánal, mútal,
  návet, wíyal
Cahuilla Indian táxliswet
Cahuilla language ʔívil̃u-ʔat
calf (of the leg) kaykáyaʔka
call, to -téwan-, -wáy-ni-
call over the phone, to
  -vuk-séqay-
calm down, to -yémi-
camera tax-k^{W}áʔisne-vaʔal
camp, to make -támituk-
candy dúlsi
cane húyanaxa-t, -ʔík-ʔa,
  náxa-t

canyon pámamal̃, pánu-wen-ik, yáwaywet
care for, to -méle-
carpenter yúl-wet
carry, to -núŋu-, -ʔúʔ-
carry on, to -téyan-
carry on the back, to -túk-
carry with the hand, to -wík-
carrying net ʔíka-t
cast off skin, to -húm-
cat's claw páxal
cat-tail kúʔut
catch, to -yáw-
cave téki-š
cave in, to -lápaš-
center (of plants) pásun
ceremonial bundle máiswa-t
ceremonial official paxáʔ
chair ñáš-vel
chamise ʔúʔut
chase, to -némi-
chase away, to -kíwaʔan-, -néemi-
cheap, to become -xáyuqi-
checked, to be -téveleve-
cheek k^wáča-l
Chemehuevi Indian čemewáva
chest -táw
chew, to -míš-
cherry, wild čámiš
chia pásal
chicken xanemúu
chicken hawk spp. kísil̃, k^wáʔal, tékvet, wésanwet
chickenpox, to have -lúmu-
chief nét
child kíʔat
chill, to have a -sámam-, -síi-
chin -ʔéyewakʔa
chip, to -čípal-
chipmunk sísil̃
chirp, to čúp čúp
choke, to -čáʔ-, -kusméti-, -kustémi-
chokecherry ʔátut
cicada táčikal
circular, to be -túyva-
clap hands, to -pákin-
clay tésel, tésnat, yúuliš
claw, to -čúk-, -čúkla-
clean, to -líway-, -wákaʔan-
clean, to get -qáyi-
clear tévelve
clear, to be -táwi-
clear, to become -čáwi-, -qáyi-
clear place hátava
clear up, to -čéxi-
clench hands, to -máqʔu-
climb, to -čáwa-
climb down, to -ʔámi-
close súnči
close, to -témi-
close one's eyes, to -súpaq-, -túlu-

close one's mouth, to -náki-
clothes xḗla-l, -xelyúla
clouds wéwn-iš
cloudy, to become -yúpi-
coal túl̃
coil, to -véni-
cold qā̃la-ka, yúyma
cold, to be -če-táxal-
collapse, to -če-hémi-,
-lápaš-, -qápal-
collapse, (legs) to -če-lúyuv-
colored, (body) to get -pákaa-
comb péyna
come, to -nék-en-
come about, to -téeŋ-
come across, to -námik-
come down, to -ʔámi-
come near, to -pénipis-
come off, to -čál-, -čúvi-
come off, (tooth) to -če-wákal-
come out, to -pís-
come over, to -pénipis-
come to the edge of water,
to -ŋélew-
companion -kíl̃iw
compare, to -nánva-yax-ni-
compete, to -háayu-
competitor -káytu
constipated, to get -tépiš-
continuously múʔ
contract, (forehead) to
-l̃ímaa-
cook, to -kúl-, -séx-
cool yúyma
cool, to make -yučíwi-
cool off, to -héq-
cord káwi-ve
corn máys
corner, in the ŋáʔ-ika
cost of, at the pe-ta
cottontail távut
cottonwood tree lávalvanet
cough, to -ʔúʔuhu-
cough up, to -ke-xékin-
count, to -téwan-
cousin -ñukʔu
cover, to -két-
cover up, to -vuk-čípi-n-,
-vuk-ʔúmin-
covered, (hole) to get -čípi-
cow váakaʔ
coward yúkn-ivaš/-iwet
coyote ʔísi-l̃
crack, to -čápi-, táš-,
-pe-xéki-
cradle sí-at
cramp, to have -če-héwaš-,
-če-púkuš-, -če-súkuš-,
-če-túnuš-
crane (bird) káal, pàl
vúkivaš
crawl, to -čáwa-
crawling lúŋu-lúŋu
crazy hé-sun ʔíʔive (s.v.
sún-il̃)
crazy person lóoko

crazy, to become -kíksew-lu-
create, to -núk-
creator núk-iš, táv-iš
creature táv-at
crickets séʔl̃am
crippled háaxal̃uš, lúumiš
criticize, to -míčan-
crooked, to be -kapu-kápu-, -lika-líka-
crooked, to get -ʔéme-, -méye-
cross, to -námi-
crow ʔálwet
crowd in, to -témi-
crowded máča-ma
crowlike bird ʔálwamal̃
crumple, (house) to -lúmaš-
crush, to -pe-mátaš, -če-xémay-
cry, to -ŋáŋ-
cry, (bird) to -háawi-, -háay-
cry for sth., to -ŋáŋiva-
cup káput-mal, kávaʔma-l
Cupeño language, to speak -čáymu-
cure, to -tíŋʔay-
curly, to be -číŋal-
curve, to -méli-, -méye-
curved round, to be -čánaa-
cut, to -wék-
cut off, to -qíviš-
cut short, to be -múti-
cute sulsímima, sinsímniš

D

damage, to -ʔeléle-k^{w}-ene-
dance sulčáamaniš
dance, to -čéŋen-, -súk-lu-
dancer čéŋen-wet
dangle, to -káyaa-
dark, to get -tul-sáwaqi-
date-palm máwul
daub, to -páš-
daughter (of man) -súŋama
daughter (of woman) -púlin
daughter-in-law -mísi-k
dawn páay-iš
day támit
daybreak, to become -páay-
deaf náq ʔíʔive
death múk-wenet
debate, to -mélan-
deceased person téwka(t)
decide, to -nánva-yax-ni-
decorate, to -séʔni-
deep wáŋam
deer súk-at
deformed, born xáhil̃uš
defecate, to -máay-, -wéš-, -wíčixan-
delighted person čáčaaka
delicious kén-ma
delirous, to become -ʔíswalu-
dent, to -če-némal-
desert ʔíŋkiš, ʔíʔexi-š

desert, to -wíčixan-
diapers čéqi-vel
die, to -čúma-law-, -múk-
different súpul-aʔan
different kinds of téetewkat
different places, in
k^{w}ániva(ʔan)
difficult héspe-ma
disgusted, to feel -senmúk-,
-símm-
dig, to -wálin-
dig out, to -wátin-
diligent čaxčáaka
dime čúviwenet
dip, to -ʔík^{w}-
dip in the water, to -čúp-
dirt téma-l, -túvave
dirty sel̃áxama
dirty, to become -sel̃áxmu-
disappear, to -čúx-, -sáwaa-
discover, to -téw-
discuss, to -mélan-
disease múk-wenet
dish wáyisma-l
dislike, to -tátaxel̃ew-
dislocated, (body part) to
become -če-húya-,
-če-púluš-
dissolve, to -kéye-
distance, with háka-n
ditch wálin-at
dive, to -ʔúpi-
dizzy, to feel -puš-ŋéy-
(s.v. púč-il̃)

dizzy, to make feel -pe-láyin-
do, to -méx-
do almost, to -ʔáyaw-
do by accident, to -munávčine-
do like that, to -ʔéx-an-
doctor, to -máyew-, -tíŋʔay-
dodge, to -máʔni-
dog ʔáwal
doll ʔíʔipiš, málisap-piš,
núk-at
doll fiesta, to have -núk-
dollar péesu
done, to be -k^{w}ás-
door kímu-l
double up, to -náanme-
doubt, to -háyu-
dough ñúč-il̃
dove máxayil̃
down (of bird) píi-l̃
drag, to -wípis-
drought pàl wáx-iŋi-qalet
draw oneself together, to
-máqʔu-
dream, to -tétʔayaw-
dress ʔéla-t
dress up, to -yuméxan-
drill through, to -mu-páxul-
drink páʔ-il̃
drink, to -pá-
drink up, to -pá-ači-
drip, to -síl̃e-, -pe-típil̃-
drop, to -čávi-, -púli-
drop and splatter, to
-páčay-

drop flat, to -páš-
drown, to -ʔúx-
drunk, to get -kíkesaw-
dry, to become -wáx-
drizzle, to -sámam-
duck spp. páat, sásaymal̃em
dumb tàma ʔíʔive
dump, to -píki-n-, -wíčixan-
dust múli-š
dust devil yáyʔal
dwarf wéwelpiš
dye,to -čúpi-n

E

eagle ʔáswet, yúŋaviwet
eagle dance mánet, púne-ʔil̃
ear náq-al
ear wax yúvisʔa
early mu-támit-i, mu-túleka (in the morning)
earring, to put on -čáyu-vi-
earth téma-l
east, toward the támi-ka
eat, to $-k^{w}$áʔ- -wáyiki-, -yáŋa-
echo, to -qawenáaw-
echo sbdy, to -ʔála-
edge ŋélel-iš
edge, around támaw
edge, at the -háy-va
edge, to -ŋélew-
edge, to the ŋáy-ika
egg wéevuʔ
egoist tátaxil
elbow púvia-l
elder (person) ʔáʔaviva, ʔáʔavuʔwet
elder (tree) húnkat
embarrassed,to feel -sun-háman- (s.v. -háman-)
emerge, to -téeŋ-
emit smoke, to -míʔ-
employ, to -káwiya-
empty one ʔíŋkiš
encircling fence, to build -yáŋi-
enclosed place wámax
enclosure, ceremonial wámkiš
encourage, to -muʔíva-n-
end hému, ŋáʔ-a
end, to come to an -háy-
enemy -káytu
enough ʔáča-ma, méteʔ-ma
enough, not to be -méli-
entangled, to get -ŋáli-
enter, to -páx-
escape, to -pe-púti-
evening mávi-š
evening, towards tam-páx-ika (s.v. -páx-)
exhaust, to -háyin-
exhausted, to be -tuháyin-
exist, not to -sáwaa-
exist, to -míyax-

expect, to -kíˀiw-
expensive, to be -ŋíñan-
eye púč-il̃
eyebrow yulsével
eyelash -puš-čávay (s.v. púč-il̃)
eyelid -puš-yúvu-veˀ

F

face púč-il̃
face, to -púču-
fail to find, to -qátiw-
fail to hit/meet, to -ˀáškay-
fail to recognize, to -táˀal-
faint, to -kúl-
fall down, to -čávi-, -máni-, -púli-
fall into, to -pe-kúli-, -ŋálaw-
fall off, to -kéŋi-
fall through, to -pe-páxul-
family -táxlew
far pépiy
far away háka-n
fast čáˀča, hávu-n, héspe
fat wí-l̃
father -na, -táata
fatigue háyin-at
feast sulčáamaniš
feather wíkil̃
feces -k^{w}áˀ-a
feed, to -wáyiki-ni-
feel, to -námaan-
female ñíčil̃, yét
fever síwi-š
fever, to have -síw-
field mouse páˀiwet
fight, to -héeñiw-
fight over sth., to -náwas-
file, to -ŋávay-
fill, to -témi-, téxin-
fill up, to -kúy-, -múye-
filth -túvave
filth in eyes -puš xél̃ˀa
find, to -téw-
find oneself, to -míyax-
find out, to -ˀéˀnan-
fine ˀáča-ˀe
finger -ma-l, -ma túˀ-i
fingernail sálu-l
finish, to -čúmi-
fire kína-qal-et, kú-t, ná-qal-et
fire, to catch -náˀ-
fire, to make -náˀani-
first múluk
fish kíyul
fish, to -ˀík-
fit nánva-nek
fit, to -náki-
five namek^{w}ánaŋ
fix, to -yuméxan-
flame, to go up in -pálaw-
flap, to -wáye-

flare out, to -pánaa-
flash, to -pálavla-, -pe-tíkal-
flat, to be -lákaa-, -lápaa-, -pálaa-
flatten, to -lákaš-, -láki-
flattened, to be -taq-táqa-
flea máčil, múkaš
flee, to -híŋ-iči-
flesh -túkʔu
flick, to -pe-láwin-
flicker, to -kísal-
flicker (fire), to -pálavla-
flip off, to -pe-tékʷel-
float, to -képi-, -qípi-
flour túʔat
flow, to -wáne-
flow out, to -múye-, -páye-
flower séʔ-iš
flute, to -wíiru-
flutter, to -véley-
fly ʔáʔawet
fly, to -pe-ʔéwi-, -híŋ-, -wáye-
foam, to -páxil̃a-
fog háway-š, páxiš, páyi-š
foggy, to be -háway-, -páye-
fond of, to be -ʔáyaw-, -ʔíʔiklu-, -méle-
fold, to -če-lámi-
follow, to -kíil̃ew-, -kíin-
follow tracks, to -tépin-
follow tradition, to -némi-
following sbdy séʔŋax
fontanel híkusa-l
food wáyiki-wenet
foot -ʔi
forehead -wíyʔi
forget! méme
forget, to -sun-táwas- (s.v. -táwas-)
formed, to become -qáni-
four wíčiw
fox qáwisiš
freeze, to -tépawka-
friend -ʔamíwu-ki, -kíl̃iw
frog wáxačil̃
fruit túʔ-iš
frown, to -l̃ímaa-
frozen če-héespekuš, tépače-wet
full máča-ma
full with food, to become -púy-
fun, to have -kanávi-
funeral kúy-il̃
funny sulsímima
fur píi-l̃
further múʔan

G

gamble, to -tášl̃a-, -táxpi-
game ʔíʔk-il̃
gargle, to -líway-
gather, to -číʔ-, -yékaw-

gather wood, to -kélaw-
generous néʔwet
get away -če-kéwin-
get blocked, to -mu-témi-
get cured, to -húva-
get dark, to -mávi-
get dusty, to -múle-
get hold of, to -hívin-, -kús-
get in a crawling position, to -mu-čáwaqe-
get old, to -návax-
get over the hump, to -číʔa-pis-
get sick, to -múk-
get skinny, to -ʔíka-
get sores, to -kéye-
get together, to -máqi-, -náki-
get up, to -k^{w}éʔeqe-
get upside down, to -píki-
get water, to -páw-
get weak, to -múk-
get wet, to -kési-
girl náwišmal
give birth, to -máyl̃u-
give enema, to -múmul-
give (food), to -ʔékamax-
give (money), to -máx-
glide, to -képi-
go, to -híči-
go ahead, to -múlu-
go along with, to -kíil̃ew
go away, to -ŋíi-, -sáwaa-
go down, to -ʔámi-
go down, (the sun, water) to -xálal-
go down headfirst, to -muyéxe-
go down to the other side, to -vuk-ʔami-
go home, to -ŋíi-
go in, to -páx-
go on! wáqiš
go out, (fire) to -túq-
go over, to -vuk-ʔámi-, -námi-
go round, to -kávay-
go to a meeting, to -máqi-
go to bed, to -túk-
go up, to -čáʔaqi-
god ʔámnaʔa, dióos, -kívasaw
good ʔáča-ʔe
good luck ʔeswéerta
good-by híwña
gopherlike animal tamasésket
gourd, buffalo qáxalkut
gourmand wáyiki-vaš
goose, wild ʔálukul, láʔlaʔ (greyish)
grab, to -čúk-, -náwas-
grandchild -k^{w}ála, -qála, -súla
grandfather, maternal -k^{w}a-l
grandmother, paternal -káaka
grandmother, maternal -su, -túutu
grandparent, paternal -qaʔ

grape, wild suwánawet
grass spp. sámat, símut
grasshopper wíʔit
graveyard kúy-vaʔal
grayhaired, to become
  -méaa-
grease wí-l̃
greasewood ʔátukul, ʔúʔut
Great Bear, the čéxyaʔam
great grandparent píw-il̃
great one ʔámna-ʔa
green túkvaš-nek-iš
green (unripe) sáw-et
grimy face, to make -síŋal̃-
grin, to -séŋi-
grind, to -péy-, -téx-,
  -túla-, -túlus-, -píŋ-
grinding pestle páxwal̃
ground téma-l
ground wheat pásal
grow, to -ʔáʔavuk-, -qáni-,
  -wél-
gum sáan-at
guess, to -távan-
gun čúkinapi-š
guts sáʔi-l̃

H

hail tévaxalem
hair of body píi-l̃
hair of head yúluka-l
half kʷánaŋ
halfway ʔámiʔan
hallo! wáa
hammer, to -pe-tépeš-
hand -ma-l
handle qáwive
handsome man pašwél-iš
hang, to -távi-vi-, -wíway-,
  -yúlaa-
hang up, to -wíway-
happy, to be -čáy-
happen, to -méx-, -míyax-
hard héspe
hard time súnikat
harden, (breast) to -qáw-
hardened, to get -túpiš-
harness, to -qáwi-n-
hatch, to -čáli-
hatched púlayiš
hate, to -kʷáʔil̃e-
have, to -yáw-
have a fiesta, to -kéwe-
have a good time, to -čáy-
have an affair with sbdy's
wife, to -ʔéʔyetu-
he ʔét, péʔ
head yúluka-l
hear, to -náqma-
heart sún-il
heart of plant pásun
heat síwiš
heavy číki-ma, péle-ma
heavy wind, rain tévisiʔwet
heel -ʔi tákʔa

help, to -mámayaw-, -náxači-
herb sámat
herd, to -kíwaˀan-
here ˀípa
hey! wáa
hiccup, to -nénama-
hide láqačil̃
hide, to -néŋ-
high up ˀévan
hills muˀmúˀa-wet
hip húsi-l̃, -miš
hire, to -káwiya-
hit, to -pe-púxay-, -qáčin-,
  -pe-qépay-, -vúk-
hit against, to -pe-qáŋi-
hit splashing against, to
  -pe-qáčaw-
hitched, to be -káwi-
hoe, to -vúk-
hold, to -yáw-
hold (by hand or chain), to
  -ˀík-
hold (under the arm), to
  -kʷálma-
hole téki-š, wálin-at
hole, to have -kávi-
hole, to make -kápal-
holler, to -péleley-, -wáy-
homosexual náanxiš
honey míyel̃
hook, to -ˀík-, -ŋáli-n-
hooked, to get -qáwi-
hop, to -číŋay-
hopefully sáxalu
Hopi Indian hóopi
horn ˀáwa-l
horse kaváayu, pásukat
horsefly píˀpiš
hot, to become -síw-
hot, to feel -ˀéme-
house kí-š
how méxanuk
huddle, to -máqˀu-
hug, to -táwe-
hummingbird túčil̃
humorous sulsímima
humpbacked, to be -púksaa-
hunchbacked, to be -pe-púˀuu-
hunger kʷáywil̃
hunt, to -ˀámu-
hurry up, to -táˀatay-
hurt, to -múk-ne-
husband wélˀisew-il̃

I

ice pàl tépawkaš (s.v.
  pá-l)
if háwa, héma
if not ˀáwa
ill séken
important person yáˀexiš
in front of -múči
in the middle, to be
  -máxel̃e-
in the shade of color, to be
  -mísva-

inclination wéyi-ʔa
incline, to -čáka-, -wéyi-
incline curving, to -káyvaa-
incline forward, to
-muhúyaqi-
inclined, to be -káwlaa-
Indian shoes čáwiš
Indian soap néxiš
Indian Wells káviñiš
indigestion, to have -kúča-
inhabitant kík
initiate, to -ʔéw-lu-ni-
insert, to -čéki-n-
inside pé-tuk
intercourse, to have -kúŋlu-,
-yím-
invite, to -páx-ane-,
-wáy-ni-
iodine bush húat
iron túkvaš
iron, to -sétin-, -wáwatne-
irrigate, to -weláwali-
it ʔét, péʔ
itchy, to feel -sáqa-

J

jagged čawál
jagged, to stand -sákʷaa-
jagged, to be -čáŋaa-
jail témi-n-vaʔal
jar, water kávaʔmal
jealous, to be -náwaan-,
-tátaxel̃ew-
jerk, to - ce-méli-n-, -wéqaš-
Jimson weed kíkesew-vaʔal
join oneself, to -náki-
joke, to -ʔíʔismatu-
jump, to -híŋ-, -pe-púčaq-
jump and stick, to -čúkla-
jumping cactus čúkal
juniper, California yúyil̃
just ča, če-, péqi, túʔ
just about xúum

K

kick, to -čéŋen-, -híŋ-
kidnap, to -ʔéyetu-,
-yu-ʔíva-
kidney pípiviskun
kill, to -mék-an-, -pe-sáqin-
kind n. ʔéʔexiš
kiss, to -čúŋ-in-
kitchen kúl-vaʔal
knead dough, to -ñúš-
knee támi-l̃
kneel down, to -lépeqi-,
-méči-
knife pásivat, túkvaš
knock, to -púx-, -qáŋ-,
-téx-
knock down, to -pe-ʔétel-,
-hémi-n-, -lúmaš-
knot, to have -túči-
know, not to -túmawan-
know, to -ʔéʔnan-
know, to come to -távan-

knowledge ʔéʔnan-il̃

L

lake pàl múye-qal-et
land téma-l
language háwaway-at
language, to talk -kútaš-
lard túpič-iš
last háy-ve, séʔŋax
later máwa, séʔŋax
laugh, to -sém-
laundry soap ŋáyal
law núʔin-at
lay eggs, to -máyl̃u-
lay straight, to -péti-n-
lazy person mušʔíva-l
leader núʔin-vaš, yáʔexiš
leaf pála-t
leak, to -sát-
lean, to -muʔíka-, -muʔíva-,
  -qéyi-
lean sideways, to -kávaqi-
learn, to -ʔéʔnan-
leather láqačil̃
leave wife or child behind, to
  -ʔámi-n-
leave sbdy, to -qámi-
leaves yámil̃
left ʔíšva
leg -ʔi
lend a hand, to -mámayaw-
let go, to -ʔámi-n-
let sbdy do, to -qámi-
letter kʷáʔisne-at
level, to -čáwi-, -táwi-
level, (spherical obj.) to be
  -mal-mála-
liar čuuŋiš, tama-kéniš
lick, to -píl̃ay-
lid témi-ve
lie down, to -máx-
lie on back, to -táča-
lie on belly, to -túmakaw-
lie sideways, to -čáka-,
  -kávaqi-
lie stretching, to -péti-
lies, to tell -táatusne-
lift up self, to -čáʔaš-,
  -čáʔkav-, -kʷéʔeqe-
lift up the chin, to -ʔáku-
light n. háti-wen-et
light kʷáwawaʔ-il̃
limp, to -číŋay-
line héti-wen-et, qíipi-wen-et
lined up, to be -wíl̃i-
lion, mountain túkwet, ʔíswet
listen, to -náqma-
little, a ʔínis
live, to -híw-, -qál-
lively person čačáaka,
  kʷápi-qal-et
liver -némʔa, yávayva
living person kʷápi-qal-et
lizard spp. čáxwal,
  čúkaʔwalla, kéčiš,

kíl̃imuʔat, múl̃ak, múviʔ,
náyxal, páyul, píyʔxʷal,
tátaxsil̃, yáŋvaʔ
lock up, to -témi-
locoweed qášil̃
long wávu-ma
long, to be -pe-kʷéniš-
long ago yéwi
longish, to be -húyaa-
look, to -téeŋ-
look at, to -téew-
look at meanly, to
-ŋáŋeyaʔan-
look back, to -ʔéliš-
look for, to -hál-
look forward, to -táxʔisl̃u-
look up, to -ʔáku-
loose, to -xálʔaqe-
loose, to be -télaa-
loose, to get -léʔeley-
loose bowels, to have
-pe-síčaq-
loosen, to -če-télaš-
lose, to -táwas-
lose one's weight, to -ʔíka-
louse, body kúʔa-l, náwil̃a-t
louse, hair sáʔwal
love, to -ʔáyaw-
Luiseño language, to speak
-qáʔi-
lung yávayva

M

mad, to get -héñew-
make, to -kúl-
make fire, to -náʔani-
make fun, to -kús-
make noise, to -hée-, -mélki-,
-ŋálaw-, -ŋéneney-
make sbdy to fall, to -ʔétel-
male náxaniš
mama -píipi
man náxaniš
manzanita kélel
marked, to be -qípi-
marked with a line, to be
-wíli-
marriage wélʔisew-il̃
marriage, to propose -wáy-
marry, to -wáy-
marry a husband, to -wélʔisew-
marry a wife, to -kínaŋi-
maybe ʔesan
meal, ground téʔat
mean wélnet
mean, to behave -tátaxel̃ew-
measles, to have -lúmu-
measure, to -ñámaan-,
-ñánva-yax-ni-
meat káarne, wáʔiš
medicine tíŋʔay-piš
medicine-man púul
meadowlark ʔísal
meet, to -námik-, -pénin-
melt, to -čáx-, -kéye-, -séy-

merrymaking sulčáamaniš
mesquite bean cake, piece of
 káxat
mesquite beans méniki̇š
mesquite beans, unripe
 séwaxil̃
mesquite tree ʔíl̃
mess up, to -sák^way-
message, to -léʔaw-
messy, to be -ʔúxvey-
metate mála-l
Mexican číʔaš, sáavet
middle náwxa-l
middle, in the ʔámiʔan
midnight tékluvel
milk, to -síyči-
mimick, to -mémxive-
mince, to -čúq-
miscarriage, to have -pumi-
misfortune, to suffer
 -tewyaw-
miss, to -qatiw-
mist háway-š
mistaken, to be -ʔémiš-
mistletoe čáyal
mock, to -ʔála-, -háawi-,
 -támaw-
mockingbird muʔíkil̃,
 támaw-et
money qíč-il̃
monster čáxasiwet
month ménil̃

moon ménil̃
more más
mormon tea tútut
morning páay-iš
morning, in the túleka
morning, early in the
 mu-túleka
mortar, types of páa-l,
 palpála-wet, qáwuvaxal
mosquito muhúlil̃
mother -ye
mountain qáwiš
mouse, field yúul̃
mouth táma-l
move, to -ʔíyax-, -néy-,
 -ŋil̃áa-, -yámu-
move out, to -síyaqi-
move slowly, to -ŋísan-
move swiftly, to -múle-
much méte-n
mucus -muvi-l̃
mud yú(u)liš
multiply, to -méte-k^w-
mushroom spp. sáqapiš, tíwil̃,
 wéwelpiš, yúlal
music mélki-ni-l̃
mustache, to have -yultáma-

N

naked, to be -kívlu-
name, to -téwan-
narrow and long, (road) to be
 -wíil̃ax-

navel -ʔul
near máŋax, súnči
needlelike obj. ʔíviš
negro túl̃-ek-iš
neighbor -máŋax kík
nephew -kúmu, -mut
nice sulsímima
niece -ʔásis, -kúmu,
-máti, -mut
night túkmiyat
night, to become -mávi-
night hawk púlmiš
nightingale púlmiš
nimble person kʷáwawaʔ-il̃
nipples -píiy, túʔ-i
no kíʔi
nod, to -wéyi-
noise, big túv
noise, to make -wáy-
nonsense ʔíʔexi-š
noon tékluvel, máxel̃i-š
nose -mu-l
nostril lámsa
north témam-ka
not kil̃e
not knowing anything
temtémaʔan
not right ʔeléle-ma
notch, to -čípa-, -lékeš-
nothing ʔíʔexi-š
now ʔívʔa-x
nudge, to -pe-téxay-
numb, to become -tétvis-,
-muyéŋi-
nuts tášvaʔal

O

oak spp. kʷíñil, páwiš,
wíʔasil̃, wíʔat
oblong, to be -húyaa-
ocean pàl múumat, pàl núkat
odor, bodily -téyʔa
offering, to make -míŋkiw-,
-wíčay-, -wíwčixan-
oh! ʔáasia
oh yes! héena
old, (man) to become -náxaluvuk-
old, (woman) to become
-níšl̃uvuk-
old man náxaluvel
old woman níšl̃uvel
olla kávaʔmal, tésnat
on páʔakʷen
on hands and knees, to get
-čáwaqe-
on that account péʔiš
one súpl̃e
only péqi, túʔ
open, to -ʔáqi-, -hákuš-
open, to be -kávi-
open basket čípatma-l
open hands, to -sálaqi-
open mouth, to -wáʔaqe-
open eyes or mouth, to
-če-kʷálaʔan-
open place hátava

opening, to get -kápal-
opening, at the ŋáliva
or háa
orphan híwtiniš
other súpul
otherwise ʔáwa
ouch! ʔéte
out of mind, to be -ʔíswalu-
out of place, (leg) to be, -ŋáli-
outside kímu-ŋax
overcast, to become -yúpi-
overnight, to stay -támituk-
oversleep, to -kup-čáʔay- (s.v. -kúp-)
owe money, to -déeve-
owl kúkul, múut
owner of house -hékik

P

pain, to cause -pe-láyin-
paint, to -húmay-, -ʔíʔisne-, -k^{w}áʔisne-
palate -tuklákma
pale séken
palm, fan/date máwul
paper pepéel
paralyzed lúumiš
parch, to -téqan-
parent máyl̃u-š
partner -kíl̃iw, -táxlew
party, to have -kéwe-
pass a while, to -yéŋ-
pass away, to -sáwaa-
pass by, to -péniiči-
pass quickly, to -pe-pénew-
pasted, to be -táki-
pasted, to get -tákal-
patch up, to -tátkame- (s.v. -táki-)
pay, to -ŋíñan-
peacock pávu
peck, to -čúčuk-, -pe-čúkay-
peel, to -síʔay-, -k^{w}élel-, -če-sípi-
peek, to -húlaqan-
peek out, to -čáyaqi-
penis -wéʔi
penny sélnek-iš
peon stick pyóon
peppery qél̃ak
perfume wíči-n-vaʔal
perhaps sáxalu
perk up, to -k^{w}étel-
permit, to -yéŋin-
person táxliswet
personally -táwiš
pestle, stone páwul, tákiš
pet -ʔaš
pick, to -číkav-, -húkul-, -pe-púxay-, -yékaw-
pick fruit, to -ʔáy-, -číʔ-, -návki-
pick up, to -k^{w}áš-
pile up, to -múʔaqi-, -múʔaš-, -téʔeqe-

pinch, to -číkav-, -húkul-
pine wéxet
pine nut tévat
pipe yúlil̃
pit ténq-il̃
pitch pásnat
place to roast agave
wáqvaʔal
place where dead people live
télmekiš
plan, to -nánva-yax-ni-
plant (used for cold)
tánwivel
plant, to -wés-
plate wáyisma-l
play, to -ʔíʔk-, -kanávi-,
-málisew-, -qáwpi-
plow, to -qíyne-, -wék-
pocket káwkun-il̃
point, to -sívalu-
point at, to -máʔuni-
pointed, to be -hulhúla-,
$k^w$is-k^wíse-
poison náaviš
poke, to -qáčin-
poor súnweʔ-ma
poor person sun-súnikat
pop off, to -čál-
possibly sáxalu
pot, types of káva ʔmal,
tápaʔmal, tésnat
potato , Indian tál̃ki
pottery tápaʔmal

pound, to -čúq-, -péy-,
-túla-
power ʔíva-ʔal, téʔayawa
praise, to -mu-ʔíva-n-,
-če-qéyl̃ek^{w}ene-
pray to God, to -míisi-
precipitous, to be -túmaw-
pregnant níit
preserve, to -téyan-
press, to -sétin-
press down, to -sétaʔan-
pretend, to -tax-če-táʔal-ne-
pretty ʔélka
pretty, to be -pálaw-
prickle, to -pe-čáŋin-
priest, Catholic páadre
probably ʔesan, héma, náʔqa,
sáxalu
propose (to marry), to -kúŋlu-
proud tel̃ʔáʔayamal̃
proud of, to be -če-qélek^{w}ene-
provoked, to get -símm-
prune, to -púvuš-
pry open, to -k^{w}étel-
puberty rites, to do
-ʔéw-lu-ni-
pull, to -húlul-, -wípis-
pull off, to -húpaš-
pull out, to -če-húlin-,
-húqin-, -če-húš-
pull out (tree), to -qúyen-
pull out (weeds, etc.), to
-lúpin-

pull up, (mouth) to -séŋi-
pulverized, to get -píŋ-
pumice stone tésvaˀal
pump (water), to -wéy-
pumpkin kalaváas, néhwet
pungent qél̃ak
purse káwkun-il̃
push, to -ˀétel-, -núˀuqan-
push oneself under (ashes, etc.), to -mu-píl̃i-
put, to -ŋáqi-n-
put away, to -ˀéx-an-
put design, to -ˀíˀisne-, -k^{w}áˀisne-
put feather, to -húmsan-
put in, to -hámin-
put in order, to -táv-, -wén-
put on clothes, to -ˀéla-
put on earrings, to -čáyu-
put on hat, to -yúmuˀ-
put on shoes, to -wáqča-
put on the head, to -ˀúˀ-
put on trousers, to -páxani-
put the arm around sbdy's neck, to -káyma-, -k^{w}álma-

Q

quail spp. qáxal, teseqáxal, xáwet
quail, baby séyewet
quarrel, to -náyax-
quick doer čaxčáaka
quickly čáˀča, hávu-n
quiet, to be -čémi-, -ték-lu-
quit, to -qámi-
quiver, to -kúl-, -yúyi-

R

rabbit, cottontail távut
rabbit, jack- súˀiš
raid, to -túmaw-
rain, to -wéwen-
rainbow píyaxat
raise, to -čéˀ-eqi-
raise (child), to -wél-ne-
rake, to -wákaˀan-
rat qáwal, yúul
rather más
rattle néhmal, páˀaya-l
rattle of snake číčika-t
rattlesnake spp. mésaˀa, séwet
raw sáw-et
reach for, to -yúˀaqi-
reach somewhere, to -píš-
read, to -léer-
ready nánva-nek
recently túku
recognize, to -ˀéˀnan-
recognize, not to -túmawan-
recovered, to become -ˀáča-k^{w}-
rectum máy-va, -súyaˀa

red sélnek-iš
red clay káal
reed spp. páŋat, páxal
refugee híŋ-iči-š
refuse, to -če-kálaw-
relative míñikʔi, taxmíŋkik
remove, to -ʔéx-an-
rent from, to -téʔe-
resemble, to -ʔáyax-
rib čáwa-ʔal
ribbonwood hénil
rich ríiku
ride, to -pesyáar-
right ʔáča-ma
right hand, to one's ʔáča-ʔika
right away ʔívʔa-x
ring out, to -líwiwey-
rip, to -pákaq-, -če-péki-, -če-sáli-, -če-sáyi-
rip on the seam, to -qépel-
ripen, to -k^{w}ás-
rise up, to -wél-
rise up spinning, to -mínay-
rival -káytu
river pá-l, wáni-š
road pít
roadrunner púuiš
roast, to -wáʔ-
roast agave, to -táŋ-
roast in pit, to -téneq-
robin tis-qáxal
rock qáwiš
rock, to -ʔáqyaw-, -ŋéy-
rock to mash plant páyx^{w}al
roll, to -čénen-, -máni-, -vuk-méni-
roll in, to -píl̃i-
roof kís-vaxat
roomy, to be -háka-
root, to -púku-
ropelike thing wánal
rotten, to become -písa-
rough, to be -lúčaw-
round, to be -púmule-, -túyva-
round, to become/get -páti-, -če-púmuqe-
rub, to -mávay-
run, to -pe-ʔéwi-, -ʔíva-
run away, to -híŋ-iči-
run out, to -čúma-law-
run over dike, to -če-wákal-
run race, to -nánami-
runner yáʔik
rush in, to -pe-kúli-

S

sack kún-il̃
sad súnweʔ-ma
sadness súnikat
sage pálna-t
sagebrush, California húulvel
saliva háña-l
salt ʔíŋ-il̃

salt grass símut
salty sétax
sand ŋáči-š
sandal čáwiš
sap of mesquite tree
kʷál̃ʔit, télmu
saucepan kápatmal
say, to -kútaš-, yáx-
scarce hálave
scared, to become -yúki-
scarf páañu
scatter, to -vuk-čípi-n-,
-páčaaq-, -pe-púwi-,
-vuk-sáay-, -pe-wáʔaš-
scorpion mánisal̃, súyil̃
scrape, to -čál-, -ŋép-,
-če-sípi-, -sív-
scratch, to -ŋíl̃ay-, -sáluk-,
-xélew-
scream, to -kʷíl̃il̃a-
scrub, to -ŋép-, -ŋépel-
scrub off, to -méleka-
sea-blite ŋáyal
seat ñáš-vel
search, to -hál-
secretly čaqaʔéʔil̃, čeʔéʔnil̃
see, to -téew-
see a witch doctor, to
-púhya-
seed púč-il̃, qáxʔa
seem, to -ʔáyax-
seep-weed ŋáyal
self tax

sell, to -máx-, -vendéer-
send, to -núʔin-
send out roots, to -wála-
separate, to -wáxi-
serve mass, to -míisi-
set, (the sun) to -páx-
settle down, to -ñáš-, -ték-,
-túpa-
sew, to -ʔúlan-
shade kís-iš
shaggy, to be -sákʷaa-,
-yáŋaa-
shake, to -čéleley-, -ŋéy-,
-ŋil̃áa-
shake head, to -ŋáya-
shaken off, to be -tékʷe-
sharp, to be -táma-
shape , to -ŋávay-, -sív-
shave, to -sív-
she péʔ
shell sáva-l
shell, to -čál-, -číl̃ay-,
-táš-
sheep, mountain páʔat
shimmer, to -tévelvey-
shin -táxalxa
shine, to -háti-
shirt, to put on -wíyavi-
shoes wáqa-t
shoot, to -múx-
shoot at a small bundle, to
-l̃íl̃ʔan-
shoot through, to -mu-páxul-

shoot up, to -pe-púki-
short, to be -múti-, -tépi-, -túqi-
shoulder -sékʔa
shove, to -če-ʔétel-
show, to -ʔúne-
shrink, to -súkaa-, -če-súkul-, -če-súkuš-, -pe-súval-, -če-súyal-, -če-túnuš-
side, to one's ʔámi-ka, čáʔaw-ika, máŋax
side by side, to be -wáči-
sieve yáči-n-vaʔal
sift, to -wépin-
sifted, to get -yáči-
similar péŋki-š
sing, to -táxmu-
sing aloud, to -líwiwey-
sing against each other, to -ʔíswax-, -tátaxel̃ew-, -wéx-
sip, to -če-súlul-
sister, elder -qis
sister, grandfather's -qéx
sister, mother's elder -nes
sister, mother's younger -yes
sister, younger -náwal̃, -wáxal̃
sister-in-law -télme
sit, to -číʔa-
sit down, to -ñáš-
sit up all night, to -páay-
sit upright, to -híw-, -qál-
skillful ʔéʔniš-ka
skin sáva-l
skinny, to become -yáwi-
skunk ték^{w}el
sky túkvaš
slap, to -pe-pákin-
sleep, to -kúp-
sleepy, to be -kúkup-, -tuháyin-
slice, to -wék-
slide down, to -táyul-ki-, -xáyuqi-, -xáyuš-
slip in, to -píl̃i-
slippery, to become -táyul-
sloppy, to be -ʔúxvey-
slowly pél̃an
small ʔíniš-il̃
small change čúviwenet
smallpox, to have -lúmu-
smart ʔéʔniš-ka
smash, to -če-síčaq-
smash sth. juicy, to -ñúš-
smear, to -húmay-
smell, to -húv-
smell sth., to -húvi-
smile, to -kaskási-, -sém-yaw-, -séŋi-
smoke míʔ-at
smoke tobacco, to -píva-
smoke-tree náswet
smooth, to become -táyul-

smooth, to make -yáwan-
smother in, to -mu-píl̃i-
snag, to -če-sáyi-
sneak up on, to -ʔéyawan-
sneaky way, in čaqaʔéil̃,
čeʔéʔnil̃
sneeze, to -háʔtis-
snore, to -tálal-
snow, to -yúy-
so what! čáqapa, mínčaʔan
soak, to -čúpi-n-
soak out, to -xáš-
sob, to -če-húhkum-
soft héveve
soft-flag kúʔut
soft spot on baby's head
híkusa-l
softly pél̃en
sole (shoe) -ʔi pé-tuk-wiš
(s.v. pé-tuk)
some time ago ʔéxama
someone/-thing important
míñikʔi
somersault, to -čáxuu-,
-súwelu-
sometime mí-paʔ pa (s.v. míʔ)
somewhere mí-vaʔ pa
son -kíhma, -méxan
son-in-law -míŋkiwʔa
song táxmu-ʔat
soon, very xúum
soot kéʔmet
sore, to feel -qél̃a-

sorry for, to feel -súnwe-
soup hépal
southward kíčam-ka
spank, to -vuk-sésqame-
spark, to -kísal-, -pálaw-
sparkle, to -pe-tíkal-
sparrow ʔáqniš
speak, to -kútaš-
spectacles -púš-ŋa-viš
speculate, to -náʔmiš-
spider xʷálxʷal
spin, to -púne-, -súvale-,
-súyuy-
spin slowly, to -kávale-
spill, to -píki-n-, -síl̃e-
spirit téwlavel
spirit, great -kívasaw
spit háña-l
spit, to -čúʔan-, -ke-xékin-
spit out, to -qépax-
splash, to -pe-ŋélew-,
-pe-wíči-
splatter, to -páčay-
split, to -čápi-
split, to be -wáqi-
split up, (people) to
-pe-púwi-
spoil, to -písa-
spokesman núʔin-qal-et
spoon kúmal
spotted píintu
spotted, to be -tákal-
spread, to -wíl̃i-

spread legs over, to
-če-háalkiši-

spread open, to -pélaan-

spread out, to -pánaa-,
-vuk-sáay-

sprinkle, to -weláwali-

spring up, to -pe-wíči-

springtime táspaʔ

squash, wild néxiš

squash, to -pe-mátaš-
-če-ñúčay-, -pe-sétin-,
-če-síčaq-

squat, to -čúvaqi-, -pámuwu-

squeeze, to -če-ñúčay-, -sétin-

squirrel, ground qíŋiš

squirrel, tree síkawet

squirt, to -pe-k^wétet-

stab, to -qáčin-

stage-fright, to get -háman-

stagger, to -káwalva-, -kíval-

stand, to -číki-, -wéwen-

standing, to be -híwen-

standing in order, to be
-čéli-

stand up, (hair) to -čáŋaa-

star súʔwe-t

stare, to -ŋáŋeyaʔan-,
-téew-ŋi-

stay, to -híw-, -máx-, -yéŋ-

stay behind, to -kíya-

stay overnight, to -túk-

steal, to -ʔéyetu-

steam, to -múlul-, -múluluy-

steep, to be -túmaw-

step over, to -če-háalkiši-,
-k^wáliš-

stepmother -yes

stick húyanaxa-t, -ʔík-ʔa,
náxa-t

stick, walking čík^{w}a-pi

stick, to -pe-čáŋin-

stick, (bur) to -čúk-

stick between, to -čéqi-

stick in, to -čéki-, -číki-

stick into, to -pe-čúpaq-,
-pe-kúli-, -qáčin-

stick out, to -čáyaqi-,
-čékma-, -k^wétel-

sticker čúkal, čúŋal,
ʔíwya-l

stiff če-héespekuš

stiff, to become -čík^{w}a-,
-če-kíyʔul-, -muyéŋi-

still muʔ, péqi

still, to be -ték-lu-

sting, to -múx-

stingy person ʔísiwet

stinkbug sískiŋil̃

stir, to -múlay-, -ŋélew-,
-ŋéwen-

stomach téʔi-l̃

stoop down, to -čúvaqi-,
-k^wéyʔeqi-, -k^wéyʔeš-,
-láki-

stop, to -čémi-, -qámi-,
-pe-táki-, -ték-lu-, -wéwen-

storage basket méyenat
storage basket, to make -pénew-
storage of food télkʷaam
store, to -tétxe-, -téxin-
story háwaway-at
story, to tell -selhíiščе-
story, true ʔáʔalxe-at
straddle, to -pálkiš-
straight, to be -pe-kʷéniš-
straight ahead pétaʔwiš
straightener (of arrowshaft) patávnivaʔal
strain, to -sát-, -túp-in-
stranger léʔet
strawberry píkl̃am
strengthen, to -ʔíva-n-
stretch, to -wási-, -wáwatne-
stretch legs, to -wéwču-
stretch out, to -héti-
string káwi-ve
string, to -yúl-
striped píintu
striped, to be téveleve
stripped off, to be -kívlu-
strong, to be -ʔíva-
stubby, to be -pámuwu-
stuck, to get -ŋáqi-, -če-tépiš-
stumble, to -če-tépin-
stumble over, to -pe-číkʷal-, -máni-, -pe-tíʔal-
stump wálʔa
stunned, to get -čáŋal-
suck, to -čúŋ-
suck breast, to -pís-
suffering súnikat
suffocate, to -hikus-témi-, -kus-témi- (s.v. -témi-)
sugar písil̃
sugar bush nákʷet
sumac nákʷet, sélet
summer táwpaʔ
sunbathe, to -tám-kus-
Sunday domíŋgo
surprise (interj.) číŋaay
surprised, to be -káviiči-
surround, to -kámiš-
swarm into, to -pe-súlul-
swarm out, to -múlul-
swallow, to méŋkʷa-, -če-súlul-
sway, to -wéyi-, -yúlaa-
sweat, to -ʔéʔwa-
sweathouse hášlaʔ-il, húwiačet
sweep, to -wákaʔan-
sweet písil̃-nek
swell, to -pátiš-, -páxan-
swing, to -káyaw-
switch, to -če-séqay-
swollen páxan-iš
sword pásivat
sycamore sívil

T

table lamésa
tack, to -ŋáqi-n-
tail -k^{w}as
tail (bone's area) húsi-l̃
tail of the arrow
k^{w}áyʔanpi-š
take, to -kús-
take a rest, to -híkus-
take along, to -núŋu-
take along as lunch, to
-nútka-
take an Indian bath, to
-húneke-
take as wife, to -wáy-
take away, to -náwan-
take care of, to -k^{w}áaviču-,
-téček^{w}-, -yáw-
take care of a baby, to
-ʔáqyaw-
take meal, to -wáyiki-
take off, to -hákuš-, -húpaš-,
-k^{w}áwuš-, -k^{w}élel-
take sanbath, to -híysay-
talk, to -háwaway-, -kútaš-
talk the Cahuilla language, to
-ʔívil̃u-
tall wávu-ma
tangled up, to get -túči-
tap, to -pákin-, -téx-
tar pásnat
target mú-ivaʔal
taste, to -námaan-
tasty kén-ma
tattoo, to -číšxin-
tea spp.čah, čáŋʔalaŋiš,
tútut
teach, to -ʔúʔune- (s.v.
-ʔúne-)
tear, to -qíwiw-, -če-sáli-
tear apart, to - ce-wáqi-n-
tear down, to -qápal-
tear off, to -k^{w}áwuš-
teardrop -ʔis
tease, to -ʔíʔismatu-, -kús-
tell, to -tétiyax-, -téwan-
tell a true story, to -ʔáʔalxe-
tell lies, to -čúŋiš-l̃ew-,
-tama-kékenawk-, -táatus-ne-
(s.v. -táwas-)
tell to do, to -núʔin-
ten namečúmi
testicles téwiil̃em
than pe-ta
thank you ʔáča-ma
that guy táxat
that is why péʔiš,
súnaxwenepa
that time, at péŋa
that way, to be -ʔíyax-
thaw, to -xáš-
then púti
there péŋa
therefore hémax
thick číki-ma

thickset, to be -pámuwu-
thigh -miš
thin, to become -yáwi-
think, to -sičúmin-
thirst, with tákut piš
this ʔíʔ
this kind ʔíŋkiš
thorn čúŋal, ʔíwya-l
three páh
thread ʔíilu
thread, to -yúl-
threaten, to -sun-háhyam-
(s.v. sún-il̃)
throat kúspi-l̃
throat, inside of paxwáyvaʔa-l
throw, to -vuk-čípi-n-,
-pe-séqay-
throw (lasso), to -pe-ŋáli-
throw (stick), to -vúk-
throw away, to -ʔámi-n-,
-wíčixan-
throw flat on the ground, to
-vuk-páčay-
throw into a hole, to -ŋálaw-
thumb -maʔ ʔámnawet
thunder táwva-l
Thursday, on wíčiw-kʷal-pa
tied, to be -káwi-
tied, to get -qáwi-
tied around, to be -súti-
tick máčil
tickle, to -l̃ákay-, -séwel-
tight, to be -ŋátaš-, -lékeš-
tighten, to -súyiš-, -tépaqa-
time támit
tip hému
tip, to -ŋával-
tipsy, to be -puš-ŋéy-
(s.v. púč-il̃)
tired, to be -háyin-,
-tuháyin-
tired of, to become -senmúk-
toad, horned čálaka(t)
toes hé-ʔi túʔ-i (s.v. -tú-)
tomorrow túleka
tongue -náŋ-il̃
too tésax
tooth táma-l
top of, on páʔakʷen
tornado téneʔawka
tortilla, to make -sáw-
toss, to -ʔámi-n-
touch, to -ŋával-, -yáw-
toy málisap-piš
track -ʔi
track, to -tépin-
translate, to -péniiči-ni-
trap, to -héw-
traveler ném-et
treat, to -péniiči-ni-
tree kélaw-at
tribe -táxlew
trim, to -púvuš-
trip, to -če-tépin-,
-pe-tíʔal-
trot, to -yúʔi-

true čepév
trunk wál?a
try, to -námaan-
tuberculosis, to have
-čáčawa-
tule páŋat, pá?ul
turkey púlmiwet
turkey buzzard yúŋaviš
turn, to -méli-, -méye-
turn around, to -kávay-,
-vuk-méni-
turn into (a different shape), to -vuk-méni-
turn into (the hue indicated), to -híwla-
turn on a light, to -háti-
turn over, to -vuk-méni-
turn to, to -púču-
turtle spp. ?áyil̃, yú?ayl̃
twin číšxiniš
twist, to -kávale-,
-če-méli-n-, -méye-,
-súvale-, -súwelu-
two wíh

U

ugly ?elél-k^{w}-imal̃
uncle -kum, -mas, -tas
under pé-tuk
underbrush témaš
understand, to -náqma-
unimportant ?í?exi-š
unknown híhmay-?a
unmarried person ?íŋkiš
untie, to -čúvi-
upper ground, on ?áwta
upset one's stomach, to
-ték^{w}axa-
urinate, to -pís-, -sí?-
use as earrings, to -čáyu-

V

vanish from sight, to -čúx-
vegetable wés-at
very much héspe
vibrate, to -téveve-
visit, to -píitu-
vomit, to -pípivis-
vulva číŋil̃

W

waist tí?i-l̃
wait for, to -kí?iw-
wake up, to -k^{w}ápi-
walk, (horse) to -kúp-
walk around, to -ném-
walk with a walking stick, to
-čík^{w}a-
wall kíwniš
wander around, to -nénem-
want, to -?áyaw-, -?í?iklu-
war héeñiw-il
war dance mánet

warm tíŋ-iš, tíwma
wash, to -k^{w}íče?an-, -pášam-
wash hair, to -yúvušxu-
wash away, to -?úx-
watch, to -téew-
water pá-l
water baby k^{w}ásimayka
water dog pá?aqniwet
water, to -welávwali-
watermelon ?estú?iš, sandíya
wave, to -véley-
way pít
way back húŋa-yka
way, this/that ?éxenuk
way underneath ŋáy-ika
way up ?áwsun
weak, to get -čáŋal-
wear, to -?éla-, -xéla-
wear (shoes), to -wáqča-
weary, to be -tuháyin-
weasel temasésket
web, to -héw-
weed spp. púu?upul, sélel̃, sélet, séqnat, súul
week semáana
weigh, to -péle-k^{w}-
well ?áča-?e
well (then) púti
west qáwi-ka
wet pál-(n)ek
wet, to get -pávas-
what? híče?a
what about? ?áwa
what kind? míŋki
what on earth! hétu
wheat tríiwa?a
where? míva?
which? mí?
whip, to -mék-an-, -vuk-séqay-
whirl, to -púni-, -súyuy-
whirl around, to -súvuvey-
whirlwind kùt yáy?al, téne?awka
whisper, to -sáwa-
whistle páxal
whistle, to -k^{w}íwi-
whistler (animal) tamasésket
white téviš-nek
white man mélkiš
who? háx?i
why? míyax-wen pe
wide háka-ma, híl̃e-n
widow múk-vel
widower kínaŋa múk-iš
wiggle, to -káwalva-, -kíval-, -wáma-
wildcat túkut
wilderness ?í?exi-š
willow spp. ?ávasil̃, sáxa-t
wind yá?i
wind, to -če-méli-n-
wing wáka-t
wink, to -mák-, -pe-qítaš-
winnow, to tá?in-, -wépin-

winter támivaʔ
wish, to -sun-híisče- (s.v. -híči-)
witch dance, to perform -púwax-
witch doctor páʔvuʔl, púul
with -new
without ʔíʔive
wobble, to -láʔeley-
woman ñíčil̃
woman, young ʔélka
womb -púnʔa
wood kélaw-at
woodpecker spp. kúpanil̃, táviš
word háwaway-at, kútaš-ʔat
work, to -tuvxá-
world téma-l
worm sívuy-al
worm (with two horns) píyaxat
wormy, to become -kúʔa-
wrap around, to -húmulku-
wrestler tax-ʔámamni-vaš (s.v. -ʔámi-)
wring, to -kʷíčeʔan-
wrinkle, to -če-lámi-
wrist -ma káwʔa (s.v. káwʔa)
write, to -ʔíʔisne-, -kʷáʔisne-
wrong ʔeléle-ma

Y

yawn, to -kákape-
year táwpax-iš
yellow tésnek-iš
yellow jacket muxáavikat
Yerba mansa čívniš
Yerba santa tánwivel
yes hée
yesterday túku
yet péqi
you ʔét
young páʔuš
young girl ʔélka
young man pašwél-iš
youngest person ʔáksaʔviš
yucca blossom sével
yucca fruit nínil̃
Yucca nolina kúkuʔul
Yucca schidigera húnuvat
Yucca whipplei pánuʔul
Yuman yúumu